STUDENT'S BOOK

HUGH DELLAR AND ANDREW WALKLEY

UPPER INTERMEDIATE

OUTCOMES

HEINLE
CENGAGE Learning

Australia • Brazil • Japan • Korea • Mexico • Singapore • Spain • United Kingdom • United States

WELCOME TO *OUTCOMES*

Outcomes will help you learn the English you need and want . Each of the sixteen units has three double-pages linked by a common theme. Each double page is an individual lesson – and each teaches you some vocabulary or grammar and focuses on a different skill. The first lesson in each unit looks at conversation, the next two at reading or listening.

WRITING UNITS

There are eight writing lessons in the Student's Book, which teach different styles of writing. Each one has a model text as well as speaking tasks to do in pairs or groups. There are also extra vocabulary or grammar exercises to help you write each kind of text. In addition, there is a lot of writing practice in the *Outcomes* Workbook.

REVIEW UNITS

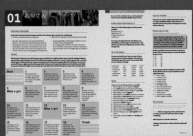

There are four Review units in this book. Here you practise the core grammar and vocabulary of the previous four units. The first two pages of each unit feature learner training, a board game, a quiz and work on collocations and pronunciation (especially individual sounds). The next two pages feature a test of listening, grammar and vocabulary. This is marked out of 80 – so you can see how you are progressing.

Clearly stated communicative goals in the unit menu, supported by grammar and vocabulary.

Grammar taught in context, with natural examples of usage and clear practice tasks.

Information on interesting bits of language common to native speakers of English.

Fuller explanations, more examples, and exercises are in the reference section at the back.

Speaking activities allow you to exchange information and ideas or comment. A longer final speaking task ends every unit.

Interesting listenings and readings. Very varied contexts .

Tasks to practise a variety of skills.

Visuals to help with new vocabulary.

---

01 ENTERTAINMENT

In this unit you learn how to:
- describe films, music and books
- politely disagree with opinions
- describe pictures

Grammar
- Talking about habits
- Adjectives and adverbs

Vocabulary
- Describing films, music and books
- Talking about pictures

Reading
- Heard it all before

Listening
- Films and the cinema
- A guided tour of an art gallery

SPEAKING

A Work in pairs. Tell each other about your interests and how you spend your free time. Do you have much in common?

GRAMMAR Habits

You are going to hear the answers eight people gave to different questions that use the structure *Do you ... much?*

A 🔊 1.1 Listen and write the questions you think were asked.

B 🔊 1.2 Listen to the following extracts from the audioscript for exercise A. Complete 1–8 with expressions and structures that show habits.
1 I don't .... during the week, though.
2 Yeah ....I take my mp3 player with me everywhere.
3 Not as much ...., because I really love it.
4 Yeah ...., to be honest. I guess I might in the summer.
5 I don't pay much attention to it most of the time. .... a big game, if there's one on.
6 Yeah, I guess so. I usually play football on a Wednesday and I go running ....
7 No, ... I tend to wait for films to come out on cable.
8 Not as much as I .... I was addicted to *The Sims* for a while, until my parents banned me. I .... sometimes play for 5 hours a day!

C Complete the following so they are true for you.
1 I ... all the time.
2 I don't ... as much as I used to because ...
3 I tend to ... at the weekends and now and again I ...
4 As a rule, I don't ... , but I will if ...
5 I used to ... a lot. I'd ...

▶ Need help? Read the grammar reference on page 136.

D Write five questions using the structure *Do you ... much?* Ask and answer the questions in pairs. Use some of the structures from exercise B to answer.

NATIVE SPEAKER ENGLISH

We often say *stuff* when we are being vague. It means *things. Stuff* is uncountable.

All kinds of stuff as well – rock, pop, even some classical.
I download quite a lot of stuff too.
I like their more recent stuff.

VOCABULARY Describing films, music and books

We use pairs of adjectives with similar meanings to emphasise what we mean. We often repeat the adverb with each adjective:

It's amazing, just really, really good.
It's just incredibly moving – incredibly sad.

A Complete the sentences with the words in the box.

| awful | commercial | dull | gripping | disturbing |
| catchy | over-the-top | weird | hilarious | uplifting |

1 It left me cold. It was typical big-budget Hollywood – very ....
2 It's very easy to sing along to – very ....
3 It's .... – just really, really funny.
4 It does nothing for me. It's quite boring, quite ....
5 I can't explain it. It's just strange – really ....
6 It's just too much for my liking – just really ....
7 You can't stop reading. It's just so exciting, so ....
8 It's good, but it's quite upsetting – quite ....
9 It's a really inspiring story, really ....
10 Don't go and see it! It's dreadful, absolutely ....

B In pairs, discuss which adjectives from exercise A describe films, books and music you know.

8 OUTCOMES

SPEAKING

A Work in pairs. Discuss these questions.
- Which of the following would you classify as art?

| graffiti | product design | furniture | pop videos |
| animation | video games | fashion | advertising |

- Are there any other things you regard as art?
- Do you have a favourite piece of art?
- Do you ever go to art galleries or exhibitions?
- What was the last one you went to? What was it like?

VOCABULARY Talking about pictures

A Look at the definitions below and discuss which adjectives describe the painting on this page.
1 If a painting has a **sombre** mood, it looks serious and sad.
2 If a painting is **lifelike**, it looks very realistic.
3 If it's **pretty**, it is nice and pleasant to look at.
4 If a painting is **dramatic**, it contains a lot of exciting action.
5 If it looks **dated**, it is no longer fashionable or relevant.
6 If it's **atmospheric**, a painting creates a special mood – such as a feeling of romance or mystery.
7 **Abstract** paintings show an artist's feelings or thoughts – rather than realistic objects or events.
8 If it's **ambiguous**, the meaning of the work isn't clear – it's open to interpretation.
9 An **intimate** painting shows private moments in someone's life.

C Cover exercise B. Complete these sentences about other paintings using words from exercise B.
1 I think it could .... be Spain or Italy in this picture.
2 Everyone looks .... they're having a really good time in this picture.
3 I get the .... they've been arguing. They .... really fed up with each other.
4 They've .... just moved in and are redecorating the whole flat, from the look of it.
5 They .... all be students. That looks .... a university canteen to me.
6 Everyone in this picture .... to be queuing or waiting for something.

LISTENING

You are going to hear a guide in an art gallery telling a group of visitors about the large painting on the right.

A Work in pairs. Describe what you can see in the paintings on the right. Use language and structures from *Vocabulary: Talking about pictures*. Then discuss these questions.
- Which of the two portraits do you prefer? Why?
- Can you see any parallels between the two works?

🔊 1.4 Listen and answer these questions.
1 When was the painting done?
2 Who are the couple in the painting?
3 What's the relationship between this painting and the painting by Jan van Eyck?
4 Why did the painter include the lilies and the cat?
5 What happened to the couple after the painting was finished?
6 Which five adjectives from exercise A of *Vocabulary: Talking about pictures* does the guide use?

B Which of these sentences about the painting above do you agree with?
1 The dark colours create a sombre mood.
2 She looks as if she's pulling her hair out.
3 She's obviously crazy.
4 She seems to have just woken up.
5 The man in the corner appears to be praying.
6 They both look very upset. I get the impression someone's died.
7 They look like a couple. They could well be lovers.
8 It must be night-time because all the colours are so dark.

10 OUTCOMES

LISTENING

You are going to hear two people talking about films.

A 🔊 1.3 Listen and take notes on how their tastes are similar – and how they differ.

B Answer these questions about the two people. Listen again to check your ideas.
1 Do they go to the cinema much?
2 What kind of films are they into? Anything in particular?
3 Have they seen any films recently?
4 What did they think of them?

LANGUAGE PATTERNS

Write the sentences in your language. Translate them back into English. Compare your English to the original.
It's (not) the kind of thing you can watch and just switch off.
It's (not) the kind of music you can dance to.
It's (not) the kind of film you'd take your kids to see.
It's (not) the kind of thing you'd like.
It's the kind of music my dad listens to.
It's the kind of thing they sell in airport bookshops.

CONVERSATION PRACTICE

A Work in pairs. With a different partner, have conversations starting *Do you read / listen to music / watch TV / go to the cinema much?* Ask further questions like those you heard in *Listening*. Use as much of the language from these pages as you can.

ENTERTAINMENT 9

DEVELOPING CONVERSATIONS
Disagreeing politely

When we disagree with someone's tastes, we often soften our responses using *not really, not that* and *a bit*. For example:
It's not really my kind of thing.

A Match 1–8 with the responses a–h. Then underline the expressions that use *not really, not that* and *a bit*. The first one is done for you.
1 I love 60s music. The Beatles, The Stones, stuff like that.
2 Have you seen *Saw*? I love that film. It's so scary.
3 I love fantasy – *Harry Potter* and that kind of thing.
4 I love that film. He's hilarious in it – really, really funny.
5 Don't you like opera? I love it.
6 I tend to read stuff on history or politics.
7 Have you heard any *Dover*? I love their music.
8 Have you ever read *Mona*? It's so moving. I loved it.

a Oh right. I'm not that keen on horror films. I don't really like films with a lot of blood and stuff in them.
b Oh right. I'm not really interested in serious stuff like that. I prefer something a bit lighter, something easier to read.
c Really? I'm not that keen on that kind of stuff, to be honest. I prefer something more realistic, more true-to-life.
d No, not really. I'm not that keen on classical music and I certainly can't be bothered to sit through 4 hours of it!
e Really? It didn't really do anything for me. I guess it's just not my kind of humour.
f Really? That's the kind of thing my dad listens to! I prefer something a bit more modern.
g Really? It left me cold. I just found it a bit dull, a bit boring. I didn't even finish it.
h Yeah, I like some of their early stuff, but they've gone a bit too poppy for my liking – a bit too commercial.

B Tell a partner about films, books and music you like – and why you like them. If your partner disagrees, they should use some of the underlined expressions from exercise A.

Listening exercises provide examples of the conversations you try in Conversation practice.

Many expressions and grammatical patterns in spoken English are similar to other languages. These exercises help you notice those.

This section allows you to put together what you've learnt.

Pronunciation activities are integrated with the communicative goals.

Further grammar and vocabulary points presented and developed through the unit.

GRAMMAR Adjectives and adverbs

Adjectives are often used before nouns. Also, the verbs *be, look, become, seem, get, taste,* etc. (sometimes called 'linking' verbs) are often followed by adjectives.

We use adverbs to modify a verb, an adjective, another adverb or a whole clause or sentence. Most adverbs are formed by adding *-ly* to the adjective, but some can have the same form as the adjective. Examples include *fast, hard* and *later*.

A Choose the correct form in these sentences about the listening.
1 This may strike you as a *fairly / fair* conventional portrait.
2 He's *pointedly / pointed* looking away from us.
3 The work is a very *ambiguously / ambiguous* piece.
4 It was painted *shortly / short* after their wedding.
5 It's *loosely / loose* based on a 15th century work.
6 *Unfortunate / Unfortunately,* Mr. Clark had *frequently / frequent* affairs during their five-year marriage. This played a part in their *eventually / eventual* divorce, and explains the friction that seems *apparently / apparent* between them.
7 *Sadly / sad,* Ossie Clark later fell into bankruptcy and addiction, and his life ended *tragically / tragic* when he was murdered.

B Explain your choices to a partner. Use the explanation box above to help you.

▶ Need help? Read the grammar reference on page 137.

PRONUNCIATION Adverbs describing sentences and clauses

We often emphasise the stress on adverbs that describe sentences and clauses – and pause slightly before continuing.

A Practise saying 1–6. Emphasise the stress on the adverbs.
1 Interestingly, the painting used to have a different title.
2 Actually, no-one knows who the painter was.
3 Sadly, she died at the age of only 35.
4 The painting sold last year for $18 million, but, amazingly, van Gogh himself sold none in his lifetime.
5 Incredibly, Mozart was only six when he started performing in public.
6 The painting was damaged in a fire and, unfortunately, it couldn't be restored.

B 🔊 1.5 Listen and compare how the speakers said the sentences. Then listen again and repeat them.

SPEAKING

A Work in groups of three to four. Think of a painting you like – or use the Internet to find one. You are going to present the picture to the rest of the group. First, make notes about:
· what's happening in the painting.
· the impressions / feelings you have about it.
· information about the painter and / or people in the picture (you can invent this!).
· additional comments (*sadly / interestingly / actually* etc.).

01 ENTERTAINMENT 11

LEARNING

Research suggests words need lots of revision in context if you want to be able to use them with confidence. The authors of *Outcomes* have tried hard to make sure words reappear many different times in the course. Here are **twelve** ways to learn the word *boost*.

· see it and practise it in **Vocabulary** p. 26
· look it up in the **Vocabulary Builder** p. 14
· use it in **Grammar** p. 111
· hear it in a **Listening** 4.1 p. 167
· say it in Developing Conversations p. 27
· find an example in **Grammar reference** (*so / such* p. 144)]
· read it in a **Reading** text p. 30
· write, read and listen to it in the **Workbook** Unit 4
· get it again in **Writing** p. 131
· check the grammar in **Vocabulary builder** exercises p. 17
· revise it in square 15 of the game in **Review** p. 32
· test it with **ExamView**

Outcomes VOCABULARY BUILDER

The *Outcomes Vocabulary Builder* provides lists of key vocabulary with clear explanations, examples of common collocations and exercises focusing on the grammar of the words.

MyOutcomes ONLINE

The pin code at the front of the Student's Book gives you access to a wide range of interactive, online exercises. We have created additional exercises to go with each unit from the book, so you can continue developing your English.
Visit **elt.heinle.com**

Grammar	Vocabulary	Reading	Listening	Developing conversations
• Talking about habits • Adjectives and adverbs	• Describing films, music and books • Talking about pictures	• Heard it all before	• Films and the cinema • A guided tour of an art gallery	• Disagreeing politely
• Non-defining relative clauses • The future	• Buildings and areas • Festivals and carnivals	• Ten days at the Venice Carnival	• Driving round Belgrade • Theme parks and rides	• Agreeing using synonyms
• *so, if* and *to* for describing purpose • Indirect questions	• Useful things • Word families • Problems with things	• I am ... Mr Trebus	• Asking for things • Trying to get a refund	• Explaining and checking
• *So / such* • *the..., the...* + comparatives	• The government, economics and society	• Common wealth economics for a crowded planet	• What do you think of your president? • In the news	• Responding to complaints
• *should(n't) have, could(n't) have, would(n't) have* • Present perfect continuous and simple	• Health and fitness • Football and life • Lucky escapes	• Sport – you've gotta love it!	• Unusual interests • The mad uncle	• Checking what you heard
• Modifiers • *have / get* something done	• Where you stayed • Understanding idioms	• Emails from Hong Kong	• Did you go away anywhere? • Accommodation problems	• Negative questions
• Narrative tenses • Participle clauses	• Weather and natural disasters • Plants and trees	• Animal issues	• Experiences of extreme weather • Plant life	• Exaggerating
• Modals + present and past infinitives • Nouns and prepositions	• Crimes • Agreeing and disagreeing	• Laying down the law	• Different kinds of crimes • A radio phone-in programme	• Comments and questions

DEVELOPING CONVERSATIONS
Disagreeing politely

> When we disagree with someone's tastes, we often soften our responses using *not really*, *not that* and *a bit*. For example:
> *It's not really my kind of thing.*

A **Match 1–8 with the responses a–h. Then <u>underline</u> the expressions that use *not really*, *not that* and *a bit*. The first one is done for you.**
1. I love 60s music. The Beatles, The Stones, stuff like that.
2. Have you seen *Saw*? I love that film. It's so scary.
3. I love fantasy – *Harry Potter* and that kind of thing.
4. I love that film. He's hilarious in it – really, really funny.
5. Don't you like opera? I love it.
6. I tend to read stuff on history or politics.
7. Have you heard any *Dover*? I love their music.
8. Have you ever read *Mona*? It's so moving. I loved it.

a. Oh right. <u>I'm not that keen</u> on horror films. I don't really like films with a lot of blood and stuff in them.
b. Oh right. I'm not really interested in serious stuff like that. I prefer something a bit lighter, something easier to read.
c. Really? I'm not that keen on that kind of stuff, to be honest. I prefer something more realistic, more true-to-life.
d. No, not really. I'm not that keen on classical music and I certainly can't be bothered to sit through 4 hours of it!
e. Really? It didn't really do anything for me. I guess it's just not my kind of humour.
f. Really? That's the kind of thing my dad listens to! I prefer something a bit more modern.
g. Really? It left me cold. I just found it a bit dull, a bit boring. I didn't even finish it.
h. Yeah, I like some of their early stuff, but they've gone a bit too poppy for my liking – a bit too commercial.

B **Tell a partner about films, books and music you like – and why you like them. If your partner disagrees, they should use some of the <u>underlined</u> expressions from exercise A.**

LISTENING

You are going to hear two people talking about films.

A 🔊 1.3 **Listen and take notes on how their tastes are similar – and how they differ.**

B **Answer these questions about the two people. Listen again to check your ideas.**
1. Do they go to the cinema much?
2. What kind of films are they into? Anything in particular?
3. Have they seen any films recently?
4. What did they think of them?

LANGUAGE PATTERNS

> Write the sentences in your language. Translate them back into English. Compare your English to the original.
> It's (not) the kind of thing you can watch and just switch off.
> It's (not) the kind of music you can dance to.
> It's (not) the kind of film you'd take your kids to see.
> It's (not) the kind of thing you'd like.
> It's the kind of music my dad listens to.
> It's the kind of thing they sell in airport bookshops.

CONVERSATION PRACTICE

A **Work in pairs. With a different partner, have conversations starting *Do you read / listen to music / watch TV / go to the cinema much?* Ask further questions like those you heard in *Listening*. Use as much of the language from these pages as you can.**

SPEAKING

A **Work in pairs. Discuss these questions.**
- Which of the following would you classify as art?

graffiti	product design	furniture	pop videos
animation	video games	fashion	advertising

- Are there any other things you regard as art.
- Do you have a favourite piece of art?
- Do you ever go to art galleries or exhibitions?
- What was the last one you went to? What was it like?

VOCABULARY Talking about pictures

A **Look at the definitions below and discuss which adjectives describe the painting on this page.**
1 If a painting has a **sombre** mood, it looks serious and sad.
2 If a painting is **lifelike**, it looks very realistic.
3 If it's **pretty**, it is nice and pleasant to look at.
4 If a painting is **dramatic**, it contains a lot of exciting action.
5 If it looks **dated**, it is no longer fashionable or relevant.
6 If it's **atmospheric**, a painting creates a special mood – such as a feeling of romance or mystery.
7 **Abstract** paintings show an artist's feelings or thoughts – rather than realistic objects or events.
8 If it's **ambiguous**, the meaning of the work isn't clear – it's **open to interpretation**.
9 An **intimate** painting shows private moments in someone's life.

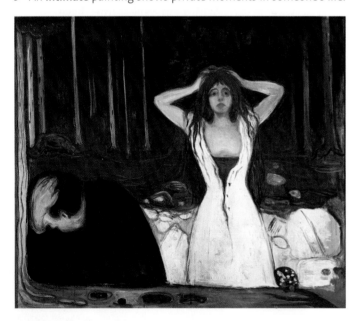

B **Which of these sentences about the painting above do you agree with?**
1 The dark colours create a sombre mood.
2 She looks as if she's pulling her hair out.
3 She's obviously crazy.
4 She seems to have just woken up.
5 The man in the corner appears to be praying.
6 They both look very upset. I get the impression someone's died.
7 They look like a couple. They could well be lovers.
8 It must be night-time because all the colours are so dark.

C **Cover exercise B. Complete these sentences about other paintings using words from exercise B.**
1 I think it could .... be Spain or Italy in this picture.
2 Everyone looks .... they're having a really good time in this picture.
3 I get the .... they've been arguing. They .... really fed up with each other.
4 They've .... just moved in and are redecorating the whole flat, from the look of it.
5 They .... all be students. That looks .... a university canteen to me.
6 Everyone in this picture .... to be queuing or waiting for something.

LISTENING

You are going to hear a guide in an art gallery telling a group of visitors about the large painting on the right.

A **Work in pairs. Describe what you can see in the paintings on the right. Use language and structures from *Vocabulary: Talking about pictures*. Then discuss these questions.**
- Which of the two portraits do you prefer? Why?
- Can you see any parallels between the two works?

B **1.4 Listen and answer these questions.**
1 When was the painting done?
2 Who are the couple in the painting?
3 What's the relationship between this painting and the painting by Jan van Eyck?
4 Why did the painter include the lilies and the cat?
5 What happened to the couple after the painting was finished?
6 Which five adjectives from exercise A of *Vocabulary: Talking about pictures* does the guide use?

GRAMMAR Adjectives and adverbs

> Adjectives are often used before nouns. Also, the verbs *be, look, become, seem, get, taste*, etc. (sometimes called 'linking' verbs) are often followed by adjectives.
>
> We use adverbs to modify a verb, an adjective, another adverb or a whole clause or sentence. Most adverbs are formed by adding *-ly* to the adjective, but some can have the same form as the adjective. Examples include *fast, hard* and *later*.

A **Choose the correct form in these sentences about the listening.**

1 This may strike you as a *fairly / fair* conventional portrait.
2 He's *pointedly / pointed* looking away from us.
3 The work is a very *ambiguously / ambiguous* piece.
4 It was painted *shortly / short* after their wedding.
5 It's *loosely / loose* based on a 15th century work.
6 *Unfortunate / Unfortunately*, Mr. Clark had *frequently / frequent* affairs during their five-year marriage. This played a part in their *eventually / eventual* divorce, and explains the friction that seems *apparently / apparent* between them.
7 *Sadly / sad*, Ossie Clark later fell into bankruptcy and addiction, and his life ended *tragically / tragic* when he was murdered.

B **Explain your choices to a partner. Use the explanation box above to help you.**

▶ **Need help? Read the grammar reference on page 137.**

PRONUNCIATION Adverbs describing sentences and clauses

> We often emphasise the stress on adverbs that describe sentences and clauses – and pause slightly before continuing.

A **Practise saying 1–6. Emphasise the stress on the adverbs.**

1 *Interestingly*, the painting used to have a different title.
2 *Actually*, no-one knows who the painter was.
3 *Sadly*, she died at the age of only 35.
4 The painting sold last year for $18 million, but, *amazingly*, van Gogh himself sold none in his lifetime.
5 *Incredibly*, Mozart was only six when he started performing in public.
6 The painting was damaged in a fire and, *unfortunately*, it couldn't be restored.

B 🎵 1.5 **Listen and compare how the speakers said the sentences. Then listen again and repeat them.**

SPEAKING

A **Work in groups of three to four. Think of a painting you like – or use the Internet to find one. You are going to present the picture to the rest of the group. First, make notes about:**
- what's happening in the painting.-
- the impressions / feelings you have about it.
- information about the painter and / or people in the picture (you can invent this!).
- additional comments (*sadly / interestingly / actually* etc.).

READING Part 1

A Work in pairs. Discuss these questions.
- Have you ever read a book or seen a film and thought the plot was very similar to another film / book?
- Which films / books were they? How were they similar?
- Did it bother you? Why? / Why not?

B On the next page is the first part of an article about common plots. Read it and then answer the questions in pairs.
1 Why does the writer claim we often find films predictable?
2 What are the main stages of the *Overcoming the Monster* plot? Can you think of any other similar stories?
3 Can you think of any examples of:
- famous monsters / baddies?
- fatal flaws that monsters / baddies have?
- the kinds of huge challenges heroes can face?

READING Part 2

Christopher Booker identified seven basic plots – and you have seen one outline. Work in three groups, A, B and C. Each person in each group will now read two more basic plots.

A **Group A:** read the text in File 1 on page 156.
Group B: read the text in File 16 on page 161.
Group C: read the text in File 12 on page 159.

B Work with students from the other two groups. Tell each other as much as you can about the plots you read about.

C In the same groups, try to remember in which plot someone:
1 seeks revenge.
2 is living in a society under threat.
3 gets away with a crime.
4 is wrongly accused of something.
5 makes an initial breakthrough before facing a series of setbacks.
6 wears a disguise.
7 enters a downward spiral.
8 slowly comes to recognise their own flaws.
9 is bullied.
10 is transported to a totally different social setting.
11 has to resist the temptation to join the forces of darkness.
12 gets separated from a group, a friend or a partner.

D Complete the sentences about books and films with words from exercise C.
1 The kids find a magic door and when they go through it, they are .... to a magical new world.
2 Once his wife leaves him, the main character enters a downward .... of drink and drugs.
3 As a child, the main character sees the murder of his father. As an adult, he is determined to seek ....
4 He gets .... from the group he's travelling with in a crowded station – and that's when it all starts going wrong!
5 The hero is a computer-obsessed teenager who wears glasses – and who's .... by the big kids in his school.
6 The main character tries hard to resist the .... of his new secretary, but in the end he fails!

SPEAKING

A Work in pairs. Discuss these questions.
- Do you know any of the stories shown in the pictures?
- What do you think of them?
- Which of Christopher Booker's seven basic plots do you think fit the stories you know? Why?
- Can you think of any films / books / stories that don't have one of the seven basic plots?

B Now think of a book, film or story you know well that has a similar plot to one of Christopher Booker's seven basic plots. Tell a partner as much of the story as you can. Can your partner guess what you are talking about?

HEARD IT ALL BEFORE

Ever been watching a film or reading a book and had the feeling you've heard it all before? You know the boy's going to get the girl, the baddie – the bad guy – is going to be killed, or the team will win their last game. What's really surprising is that we don't have this feeling more often, because according to the writer Christopher Booker, nearly all stories are based around just seven basic plots. Each kind of plot features the same character types and the same typical events over and over again.

Take the first plot, which he calls *Overcoming the Monster*. There are ancient stories like the Greek myth of Theseus killing the monstrous Minotaur and Biblical stories like David defeating the giant Goliath. More recently, we've had *Dracula*, the films *Jaws* and *Star Wars* and thrillers like James Bond, where the monster is a baddie who wants to rule the world. All these stories contain almost exactly the same elements.

In this plot, there's a community threatened by a monster – and a hero who is called to save them. The hero prepares to meet the monster, a process which often includes being given some special weapon or being told of a particular weakness that the monster has – its fatal flaw. To begin with, as the hero approaches where the monster lives, everything goes according to plan. However, when the hero finally sees the monster for the first time, they realise the huge challenge they face. Things start to go wrong and they end up trapped. They're about to be killed when at the last moment they make an amazing escape. They then succeed in destroying the monster – usually with the help of the special weapon they've been given or by taking advantage of the monster's only weakness.

It makes you wonder if any story is really original.

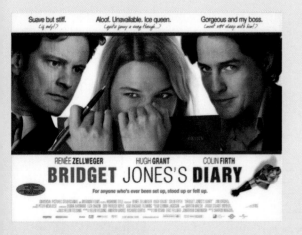

02 SIGHTSEEING

In this unit you learn how to:
- show people around your town / city
- describe places in more detail
- agree using synonyms
- talk about theme parks and rides
- hear short forms more easily

Grammar
- Non-defining relative clauses
- The future

Vocabulary
- Buildings and areas
- Festivals and carnivals

Reading
Ten days at the Venice Carnival

Listening
- Driving round Belgrade
- Theme parks and rides

SPEAKING

A Imagine the following people are coming to visit your town / city on holiday for a week.
- a school trip of twenty 13-year-olds
- four 18-year-olds
- a young couple with two kids
- a retired couple

Decide where you would recommend they go. Think about sights to see, restaurants, nightlife, cultural activities, shops, and so on.

B Work in groups. Explain your ideas.

LANGUAGE PATTERNS

Write the sentences in your language. Translate them back into English. Compare your English to the original.

Where would you recommend they go?
So what would you recommend I do?
Can you recommend any good shops?
Can you recommend a good hotel?
A friend of mine recommended that I try the Old Town.
My brother recommended that we book in advance.

VOCABULARY Buildings and areas

A In pairs, look at the words below and decide:
- if they describe buildings, areas or both.
- if they are positive or negative descriptions.

up-and-coming	stunning	trendy	grand
rough	affluent	high-rise	hideous
run-down	residential	deprived	historic

B Complete the sentences with the correct form of the verbs in the box.

| base | date back | dominate | open up |
| soar | knock down | steer clear | renovate |

1 It's really run-down. It really needs ....
2 It's a rough part of town. I'd .... of it after dark.
3 It's very historic. It .... over 300 years.
4 It's an up-and-coming area. Property prices round there .... at the moment.
5 It's hideous! It's so ugly! It really should be ....
6 It's very trendy. Loads of new boutiques and cafés .... round there recently.
7 It's very affluent. All the embassies are .... there.
8 It's a very grand building. It .... the square.

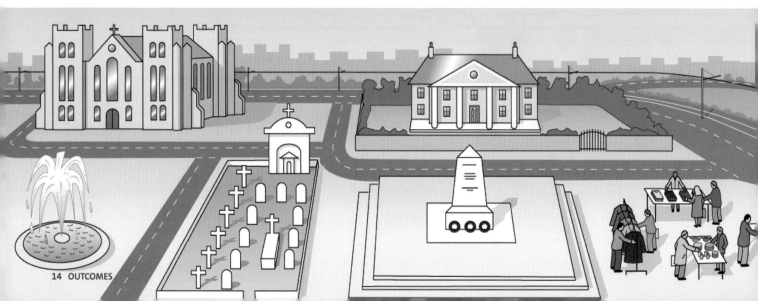

LISTENING

You are going to hear a Scottish woman, May, talking to a Serbian woman, Ivana, as they drive through Belgrade.

A 🔊 **2.1 Listen and take notes on what you hear about each of the following places. Then compare your ideas in pairs.**

New Belgrade	
the Arena	*Big concerts / sports events held there. One of the biggest entertainment venues in Europe.*
the River Sava	
Manakova Kuca	
St. Mark's Church	*Built late 1930s – on site of older church. Contains tomb of a great Serbian emperor.*
Kalemegdan Fortress	
the Victor monument	
Dedinje	

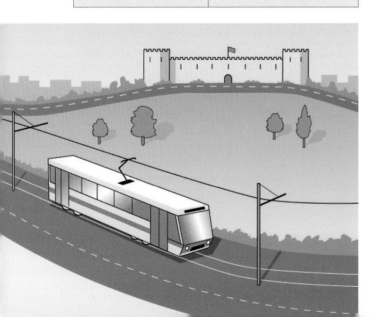

GRAMMAR

> Non-defining relative clauses add extra information to a sentence. This information is not essential. The clauses always follow a comma. They start with words like *which, most of which, by which time, where, when, whose, who,* etc.
>
> Over to the right is the Arena, *where all the big concerts and sports events are held.*

A Rewrite each of the pairs of sentences below as one sentence. Use non-defining relative clauses starting with the words above.
1 It contains the tomb of Stefan Dusan. He was perhaps the greatest Serbian emperor.
2 We're coming up to Dedinje. Dedinje is one of the more affluent parts of the city.
3 Just behind us, over to the right, is the Arena. All the big concerts and sports events are held there.
4 I went to school with a woman called Zora. Her son plays professional football in England now.
5 I started working in that office over there in 2003. Even then, the area was already starting to boom.
6 We produce bathroom tiles. We export most of them to northern Europe.

▶ **Need help? Read the grammar reference on page 138.**

DEVELOPING CONVERSATIONS
Agreeing using synonyms

> When people give opinions, we can show we agree by using a synonym.
>
> A: What a lovely day!
> B: Yeah, it's nice, isn't it?

A In pairs, take turns saying and agreeing with the opinions below. Agree using synonyms.
1 That's a really hideous building!
2 All the houses round here are amazing.
3 That church is incredible!
4 The river looks wonderful, doesn't it?
5 This is pretty run-down, isn't it?
6 This seems like quite a wealthy area.

CONVERSATION PRACTICE

A Either imagine you are driving a friend round the town shown on these pages or write the names of – or draw – places you know. Think of details about the places. Decide why they are important. Role-play a similar conversation to the one you heard in *Listening*. Then swap roles.

VOCABULARY Festivals and carnivals

A Which of the words in the box can you see in the photographs on the next page?

a fireworks display	a costume	a parade
a steel drum band	a float	a sound system
a bonfire	a mask	silly string
confetti		

B Match the nouns from exercise A to the groups of words they go with.
1   make your own ~ / wear a ~ / hide behind a ~
2   build a ~ / ride on a ~ / a ~ in the shape of a fish
3   spray ~ everywhere / get covered in ~
4   set up a ~ / a really loud ~ / hire a ~
5   dress up in a ~ / a very ornate ~ / wear national ~
6   make a ~ / sit round a ~ / throw wood on a ~
7   listen to a ~ / form a ~ / play in a ~ / book a ~
8   watch a ~ / a spectacular ~ / cancel a ~ / miss a ~
9   hold a ~ / take part in a ~ / a ~ through town
10   throw ~ / be showered with ~

C Tell a partner about a time you saw / wore / used five of the nouns from exercise A. Explain where you were and what happened.

READING

You are going to read an e-mail about the Venice Carnival.

A Before you read, discuss the question in groups.
- What do you know about Venice? Think about its history, its location, its sights and its carnival.

B Read the email on the next page and add the relative clauses below in the right gaps.
a   which are very ornate and beautiful
b   during which time people fasted
c   which I hope you enjoy
d   which would've been almost impossible
e   which can give you a real shock
f   which are these pastry things full of cream or custard or nuts
g   where they hold the big costume parade
h   which is great
i   who I'm sure you remember
j   who used to look after the dead and dying

C Decide if these sentences about the e–mail are true (T) or false (F). Then look back and underline the sentences that support your decisions.
1   Chiaki, Kyeong Jin and Nina all studied together.
2   Hotels are a bit more expensive during carnival.
3   Chiaki preferred the modern costumes.
4   Carnival celebrates the end of Lent.
5   Traditionally, people ate a lot less during Lent.
6   Chiaki sprayed some strangers with silly string.
7   She was shocked at the way people behaved.
8   Chiaki plans to send more photos.

D Find words in the email that mean the same thing as the words in *italics* in 1–8.
1   It was very kind of Nina to *let me stay at her house for free*.
2   The city was completely *full of* tourists.
3   It's *not surprising* most costumes look so good.
4   The locals generally *continue* with traditional costumes.
5   The Plague Doctor costume is quite *scary and threatening and evil*.
6   The food is delicious, but *high in calories*.
7   Venice is completely *changed in a good way* during carnival.
8   People *light and explode* fireworks all the time.

E Work in pairs. Discuss these questions.
- Do you have a carnival or festival in your town / city / area?
- Do you usually go to it?
- What does it involve? Which of the words from *Vocabulary* can you use to describe what happens?
- Have you ever been to any other carnivals or festivals? Where? When? What were they like?

F Write an email to a friend about your time at a carnival / festival in your town / city – or about another carnival / festival you have been to. Before you start writing, think about:
- the history of the event
- how long it lasted
- what the food / drink was like
- what you saw / did
- what you enjoyed best
- any problems you had
- what photos you are sending

To KyeongJin@hotmail.ml

Subject Re: Hello there

Hi Kyeong Jin,

I hope this finds you well. I'm really sorry I haven't written for so long, but the beginning of the year was really busy for me – and then I went off to Venice for the carnival. In fact, I only got back to Boston last night!

Venice was absolutely amazing. You would've loved it. I stayed with Nina,¹ .... from uni. It was really kind of her to put me up – and it meant I didn't have to struggle with trying to find a hotel, ²...! The city was completely packed with tourists for the whole ten days, and prices really shoot up.

Nina lives with her family, about ten minutes' walk from the main square, ³... on the first day. Some of the costumes were just incredible – people spend months and months preparing, so it's no wonder they look so good, really. Lots of tourists were dressed-up in all kinds of crazy outfits – giant rabbits, pirates, even hot dogs – but the locals tend to stick to traditional costumes, ⁴..., and they all wear masks as well. My favourite costume is called the Plague Doctor. It's really scary and sinister and I was told it's based on real doctors, ⁵... when the plague hit Venice.

Apparently, *carnevale*, the word the Italians use, comes from Latin and means 'farewell to meat'. Traditionally, the carnival took place in the week leading up to Lent, the 40 days before Easter, ⁶ .... That's why food is really important during carnival, and I ate lots and lots of *frittelle*, ⁷... – fattening, but really delicious!

Venice is as beautiful as everyone says: very romantic and atmospheric. All through the carnival, though, it's transformed as they have big fireworks displays, bonfires, parties and so on, and all the kids throw confetti everywhere and spray shaving foam or that silly string stuff everywhere, ⁸... – unless it lands on you! Mind you, we ended up buying some ourselves and joined in the fun! Attack is the best form of defence, right? People also set off fireworks all the time, ⁹... if you're not expecting it. I nearly had a heart attack a couple of times.

I've attached a few photos, ¹⁰... . I was going to send more, but I didn't want to make your computer crash like I managed to last time! I've uploaded loads more onto my website, if you fancy having a look.

Anyway, hope to hear from you soon.

All the best,
Chiaki

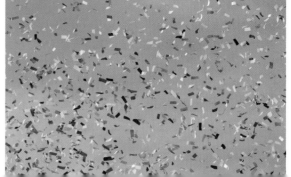

SPEAKING

A Rank the pictures above from 1 (like most) to 8 (like least). Explain your choices to your partner. You might want to use some of this language:

> I'm scared / terrified of heights.
> It looks exciting / scary / terrifying / fun / a bit tame / boring.
> I love things that spin round / go fast / go upside-down / you slide down.
> I'd get splashed / dizzy / sick / tired / bored.
> It'd really set your pulse racing.
> You'd get a great view.

LISTENING

You are going to hear six short extracts with people talking about rides and theme parks.

A ◈ 2.2 Listen and decide which pictures above are most similar to the attractions the speaker(s) in each extract are talking about.

B Listen again and decide which speaker is:
1 protesting about a proposal
2 promoting something
3 talking about a forthcoming trip
4 feeling unwell
5 relating an experience
6 complaining about having to do something

C Explain your choices to a partner and see if they agree.

D In pairs, try to complete these collocations from the extracts. Look at the audioscript on page 165 to check.
1 The riders are .... into seats.
2 They .... 20 metres down into total darkness.
3 There are no height .... on the boats.
4 I was holding really ....
5 It falls really .... – like almost vertical.
6 It has all these loops and .... and turns.
7 The company is applying for planning ....
8 We're .... a campaign.
9 They put a further .... on water resources.
10 They .... armour.

E In groups, discuss the questions.
1 Have you ever been to an amusement park / fairground? When? Where? What rides did you go on? Did you do anything else? Was it good?
2 Have your parents ever done anything that you thought was unfair? What?
3 What different strains could tourism put on society or on the environment?

GRAMMAR The future

> Remember there's no one form to talk about the future in English. At different times we use the present simple, the present continuous, *be going to* + verb, *will*, *might*, *shall*, *have got to*, *be due / bound to*, etc.

A The following sentences contain incorrect uses of future forms. In pairs, try to correct them.

1 This year we *introduce* a new ride.
2 It's *bound to* officially open in June.
3 I can tell you it's *really setting* your pulse racing.
4 What *do* we go on next?
5 You *will* come with us next time. It's so cool.
6 This is *due to worsen* the situation in the future.
7 Still, I *go* to the medieval show anyway.
8 I think I *will* be sick!
9 I *get* you a tissue.

B Compare your ideas with the audioscript on page 165. Explain the uses of the different forms.

▶ Need help? Read the grammar reference on page 139.

C In 1–6, one or two of the sentences are incorrect. In pairs, discuss your choices.

1 a The move will improve things in the future.

> Sometimes different forms can be used without changing the meaning. For example, *you can use will or be going to* for predictions, but not the present continuous.

   b The move is improving things in the future.
   c The move is going to improve things in the future.
2 a We're going to meet some friends later.
   b We're meeting some friends later.
   c We meet some friends later.
3 a I think I'll faint.
   b I think I'm going to faint.
   c I'm due to faint.
4 a Don't worry. I'll pay for this.
   b Shall I pay for this?
   c It's OK. I pay for this.
5 a You come with us next time.
   b You'll have to come with us next time.
   c You've got to come with us next time.
6 a I might go to the shops later, so I'll get the paper then.
   b It's possible I go to the shops later, so I'll get the paper then.
   c When I go to the shops later, I'll get the paper.

D Some verbs are often used in the present continuous to describe plans and feelings about the future. Complete the short text with the correct verbs in the present continuous.

think	plan	hope	expect	dread	look forward

I [1].................... really .... to having some time off in the summer, because I've been studying really hard. I [2]....................... of going to Germany in August to see some friends I met while I was studying there. I've spoken to a friend in Stuttgart and he [3]........................ already .... to rent a car and drive me round the country! We [4]....................... also .... to see Oasis in concert if we can get tickets, because they're playing in Berlin on the 25th. Of course, it still depends a bit on how my exams go. It's not that I [5]....................... to fail or anything, but they are quite tough and I do get pretty nervous. Actually, to tell you the truth, I [6]....................... them and I can't wait for the academic year to end!

PRONUNCIATION Elision and linking

A 🔊 2.3 Listen to the sentences from *Listening* and write what you think you hear. Then compare your ideas in pairs. What are the formal full forms in each case?

You get really nervous, you know, with anticipation [1]........................ it goes quite slowly and I was holding really tight and going 'This is [2]....................... be awful. I [3]....................... get off.'

> In spoken English, grammar structures and other words often get shortened and joined together. For example, we say *wanna*, *'cos*, *gonna*, *gotta*, *shoulda*, etc. instead of *want to*, *because*, *going to*, *(have) got to*, *should have*, etc. However, don't use these forms in formal writing.

B 🔊 2.4 Listen and repeat what you hear.

C Listen again and write the sentences with their correct full forms.

SPEAKING

A Work in groups. Tell each other about:
- something you're expecting to happen soon
- something you're hoping to do in the not-too-distant future
- something you're thinking of doing in the next week
- something you're planning to do when you next have a holiday
- something you're dreading
- something you're really looking forward to

Your partner should ask questions to find out more.

03 THINGS YOU NEED

In this unit you learn how to:
- talk about a wide range of objects
- describe what things are for
- explain what's wrong with things you've bought

Grammar
- *so, if* and *to* for describing purpose
- Indirect questions

Vocabulary
- Useful things
- Word families
- Problems with things

Reading
- I am ... Mr Trebus

Listening
- Asking for things
- Trying to get a refund

VOCABULARY Useful things

A Look at the pictures in File 15 on page 160 and discuss the questions.
1 Are there any things you've never used? Why not?
2 Which of the objects do you use: all the time / regularly / now and again / hardly ever?
3 Do you have any of these things on you now? Which of the things do you have at home?
4 Which of the things did you NOT know in English before?

B In groups, add as many of the things on page 160 to the categories below without looking at the pictures. Which group can remember the most words?
- the office / study: ....
- the kitchen: ....
- clothes: ....
- DIY: ....
- first aid: ....

NATIVE SPEAKER ENGLISH

DIY

DIY stands for *do-it-yourself*. DIY means all those jobs in the house which it's cheaper to do yourself – like painting, mending things, putting up shelves, etc.

I'm not very good at DIY. I'd rather pay someone else to do the work in my house. My dad gets in a bad mood when he does DIY.
There's a DIY store down the road.

C Work in pairs. Test each other by asking the questions below. Use as many words from page 160 as you can.

Student A: look at page 160
Student B: keep your book closed
Student A: ask: What do you need
- to tie things together?
- to put up a poster or a notice?
- to wash and hang up your clothes to dry?
- if there's a crack in your roof and it's leaking?
- so you can mend a rip in your clothing?

Student B: look at page 160
Student A: keep your book closed
Student B: ask: What do you need
- to keep papers together?
- to put up a picture on the wall?
- to prevent something rubbing or to protect your body?
- if you knock over a cup and it smashes on the floor?
- so you can see better in dark places?

GRAMMAR *so, if* and *to* for describing purpose

A Look back at *Vocabulary* exercise C and see how *so, if* and *to* were used to show the purpose of things. Then complete the following sentences.
1 I need some tape .... put up a poster on the wall.
2 Can I have a cloth .... I can wipe the table?
3 It's a thing you can put on your heel .... your shoe's rubbing.

▶ Need help? Read the grammar reference on page 140.

B Why would you use or need the following things? Think of one common and one less common purpose for each. For example:
a cloth
You use it to wipe the table after you've had dinner.
If you can't open the top of a jar, you can put a cloth over the top so you can grip it better.

| a thread | a nail | a bandage | a lighter | a bucket |

DEVELOPING CONVERSATIONS
Explaining and checking

A ⏺ 3.1 **Listen to two conversations. Which of the things in the pictures below are they talking about?**

Look at the ways the speakers explained things:
A: *That stuff – it's a bit like chewing gum or something*
A: *They have a sort of springy gate thing*

You can check you understand using these patterns:
B: *What? You mean blu-tac?*
B: *What? You mean the thing you use to connect yourself to the rope?*

B **Think of things that you don't know the name of. Use some of the words above to explain them to a partner. Your partner should check they have understood and draw what you have explained.**

LISTENING

You are going to hear a conversation where a man asks for something.

A ⏺ 3.2 **Listen and answer these questions**
1   What does he want?
2   What for?
3   What does he use instead?
4   What else does he need – and why?

B **Work in pairs. Try to complete the sentences from the conversation. Then listen again to check your answers.**
1   I don't think there's one here. .... use a knife?
2   You need a stick .... to push it down.
3   Would a pencil .... ?
4   It wouldn't be ....
5   What about a wooden spoon? .... the handle.
6   Yeah, that .... do.
7   Don't worry about it. These ....
8   You might want to rub some salt into that shirt or ....

SPEAKING

A **Discuss the questions in groups.**
•   Can you think of a situation where you didn't have the things you needed and you had to improvise or make do?
•   Do you know any ways of removing these kinds of stains?

wax	oil	coffee	grass	paint

CONVERSATION PRACTICE

You are going to take turns to ask for different things and to solve different problems.
Student A: look at File 17 on page 161.
Student B: look at File 21 on page 162.
Then use this guide for each conversation:

Have you got ....?	
	Sorry .... *What do you want it for?*
Explain situation	
	Offer alternative: *Will a ... do? / Can't you use..?*
Accept – or explain why not	
Continue the conversation till you find a good solution.	

SPEAKING

A Look at the photos below of some things that people collect. Write six questions you could ask someone who collects things like this.

B Tell a partner about something you collect / used to collect. Your partner should ask the six questions they wrote. They might need to change the grammar of the questions. If you've never collected anything, use the pictures for ideas.

READING

A Read the blog about a man called Mr Trebus and answer the questions.
1 What did Mr Trebus collect?
2 How does the blogger say he is similar to Trebus?
3 What reasons are given for Trebus and the blogger keeping things?
4 Are you at all similar to Trebus and the blogger?

B Correct these sentences about Mr Trebus. Look at the blog again if you need to.
1 His house became a fire **hazard**.
2 He was a **veteran** of the Vietnam War.
3 He was a navy **commander**.
4 The **trauma** of his father's death caused his obsession.
5 He **settled** in Birmingham after the war.
6 He **sorted** the junk into piles of different colours.
7 He **acquired** a number of valuable paintings.
8 The neighbours complained about **infestations** of cockroaches.
9 He **resisted** arrest by the police.

C Now translate the words in bold into your language.

VOCABULARY Word families

A In groups, think of words ending with these suffixes and then answer these questions
• Which of these suffixes do NOT form nouns?
• What kind of words do these other suffixes form?

-al	- ise	-ion	-less	-ness	-y	-ity	-ism	-ment	-ious

B Complete 1–8 with the nouns from the blog based on the underlined words.
1 He's <u>obsessed</u>   have an ....
2 He's been <u>evicted</u>   face ....
3 He's <u>cautious</u>   show great ....
4 I'm <u>afraid</u>   overcome my .... of flying
5 He's well-<u>intentioned</u>   have good ....
6 I'm very <u>optimistic</u>   be full of ....
7 He's really <u>mean</u>   it's pure ....
8 He's <u>pessimistic</u>   despite the ....

C In what ways are Mr Trebus and / or the blogger:

obsessive?	well-intentioned?	pessimistic?
optimistic?	cautious?	mean?

D Do you – or does anyone you know – have these characteristics? Give examples of their behaviour.

SPEAKING

A Read the comments which have been added in response to the blog. Decide which you like or agree with most. Discuss your choice with a partner.

B Write your own comment to add to the blog. It could be your opinion of the blog / the blogger, an example of Trebus-like behaviour or a comment about one of the other comments.

C Pass your comments round the class and discuss them. Which comment or comments do you like the most / least? Why?

I am ... Mr Trebus

Some years ago, an 80-year-old Polish war veteran hit the headlines when the local council forced him out of his own house in London because it had become a health hazard. Mr. Trebus, who'd had to leave his hometown in Poland after Germany invaded at the beginning of the Second World War, later served as a tank commander in the British army. Perhaps it was the trauma of what he lost when he left Poland that caused his obsession – who knows? – but after he settled in London, he began collecting all kinds of things. He would tour the local neighbourhood recovering things from bins that others had seen as mere rubbish. He then took this junk home and sorted it into piles of similar things: a room packed with vacuum cleaners, a corner for old doors, another for windows. He also managed to acquire practically every record Elvis Presley ever made.

However, as he filled his house, his wife left him and the neighbours increasingly complained about rat infestations. By the time the council came to evict the old man, he had just a tiny space in his kitchen to live in, surrounded by stacks of old newspapers and children's toys. Yet he resisted eviction, accusing the local council of acting like dictators and arguing that everything he kept was useful

He was clearly over-the-top, but let's face it, there's a bit of Mr. Trebus in most of us. How many collectors do you know? Personally, I have boxes of old comics in the attic, which I don't read, but can't get rid of. Who hasn't made some impulse purchase which has then been left lying in some cupboard for years? How many of you have a drawer like mine in the kitchen: a drawer full of caution and fear, stuffed with good intentions (albeit unfulfilled); packed with optimism and meanness and, of course, all rubbish? In my drawer, there are a number of instructions and guarantees for things I've bought over the years, just in case they break down or I forget how to use them. Considering one of these was for a chair, that shows a good deal of pessimism – I mean, what can go wrong with a chair? There are also a large number of dead batteries which I've been meaning to take to the recycling centre and a number of leaflets – one about a local gym I still haven't joined, THREE about sponsoring a child in a developing country and several advertising a local takeaway which has now closed down. There are various odd screws, nails and pins (I'd have to buy new packs if I didn't keep them), a broken cup (I must buy some glue to stick it back together), and finally a large number of foreign coins, quite a few preceding the introduction of the euro (they might be collector's items one day, they might be valuable!).

I AM...

- ▶ ... Fernando Alonso
- ▶ ... Frankenstein
- ▶ ... that man talking to a tree
- ▶ ... an estate agent
- ▶ ... the man at a customer call centre
- ▶ ... Winona Ryder
- ▶ ... George W Bush
- ▶ ... a petty criminal

Comments

☞ **Redyellowblue**	Come on! Get a life! Just throw it all out!
☞ **Dani79**	Nice blog. On top of my cupboard, there's a box of stuff I did when I was at primary school. I read your blog and I thought 'what do I need it for?' But then I looked at those cute drawings, my funny handwriting and ... I couldn't get rid of it and put the box away again. Don't feel guilty about it!
☞ **TimothyR1975**	So we're all a bit like Trebus, but it's difficult to sympathise when you live with someone like my flatmate, who has three hundred pairs of shoes. Are you suggesting I should just put up with it?
☞ **Hardasnails**	I blame DIY. You want to put up one shelf and you need a whole garage of tools to do it. I thought I had solved this when I bought a three-in-one power tool, which could make holes, cut things and put in screws, but in fact it never really worked. So now I have that tool, plus the drill, saw and set of screwdrivers I had to buy to replace it.
☞ **Greengoddess**	Trebus showed how wasteful human beings are! He's a hero!

SPEAKING

A **Work in groups. Look at the reasons people had for taking things back to a shop and then discuss questions 1–4.**

It was a present from a friend and I didn't really like it.

There was something wrong with it.

I realised after I'd bought it that I could get the same thing cheaper elsewhere.

It wasn't the same as the sample I'd seen in the shop.

I really liked it when I was in the shop, but by the time I got it home, I'd changed my mind.

It didn't actually fit me as well as I thought it did when I was trying it on in the shop.

None of my friends liked it very much.

It didn't match the description I'd read in the shop.

1 In which of the situations do you think the shop has an obligation to refund the customer?
2 Have you ever returned something for these or any other reasons?
3 What did you actually say when you went to the shop to return the goods?
4 What was the result? Did you get your money back or what?

LISTENING

You are going to hear a man trying to return something to a shop.

A 🔊 3.3 **Listen and answer these questions.**
1 What does the customer want to return? Why?
2 How successful is he?

B **Work in pairs. Decide if these sentences about the conversation are true or false. Can you remember what was actually said? Listen again to check your ideas.**
1 The tie was a Christmas present.
2 It was purchased last week.
3 The man doesn't think the tie suits him.
4 He's brought the receipt with him.
5 He knows his girlfriend paid for the tie by cheque.
6 The shop assistant tries to calm the man down.
7 The tie cost almost twenty pounds.

C **Tell a partner what you would you do next if you were the customer.**

D 🔊 3.4 **You are going to hear two different possible endings to the conversation. As you listen, think about these questions.**
1 Which one is most similar to how you would react?
2 In which ending does the customer sound:
   frustrated?   anxious?
   resigned?   sarcastic?
3 Which is the better way of dealing with the situation? Why?

LANGUAGE PATTERNS

Write the sentences in your language. Translate them back into English. Compare your English to the original.
Without meaning to be rude – how can you be sure it actually came from us?
Without wishing to be too unkind, he's not very clever.
I do it without letting my girlfriend know.
We can't really take it back without proof of purchase.
He went without food for ten days
They went without the children.

GRAMMAR Indirect questions

> When you want to be polite or if you think the other person might not know the answer, make indirect questions like this:
>
> *Would / Do you happen to know... ?*
> *Do you know ... ?*
> *Do you think ... ?*
> *I was wondering ...?*
>
> The rest of the question (after *if / where / who*, etc.) follows the normal word order found in statements (noun followed by verb).
>
> *Would you happen to know how your girlfriend paid for it?*
> *Do you know if it was by cheque or by credit card?*

A **Make the two indirect questions in the box above into direct questions.**

B **Rewrite the direct questions below as indirect questions, using the sentence starters given.**
1 How long does the guarantee last?
Do you happen to know .... ?
2 Sorry. Where are the toilets?
Sorry. Do you know .... ?
3 Excuse me. Do you sell wire?
Excuse me. Do you know .... ?
4 Hello. Could I speak to the manager?
Hello. I was wondering .... ?
5 When will the sofa be delivered?
Would you happen to know
.... ?
6 Sorry to bother you, but could you bring me the next size up?
Sorry to bother you, but do you think
.... ?

C **Match the responses below to the questions above.**
a Yes. There should be some in the hardware department on the second floor.
b I'm not sure, actually, but it's usually at least a year.
c If you go up the stairs, the ladies' is on your left.
d Of course. I'll just grab you one from the racks.
e It says on the computer it should go out tomorrow.
f Certainly. I'll put you through now.

D ♨ **3.5 Listen and check your answers. Practise asking and answering the questions. Try to sound polite.**

▶ Need help? Read the grammar reference on page 140.

VOCABULARY Problems with things

A **Complete the sentences with the words in the box.**

outfit	part	flash	strap	screen

1 The .... keeps freezing every time I turn it on.
2 There must be a .... missing. I've looked everywhere for it, but can't see it anywhere.
3 The .... doesn't work properly, so all the pictures always come out too dark.
4 It doesn't go with the rest of the .... I want to wear.
5 The first time I used it, the .... broke!

cracked	scratched	ripped	allergic	funny

6 It makes a really .... noise when I change gears.
7 I had some kind of .... reaction to it. It gave me a horrible itchy rash.
8 It's .... Look. There's a big hole from here to here.
9 It's .... Every time I try and play it, it jumps.
10 It's .... Look! It leaks whenever I put water in it.

B **Match the problems above to the people in the pictures on the opposite page.**

C **Have you ever had any of these problems with things you have bought?**

SPEAKING

You are going to role-play some conversations between the shop assistant and the different customers in the picture on the opposite page.

A **Before you start, look through the audioscripts about the customer trying to return the tie on page 166 and underline any expressions you want to use.**

B **Now have the conversations. Take turns at being different customers. Use as much language from these pages as possible.**

04 SOCIETY

In this unit you learn how to:
- talk about the government and their policies
- talk about how the economy is doing
- respond to complaints
- discuss social issues

Grammar
- *So / such*
- *the..., the...* + comparatives

Vocabulary
- The government, economics and society

Reading
- Common wealth economics for a crowded planet

Listening
- What do you think of your president?
- In the news

VOCABULARY
The government, economics and society

> We often use *they* and *their* to refer to the government – or to other groups of officials like the council, the police, etc.
>
> *The government's OK. They've done a lot to improve education. We're beginning to see the effects of their policies.*

A Use the extra information in 1–11 to guess the meanings of the words in **bold**.

1 The government's made a huge **difference** since they came to power. They've done a lot to help the poor.
2 Crime is almost **non-existent**. You can leave your front door unlocked at night if you want to.
3 There's a **recession**. The economy's in a total mess.
4 They're **soft** on drugs. They should introduce stricter penalties.
5 A lot of companies have **gone bankrupt** recently, so unemployment's going up.
6 The economy's **booming**. Lots of new businesses are starting up and plenty of new jobs are being created.
7 With so little rain, there are a lot of water **shortages** so the government's investigating new policies to help.
8 Inflation has really **shot up** over the last year or so. Everything's suddenly much more expensive.
9 Their policies have **boosted** our **standing** in the world. Other countries see us as more important than before.
10 Their policies are **undermining** national unity. It's made society less stable. They could destroy the country if they continue.
11 People are struggling **to make ends meet**, because wages are so low and the cost of living's so high.

LANGUAGE PATTERNS

> **Write the sentences in your language. Translate them back into English. Compare your English to the original.**
> They've done a lot to help the poor.
> They're doing a huge amount to fight corruption.
> They haven't done enough to boost the economy.
> They've done little to combat rising crime.
> They're not doing anything for young people.

B In groups, discuss whether you think the sentences are true or false for your country, and explain why.

LISTENING

You are going to hear two university students from different nations talking about politics and issues in their countries.

A ♦ 4.1 Listen and take notes on the political and economic situation in each country? Whose country sounds like it's in a better situation? Why?

B Try to complete the sentences with the missing prepositions. Listen again to check your answers.

1 Whenever I see him .... TV he comes across as being OK.
2 He's done nothing .... people like me – just put up tuition fees for students.
3 Tell me .... it! I'm going to be so far .... debt by the time I graduate, I'll be paying it back for years.
4 They've been so concerned .... supposedly 'green' laws ...
5 Can't you vote .... them?
6 The opposition are so busy fighting .... themselves ...
7 I know what you mean, but there must be someone worth voting ....
8 ... our government has done a few controversial things – stuff I didn't agree ....
9 They've done a lot to cut back .... bureaucracy too.

C Discuss these questions in pairs.
- Tell your partner about recent votes (elections / things at school / things on reality TV or talent shows, etc.). Who won? Did you vote?
- Can you think of any recent controversies in the media?
- Have you heard of anyone who had problems with bureaucracy and administration?

GRAMMAR *so* and *such*

A Complete the grammar rules that follow the example sentences from *Listening* by choosing the correct words.

The opposition are so busy fighting among themselves, they're not going to make any difference.

There's such a skills shortage that companies are paying really good money now.

> *So* and *such* are often used to link cause and result. In the part of the sentence describing the cause, use ¹*so / such* before an adjective, adverb or words like much or many. Use ²*so / such* before a noun – or adjective plus noun. You ³*have to / don't have to* start the result clause with that – especially in spoken English.

▶ **Need help?** Read the grammar reference on page 141.

B Complete each sentence starter with *so* or *such*.
1 The government is .... worried about its falling popularity ...
2 Food prices have gone up .... quickly ...
3 Most people have to work .... long hours ...
4 The police made .... a mess of the investigation ...
5 The area ended up being .... polluted ....
6 The government minister was involved in .... a terrible public scandal ...

C In pairs, write a possible ending to each sentence. Then compare your ideas with another group.

D Have you heard any news stories similar to 1–6 in exercise B? What happened in the end?

DEVELOPING CONVERSATIONS
Responding to complaints

> When someone is complaining, we often show we agree by saying *I know* or *Tell me about it* and then adding a comment. When we disagree, we soften our response like this:
>
> ....
> *I know what you mean, but ...*
> *Well, maybe, but ...*

A Match the complaints in 1–6 to the responses.
1 I don't know how people can make ends meet.
2 The job market is so competitive at the moment.
3 The pace of life is so fast here.
4 There's so much crime, you can't go out at night!
5 They haven't done anything to boost tourism.
6 This country is so bureaucratic!

a I know! It's exhausting. I feel like I spend my life just rushing around.
b Tell me about it! I can only just get by and I've got a good job.
c Tell me about it! I had to fill in four forms in three different places to get a work permit!
d I know what you mean, but if you're prepared to be flexible there's plenty of work.
e Well maybe, but it's not like that everywhere. If you avoid certain areas, it's perfectly safe.
f I know what you mean, but look what they've done to improve poor areas. That's great.

B Work in pairs. Think of one extra possible way of responding to sentences 1–6.

C Take turns responding to the sentences below.
1 They're destroying the environment!
2 It's so expensive to travel abroad at the moment.
3 All politicians are corrupt.
4 The government's soft on terrorism.
5 They're doing nothing to improve state schools.
6 The government is undermining democracy.

CONVERSATION PRACTICE

A Work in pairs. Role-play a similar conversation to the one you heard in *Listening*. Look at File 8 on page 157. Decide who will take which role and then follow the instructions.

SPEAKING

A Rank these social issues from 1 (most important) to 10 (least important) in your society.

> gender discrimination
> homelessness
> family size
> domestic violence
> bullying in schools
> school dropout rates
> the destruction of the environment
> drug and alcohol abuse
> family breakdown
> racism

B Explain your choices to a partner.

LISTENING 1

You are going to hear five short news extracts.

A 🔊 4.2 Listen and decide which of the issues from the box above is discussed in each one.

1 ....
2 ....
3 ....
4 ....
5 ....

B Work in pairs and discuss which of the five extracts you think mentions:
a someone being assaulted.
b people welcoming some news.
c people being at risk.
d someone winning damages.
e someone being prevented from carrying out major development work.

C Listen again to check your ideas.

D Add the verbs in the box to the nouns they were used with in the news extracts. Then look at the audioscript on page 167 to check.

claim	become	conduct	uphold
be denied	launch	suffer	win

1 .... a new initiative
2 .... her case
3 .... promotion
4 .... investigations
5 .... several broken bones
6 .... victory
7 .... a claim
8 .... a grandmother

E Work in pairs. Discuss these questions.
- Tell your partner about any similar stories you've heard about the social issues in *Listening 1*.
- Do you know any people with big families? How would you feel about being in a family with 17 kids? What would be difficult about it? What would be good?
- Are security cameras used widely in your country? Should there be more or less? Why?
- Can you think of any initiatives that your government or other authorities have launched recently?

Listening 2

You are going to hear two friends discussing one of the stories from the news extracts.

A 🎧 **4.3 Listen and answer these questions.**
- Which story do they talk about?
- What do they agree on?
- What do they disagree about?
- Who do you agree with more? Why?

NATIVE SPEAKER ENGLISH

Mind you

In speech, we often use *mind you* to mean *however*. It makes what has just been said less strong or true.

A: *They deserved to lose all that money.*
B: *Yeah. Mind you, it was a lot.*

It's good that there's a new initiative. Mind you, the last one didn't work very well.

He shouldn't have hit him. Mind you, he was badly provoked.

B **Which of the following sentences did you hear used in the conversation? Listen again if you need to.**
1 It was shocking what happened to her.
2 It just seems a bit excessive.
3 It's great to see that people power can actually work!
4 It makes you wonder what's gone wrong with the world.
5 It was such typical double standards!
6 That's good news for a change!
7 I don't know how they manage.
8 At least they're doing something about it at last!
9 You can't have everything in life, can you?
10 It's a bit of a worry.
11 It's lucky it was caught on film.
12 That kind of thing shouldn't be tolerated.

C **Which of the sentences above could be used to talk about the other four news stories?**

Pronunciation Stressing *and* and *or*

When we say *and*, we usually use the weak form /ənd/. However, we sometimes use the strong form /ænd/ to draw attention to the different ideas in a sentence or to emphasise a contrast. We can also stress *or* to emphasise that it is impossible for both ideas in a sentence to be true.

A 🎧 **4.4 Listen to these sentences without and with the stress on *and / or*. Repeat them.**
- They told her, 'You either have kids or you can get promoted.'
- I mean, they can have a career and a family

B **Work in pairs. Practise saying these sentences in two ways – without and with the stress on *and / or*.**
1 It's not easy to be environmentally friendly and save money.
2 You can't eat here at eight and have dinner with them at nine!
3 You can't believe in progress and believe in tradition. It's just not possible!
4 Surely you can enjoy shopping and reading gossip magazines and have a brain!
5 Either you believe in God or you believe in science.
6 Either they cut taxes or they increase public spending. They can't do both!
7 You can either have a job you enjoy or you can get rich.
8 You're either part of the problem or you're part of the solution.

C **Do you think the sentences above are true? Why? / Why not?**

Speaking

A **Work in pairs. Write a short conversation in pairs about one of the other four news stories you heard in *Listening 1*. Start by asking: *Did you see that thing on the news / in the paper about ... ?* Answer by giving a comment about how you feel about it. Then continue the conversation by agreeing / disagreeing and adding a comment. Use at least one sentence from exercise B in *Listening 2*. Try and use two other pieces of language from these pages.**

B **Act out your dialogue to another pair.**

You are going to read an article about the economist Jeffrey Sachs and global problems.

A **Before you read, look at the words from the text in the box below. Look up any words you do not know in the *Vocabulary Builder*. Then put the words into the categories you think they should go in.**

family planning	measures	birth rate	crop yields
child mortality rate	donors	poverty	seeds
scarce resources	project	soil	deprived

Population

....

....

....

Farming

....

....

....

Underdeveloped countries

....

....

....

Aid

....

....

....

B **Explain your choices to a partner. Do you have the same lists?**

C **Read the article and answer these questions.**
- Which global issues is Jeffrey Sachs mainly concerned with?
- What solutions does he suggest?
- Did you learn anything new from the article?
- Do you share Sachs' optimism? Why? / Why not?

D **Work in pairs. Explain what the article said using the words in Exercise A.**

INTERNATIONAL NEWS

Common wealth economics for a crowded planet

Jeffrey Sachs is an optimist. In summarising the state of the planet – rising population, widespread conflict, one-sixth of the planet suffering extreme poverty and hunger, global warming, AIDS and malaria pandemics – Sachs may paint a bleak picture, but he believes that all of these problems can be overcome in relatively straightforward ways and at relatively little cost. That's because the root causes of all these problems are interconnected and essentially man-made.

Take child mortality. Perhaps surprisingly, the higher the child mortality rate, the higher the birth rate. A booming population puts a greater strain on already scarce

resources, so farmers have to work harder to produce enough food for all, which means children are often put to work in the fields or at home. This, in turn, stops children getting the education which will allow them to learn, among other things, about better farming techniques, which would boost crop yields and provide more food to eat and sell. So one very basic solution would be to provide every child in poverty with an anti-mosquito bed net. Malaria is a huge cause of death in children and the bed nets would largely prevent the disease, even if it can't be wiped out altogether. Fewer children dying of malaria would help reverse the downward spiral just described, because the more secure parents feel about their children surviving, the fewer children they have.

However, it is implementing a combination of measures at the same time which truly makes a difference: free school meals boost school attendance and improve health; supplying fertilizers to improve soil and better seeds provides even better harvests; access to family planning further controls the birth rate; basic health care and clean water supplies, prevent more lethal diseases

These ideas are already being successfully put into practice in a number of so-called 'Millennium Villages' in some of the most deprived areas in the world. The cost of

the project is just $110 per person per year, of which $50 comes from donors and the rest from a mixture of local and national governments and the villagers themselves.

So if it's so simple why hasn't it been done before? What about all the aid that has been given to Africa and the underdeveloped countries of the world? Has it been lost to corruption? Sachs argues that the real problem is not corruption, but the fact that rich governments have promised such a lot, but actually given so little. They agreed to give 0.7% of national income in aid, but only five countries have met that target. He suggests current aid is $24 billion per year, which translates as just ten dollars per person – not nearly enough to implement the combined measures. He sets this against military spending, which in the USA alone, has reached $700 billion in some years.

So while Sachs sees an unprecedented opportunity to end poverty forever, he also raises an alarm that this could be the last chance we have: "The longer we wait, the greater is the suffering and the larger are the long-term costs."

Jeffrey Sachs is the author of The End of Poverty and The Common Wealth, published in the UK by Penguin. You can donate to Millennium Villages at www.millenniumpromise.org

GRAMMAR *the..., the...* + comparatives

A Complete the sentences with the comparatives used in the article.

1 The .... child mortality rate, the .... the birth rate.
2 The .... parents feel about their children surviving, the .... children they have.
3 The .... we wait, the .... is the suffering and the .... are the long-term costs.

> We use this pattern to show how an increase or decrease in something causes a related change in something else.

B Complete the sentences with one word in each gap.

1 .... richer the country, ... lower the birth rate.
2 The better educated people ...., the .... they are likely to earn.
3 The stronger .... economy, the .... unemployment there is.
4 The hungrier people are, the .... desperate they tend to be .... the more conflicts .... will be.
5 The more women there .... in government, the .... it is for the country.
6 The happier people are, the .... illnesses they ....

▶ Need help? Read the grammar reference on page 141.

C Work in pairs. Discuss how the following could affect the situation in the kinds of countries Jeffrey Sachs describes in the article. Use *the..., the ...* + comparatives.

military spending	farming techniques
foreign aid	access to the Internet
corruption	public awareness in rich countries
roads	family planning

D Work in pairs.
Student A: read File 2 on page 156.
Student B: read File 11 on page 158.
Then role–play the conversation.

SPEAKING

A Read the ideas on the right about events connected to Millennium Promise. Then do the following in pairs:

- In each case, say if you would go to the event and explain why / why not.
- Agree on which are the two best ideas below and try to think of one more idea. Explain your choices.

B Now work in groups. All of you should agree on one activity to help Millennium Promise. When you have chosen the activity, discuss when and where to do it, how to advertise it, and who should do what.

Here are some ways you can help Millennium Promise, but if you have any other ideas we'd love to hear about them. Remember, it's not just about money – it's also about education. The more people are aware of the problems and the solutions to poverty, the more people will get involved, and the more pressure there will then be on government to fulfill their promises.

❶ SCREEN A FILM
Films that touch on the issues of development such as *Blood Diamond* can be a great way of raising awareness about extreme poverty as well as being entertaining.

❷ HOLD AN AUCTION OR SALE
Get rid of all that stuff you no longer use and raise money at the same time. You could also get local businesses to contribute gifts to sell.

❸ SKIP A MEAL FOR EXTREME HUNGER
Go without lunch once a month and donate the money you save. Get your whole school or company to do the same.

❹ PARTY FOR POVERTY
You don't always have to be serious when fighting poverty. It's something to celebrate! Organise a party and raise money from tickets and donations on the night.

❺ SOME OTHER IDEAS:
Sponsored sports: sponsors pay you to walk 10km, run or… .
Food events: bake cakes, make a paella, have a barbecue or… .
Arts events: Put on a concert or play or …
Online: start a campaign, use a social networking site , send e-cards, or… .

LEARNER TRAINING

Look at the statements about learning vocabulary. Then discuss these questions in small groups.

1 Are there any statements that surprise you?

2 What are the implications of each statement for learning?

- Educated native speakers know around 17,000 word families – base words plus words formed from this base.
- Normally, you have to see / hear and understand a word anything from six to eleven times before you can use it!
- You may remember some words more quickly if you link them to a word in your own language or a mental picture.

- People forget 50% of what they learned after one hour. – and after a week they forget 80%.
- On average, people remember seven items at any one time. These items could be pairs of words or expressions.
- People remember more at the beginnings and endings of lists.

GAME

Work in pairs. Student A use *only* the green squares; student B use *only* the yellow squares. Spend 5 minutes looking at your questions and revising the answers. Then take turns tossing a coin: Heads = move one of your squares; Tails = move two of your squares. When you land on a square, your partner looks at the relevant page in the book to check your answers, but *you don't*! If you are right, move forward one space (but don't answer the question until your next turn). If you aren't right, your partner tells you the right answer, and you miss a go. When you've finished the game, change colours and play again.

Start

1 *Native English note* p. 8: if you can say what the *Native English* note was and give an example, throw again.

2 *Grammar* p. 8: tell your partner five habits about now and the past, using five different structures.

3 *Vocabulary* p. 8: say eight words and two expressions to describe films and music.

4 *Pronunciation* p. 11: say five things about yourself or your family using an adverb to describe the sentence clause.

5 Miss a go!

6 *Vocabulary* p. 14: say eight adjectives and two verbs to describe areas and buildings.

7 *Developing conversations* p. 15: your partner will say 1–6 and you must agree with a synonym.

8 *Native English note* p. 16: if you can say what the *Native English* note was and give an example, throw again.

9 *Grammar* p. 19: say six things about the future, using a differe structure each time and without using *will*.

10 *Vocabulary* p. 20: your partner will ask you about all ten descriptions in exercise C. You must get at least eight correct.

11 *Native English* note p. 20: if you can say what the *Native English* note was and give an example, throw again.

12 Miss a go!

13 *Vocabulary* p. 22: your partner will say the underlined words and you must give all the nouns.

14 *Grammar* p. 25: ask fo indirect questions to your partner, using fo different ways of start the questions.

15 *Vocabulary* p. 26: say eight of the words and phrases in bold to describe the economy, etc.

16 *Native English* note p. 29: if you can say what the *Native English note* was and give an example, throw again.

17 *Developing conversations* p. 27: your partner will read 1–6 in part A. You must agree and disagree in four ways. Add your own further comment.

18 *Grammar* p. 31: say four *the ... the* comparatives about: coffee, the economy, cars / roads, school / education.

Finish

For each of the activities below, work in groups of three. Use the *Vocabulary Builder* if you want to.

CONVERSATION PRACTICE

Choose one of the following *Conversation practice* activities.
Entertainment p. 9
Sightseeing p. 15
Things you need p. 21
Society p. 27

Two of you should do the task. The third person should listen and then give a mark between 1 and 10 for the performance. Explain your decision. Then change roles.

ACT OR DRAW

One person should act or draw as many of these words as you can in three minutes. Your partners should try to guess the words. Do not speak while you are acting or drawing!

your pulse	rub	a bonfire	a slide
a hammer	tiles	armour	float
rush around	spray	cracked	a peg
a stapler	leak	a strap	splash
upside down	sort	thread	a mop
fireworks	stain	ripped	plunge

QUIZ

Answer as many of the questions as possible.
1 What might you do if a song's very **catchy**?
2 Is an **ordeal** a good or bad thing to go through?
3 Say three different kinds of thing you might **seek**?
4 Why might you need a **disguise**?
5 What happens if you **fulfil** an ambition or a dream?
6 Why might you **steer clear of** an area or a person?
7 What's the opposite of a **stunning** building?
8 Say three things you could **launch**?
9 How do you **acquire** things?
10 What do you do if you **settle** in a town or city?
11 What things use or contain **wire**?
12 What kind of things might **leave you cold**?
13 What's a well-known **landmark** where you live?
14 Say three things you use to **join together** bits of wood?
15 How might a politician **boost** their **standing** with voters?

COLLOCATIONS

Take turns to read out collocation lists from Units 1–4 of the *Vocabulary Builder*. Where there is a '~', say '*blah*' instead. Your partner should guess as many words as they can.

PRONUNCIATION
Voiced and unvoiced consonants

> Some consonant sounds (e.g. /p/ and /b/, /t/ and /d/) are made using the tongue and lips in the same way. The different sounds come from pushing more air out (/p/ and /t/) or from using your voice (/b/ and /d/ – you can feel your vocal cords vibrating if you touch your throat as you say these sounds).

A Practise saying the consonants below. Push air out for the first consonant; feel your vocal cords vibrate for the second.
  1 /f/   /v /
  2 /p/   /b/
  3 /t/   /d/
  4 /s/   /z/
  5 /ch/   /dj/
  6 /k/   /g/

B In your groups, practise saying these phrases. Who do you think has the best pronunciation? Try and copy that person!
  1 a leave a leaflet
     b a veteran farmer
  2 a a property boom
     b combat poverty
  3 a dreading the trip
     b the battery's dead
  4 a cause widespread disease
     b use up scarce resources
  5 a change the bandage
     b achieve justice
  6 a a government campaign
     b stick it together with glue

DICTATION

You are going to hear a short extract from one of the texts you read in 1–4. You will hear it only once.

A 🔊 R 1.1 Work in your groups. Listen and take notes on what you hear. You won't have time to write everything.

B Work together to write the whole text.

C Compare what you have written with the audioscript on p. 167.

LISTENING

A ⟳ R 1.2 **Listen to five people mentioning art / painting. Match jobs a-f to speakers 1–5. There is one job that you do not need.**

a ... an artist
b ... a charity worker
c ... a DIY expert
d ... a politician
e ... a security guard
f ... a shop assistant

B **Listen again and match items a–f to speakers 1–5. There is one item that you do not need.**

a ... expressing feelings about their job
b ... expressing disagreement with something
c ... explaining a company policy
d ... updating people on progress
e ... making a complaint
f ... giving advice

[... / 10]

GRAMMAR

A **Decide if both options are correct – or if only one is.**

1 I spent two months in Greece, *which / that* is where I met Giovanni, by the way.
2 I don't really know the restaurants round there. We *use to / usually* stick to our area when we go out.
3 To be honest, I don't go as much as I *used to / should*.
4 We didn't get back till 9, *by which / during* which time it was a bit late to come over and see you.
5 Do you know *if / whether* there's a discount for students?
6 I had a few jobs, *some / none* of which were any good.

[... / 6]

B **Rewrite the following sentences using the words in CAPITALS, without changing the basic meaning.**

1 I'm sure they'll win. They always do.
   They .... win. BOUND
2 I can't find anything in here. It's such a mess.!
   It's .... I can't find anything in here. MESSY
3 I have to make a speech. It's going to be awful!
   I .... the speech. DREADING
4 There's a slight possibility of rain this afternoon.
   It .... this afternoon. POSSIBLY
5 She will help out sometimes, but not that often.
   She only helps out .... WHILE
6 I usually stay in on Friday nights.
   I .... out on Friday nights. TEND

[... / 6]

C **Find the six incorrect sentences and correct them.**

1 We're thinking in buying a new computer.
2 I always carry a pen for to write ideas down when they come to me.
3 They're so welcoming people that it's easy to make friends.
4 There were lots of rides, which most of them were really great.
5 I was fed up that I only got 50%, because I'd worked really hard.
6 There was so few traffic it only took an hour to get here.
7 Can you tell me what time the store shuts?
8 The masks people wear in the carnival look weirdly.

[... / 8]

LANGUAGE PATTERNS

Complete the sentences with one word in each gap.

1 It's not the kind of film I .... let my kids watch.
2 It's the kind of thing my mum listens ....
3 Where would you recommend I .... to?
4 Can you recommend .... good restaurants?
5 .... wanting to be nosy, what's that thing round your neck?
6 They were exhausted because they .... without sleep for 36 hours.
7 They're doing a huge .... to improve living standards.
8 They've done little .... pensioners.

[... / 8]

PREPOSITIONS

Complete 1–8 with the correct prepositions from the box. You will need to use some preposition more than once.

on	at	to	in

1 Losing his job put a big strain .... his marriage.
2 The company's .... risk of going bankrupt.
3 To be honest, I'm not that keen .... pop music.
4 The employment tribunal ruled .... her favour.
5 There's access .... the Internet in all the rooms.
6 I go there once .... a while, but not that often.
7 I've heard they're really badly .... debt.
8 The initiative is aimed .... people on low incomes.

[... / 8]

WORD FAMILIES

Complete the sentences with the correct forms of the words in CAPITALS.

1 The economy is still in recession, but there are some grounds for .... OPTIMISTIC
2 We've started yoga classes at work, aimed at reducing .... and stress. ANXIOUS
3 When investing money on the stock market, you always need to proceed with .... CAUTIOUS
4 *Fame Academy* has become a bit of an .... in our house. We never miss an episode. OBSESSED
5 Apparently, she was awarded something like twenty thousand euros in .... for the way she was treated. COMPENSATE
6 Starting a business can be a .... nightmare. There are so many rules and regulations. BUREAUCRACY
7 Do you think the attack could have been .... motivated? RACE
8 They've been granted planning .... to build a new theme park just down the road. PERMIT

[... / 8]

COLLOCATIONS

Complete the collocations in 1–8 with a word from the box.

| temptation | hazard | spiral | challenge |
| interpretation | setback | target | controversy |

1 suffer a major ~ / experience a temporary ~
2 try and resist the ~ / finally give in to (the) ~
3 face a huge ~ / rise to the ~
4 pose a fire ~ / minimise the potential health ~
5 be open to various ~s / present an alternative ~
6 set a sales ~ / meet their projected ~s
7 cause a huge amount of ~ / be surrounded by ~
8 lead to a downward ~ / try to halt the ~ of violence

[... / 8]

PHRASAL VERBS

Complete 1–10 with the correct forms of the verbs in the box.

| cut | shoot | join | come | go |
| put | dress | have | stick | set |

1 I .... nothing **against** the government taxing people, as long as the money is spent wisely.
2 For carnival, we all .... **up** as zombies! We looked ridiculous!
3 I know it'd be nice to stay an extra day, but I think we should .... **to** our original plan and leave on Tuesday.
4 The cost of flying has .... **up** recently. It's twice what it was last year.
5 Some friends .... us **up** for the night when we were in Rome so we didn't have to pay for a hotel.
6 People were .... **off** rockets in the crowd. It was quite scary!
7 It was great. Somebody had set up a sound system outside their house and everybody just .... **in** the dancing.
8 Did you see that film *X-Factor* that .... **out** last year?
9 I've .... **back** a lot. I spend half as much as I used to.
10 I'd change the shoes if I were you. They don't really .... **with** the outfit.

[... / 10]

VOCABULARY

Complete the words in the text. The first letter(s) are given.

Don't Take No is a wonderful film, [1]loo........................ based on the life of Shireen Williams, a blind civil rights campaigner. It shows her early life of [2]po........................ in a deprived area of the city, where she was [3]sub... to abuse because of her race and disability. After largely educating herself, she is refused work and, as a result, takes her claim to court where it is [4]up........................ . After this victory, she starts a widespread campaign to [5]com........................ discrimination, which leads her to government. It's a gripping film without a [6]du........................ moment, and although some of the early scenes are quite disturbing and difficult to watch, overall it's a really [7]upl........................ story which shows how you can [8]ov........................ any difficulties that are thrown at you.

[... / 8]

[Total ... /80]

In this unit you learn how to:
- talk about what you do in your free time
- talk about how fit you are
- talk about lucky escapes
- check you heard things correctly

Grammar
- *should(n't) have / could(n't) have / would(n't) have*
- Present perfect continuous and simple

Vocabulary
- Health and fitness
- Football and life
- Lucky escapes

Reading
- Sport – you've gotta love it!

Listening
- Unusual interests
- The mad uncle

SPEAKING

A **Look at the statements below and decide:**
1 which are true for you.
2 which are true for other people you know.

- I'm a member of a sports club.
- I take part in a music or drama group.
- I do volunteer work for a charity.
- I go to dance classes to keep fit.
- I like wandering round flea markets and junk shops.
- I love doing puzzles – crosswords, Sudoku, stuff like that.
- I like sewing and knitting. I make my own clothes.
- I spend a lot of my free time on Messenger or surfing the Net.
- I go walking in the mountains whenever I can.
- At the weekend, I lie in bed till lunchtime and then just chill out at home.

B **Compare your ideas in groups. Explain as much as you can about each interest / activity.**

LISTENING

A **5.1 Listen to three conversations about free-time activities and answer the following questions for each conversation.**
1 What's the second speaker going to do?
2 How long have they been doing this activity?
3 How did they first get interested in it?
4 Is the other person interested in doing the activity? Why? / Why not?

B **Listen again and choose the correct words.**
1 What are you *up to / undo* later?
2 You've got a lovely *figure / fixture*.
3 It took me about ten minutes to get my *breath / breathe* back!
4 It's like a *master / faster* class with this top Russian fencer.
5 I'm going to have a wander round the *free / flea* market.
6 I'm just going to have a *lie-in / lying*.
7 *Fair enough / Very tough* – just the thought of doing that kind of exercise makes me sweat!
8 I took *that top / it up* because I was giving up smoking.
9 She said it'd give me something to *fit well / fiddle* with.
10 *Is it / isn't it* just full of old women, this group?

C **In pairs, discuss these questions.**
- Do you know anyone who has an unusual hobby – or have you ever discovered that someone had a hidden talent for doing something?
- How long have they been doing it?
- How did they first get interested in it?

NATIVE SPEAKER ENGLISH

What are you up to?
We often use *be / get up to* in questions to ask about what people are doing.

What're you up to later?
I haven't seen you for ages. What've you been up to?
So what did you get up to at the weekend?

VOCABULARY Health and fitness

A **Match the fitness words to 1–6**

| healthy lifestyle | flexibility | stamina |
| hand-eye coordination | speed | strength |

1   She swims around 60 lengths every day.
2   He can do the 100 metres in under 12 seconds.
3   She can touch the back of her head with her leg!
4   He can lift 50 kilos.
5   She's really good at racket sports.
6   He doesn't drink, doesn't smoke, doesn't stay out late.

B **Complete the sentences with the words in the box.**

| sweat | demanding | shape |
| breath | uncoordinated | junk |

1   He's really unfit. He works up a .... just running for the bus! It's awful to see!
2   She gets out of .... just walking up the stairs.
3   He's really out of .... He does absolutely no exercise whatsoever. He doesn't even walk!
4   I went to an aerobics class for a while, but it was too .... I couldn't keep up with the others in the class.
5   I'm so unfit. I really need to stop eating so much .... food. I'm getting fat – look at that flab!
6   I'm totally .... – just very clumsy. I'm always tripping over and bumping into things.

C **In pairs, discuss these questions.**
•   Would you describe yourself as fit or unfit? In what way?
•   Do you do anything to stay fit? What?
•   Who's the fittest / least fit person you know? Why?

DEVELOPING CONVERSATIONS
Checking what you heard

We often repeat someone's statement if we are surprised or want to check information. We add a question word at the end to turn it into a question. For example:

A: *I've got my knitting group tonight.*
B: *You've got what?*

A: *I'm going to a fencing workshop all day.*
B: *You're going where?*

A ⚡ 5.2 **Listen to the examples. What happens to B's voice in each case?**

B **Complete the mini–dialogues with similar questions to those in the examples above.**
1   A: I usually run about ten kilometres most days.
    B: ....?
    A: Ten kilometres. I'm not that fast, though.
2   A: I do capoeira on Wednesday nights.
    B: ....?
    A: Capoeira. A kind of Brazilian dance thing.
3   A: I went to a comic fair at the weekend.
    B: ....?
    A: A comic fair. They had all these old Spiderman comics there. It was great.
4   A: My mum's really into embroidery.
    B: ....?
    A: Embroidery. It's like sewing, but you make pictures or patterns with the thread on the cloth.
5   A: Well, I didn't get up till 3 on Saturday.
    B: ....?
    A: 3 o'clock. I'd had a heavy week. I needed a lie-in!

C **Work in pairs. Compare your answers and then practise reading the dialogues. Make sure your voice goes up when asking the checking questions.**

CONVERSATION PRACTICE

You are going to have similar conversations to the three in *Listening*.

A **Work in pairs.**
Student A: you are going to ask Student B about a hobby or interest.
Student B: think of an unusual hobby or interest – it can be something you really do or you can invent something for yourself!

B **Plan what you wan to say. Then have a conversation. then you have finished, change roles and start again.**

SPEAKING

A Discuss in groups the following questions:
- Do you know anyone who is a big sports fan? In what way? What team(s) do they support?
- Why do you think football has become the most popular world sport? Do you like it? Why? / Why not?

VOCABULARY Football and life

A Check any words in **bold** that you don't understand in the *Vocabulary Builder*. Then discuss in groups:
- what other sports they could be used in.
- how 7–13 can be used about non-sporting things.

1. He got **sent off** for hitting another player in the face.
2. The **goalkeeper** was a hero after he saved the penalty.
3. He **fouled** him and the referee gave a free kick.
4. They almost scored – they hit a **post** and the **bar** twice.
5. Honestly, the defender hardly touched him. He **dived**.
6. We got **thrashed** 6–0. We've never lost so badly.
7. It was a really **close** game – they won 1–0 in injury time.
8. The defender **tackled** the striker before he could shoot.
9. He's really **greedy**. He never passes – just shoots.
10. He was **substituted** in the first half when he got injured.
11. They got **promoted** to the Premier League last season.
12. They were struggling so the club **sacked** the **manager**.
13. If you ask me, the game was **fixed**. The referee gave some very dubious decisions. He **disallowed** two goals.

B Use five of the words in bold to talk about things that have happened in sport or in other areas of life.

READING

A Work in pairs. Discuss these questions.
- Is sport an important part of life? Why? / Why not?
- Make a list of all the possible benefits of doing or watching sport. Think about individuals and society.

B Read the text about why sport is good and find out if it mentions any of the benefits you thought of.

C Which of these statements do you think the writer would agree with? Explain why by referring to the text.
1. If you did a bit more exercise, you'd be more positive.
2. Forcing kids to compete undermines their confidence.
3. I can't imagine how it must feel to win an Olympic event.
4. We shouldn't encourage people to read.
5. The most important thing is to win.
6. Sports clubs keep young people out of trouble.
7. It's OK for footballers to dive or pretend to be injured.
8. I work long hours so my family has everything we want.
9. Seeing great sportsmen in action is uplifting.

D Mark the text with a ✓ where you agree with what's said, and a ✗ where you disagree, and a ? where you aren't sure. Then work in pairs to discuss your ideas.

SPORT – YOU'VE GOTTA LOVE IT

Record levels of people do no sport at all, while others will not even watch it. Jerry Travis explains what they're missing.

Healthy body, healthy mind

It's maybe obvious, but worth repeating: sport keeps you in shape. Moreover, people who are physically fit are, on average, happier. In fact, the British health service has recently experimented with giving people suffering from mild depression a course of exercise instead of drugs; gym membership rather than therapy.

Preparation for life

I'm not talking about those weird non-competitive sports that some well-meaning schools insist on: no winners, no losers and everyone gets a prize. Not only are such games dull and pointless for children, life's simply not like that. Competitive sport teaches us to cope with losing and disappointments. Sure, we're not all naturally sporty, but then I'm rubbish at crosswords. You just have to find your own level and learn to enjoy your own performance. You can feel the same sense of achievement as Real Madrid winning a game by beating an opponent who is at a slightly higher (though still low!) level than you. Similarly, I'm happy completing a puzzle others would find easy.

Social and fun

What would we do without sport? Read? Play computer games? Hang around on the street? Obviously, these aren't necessarily bad – especially reading – but the first two are hardly social, and the last not that interesting or purposeful. Playing sports helps to build relationships and teaches the importance of supporting each other whether you win or lose. I'm reminded of a lovely, funny scene in a film called *Gregory's Girl*, where two teenage characters compare injuries they've had after a bad game. Likewise, football fans enjoy sharing the pain of their team losing almost as much as the joy of winning.

Crime and morality

Just going back to hanging out on the streets, if you need proof that it's not that fun, why do so many of those kids end up committing crime? It's simply out of boredom – something which sport can often replace. So making sport more widely available is good for society. But it's also good for society in showing children the importance of rules and moral choices. Of course people cheat and perhaps you've been denied the chance to win something as a result. You think 'I shouldn't have stuck to the rules! Then I would've won'. However, the rules are the sport and you know if everyone starts cheating, the game disintegrates and stops being fun. That's how we learn the correct moral decisions in sport, but we also learn why, in life, cheats are looked down on or excluded.

Sport is life

But sport isn't just learning about life. It IS life. I play tennis. I'm essentially hopeless, regularly serving double faults or weakly hitting the ball into the net. However, there are moments when somehow everything comes together and I hit a great forehand down the line or serve a clean ace. You suddenly feel like a world-beater and it's a great feeling, even if the next ball flies miles out. Isn't life all about having those feelings? And sport – playing or watching – provides many of them. No-one looks back at the end of their life and says, 'I should've worked more. I could've bought a better car' or 'I'll never forget that time my kids watched TV'. No, what we remember are things like Usain Bolt smashing the world 100-metre record in Beijing - just thrashing everyone and actually easing up to celebrate ten metres before he crossed the line. And we're more likely to think 'I should've played with my kids more' and 'I wish I'd done more sport'.

GRAMMAR *should(n't) have, could(n't) have, would(n't) have*

A **Look at the sentences from the text and complete the rules.**

1 I shouldn't have stuck to the rules! Then I would've won.
2 I should've worked more. I could've bought a better car

> We use .... + past participle to say we failed to do something and .... + past participle to say what we did was a mistake. We can add comments to show our thoughts about the result. .... + past participle shows a certain past result and .... shows a possible past result.

B **Complete the sentence using *should've / shouldn't have* and the verbs in the box.**

stick to	be sent off	pass	be
thrash	be disallowed	buy	save

1 The keeper .... that. It went right under his body.
2 That goal .... We could've got back in the game with that goal.
3 It was my own fault. I .... skiing on the simple runs. I wouldn't have broken my leg then.
4 I know Robinho was OK in the end, but Thomas .... He could've injured Robinho's leg really badly, tackling him like that.
5 Walcott .... so greedy. Why did he shoot? He .... The other striker would've scored easily.
6 I can't believe Chelsea drew. They .... them, considering the number of chances they had. They .... that striker. He's useless. I could've scored from some of those chances he had.

C 🔊 **5.3 Listen and write down the six sentences you hear. Compare them with the audioscript on page 168 and then practise saying the sentences.**

D **Discuss what actually happened in each case.**

▶ Need help? Read the grammar reference on page 142.

SPEAKING

A **Choose one of the topics below to tell your partner about. Give details using some of the vocabulary from this unit and *should(n't) have / could(n't) have / would(n't) have*.**

- Two sporting moments you will always remember.
- Two matches you've seen where something went wrong.
- Two mistakes you've made.
- Two things famous people have done wrong.

LISTENING

You are going to hear a conversation between three people – Chloe, Molly and Kyle – talking about Molly's uncle, who is a health and fitness fanatic.

A **Look at the activities below. Then discuss the questions.**

- Have you ever done any of these activities? When?
- Which would you like to try in the future? Why? / Why not?

ballroom dancing	handstands	parachuting
rock climbing	hang-gliding	ice-skating
tai chi	windsurfing	shooting

Use these sentence frames to explain your reasons.
I think it'd be fun / amazing / really exciting.
I think I'd really enjoy it because I like other similar kinds of things.
I don't have the hand-eye coordination.
I'm not flexible *enough*.
I'd be scared of breaking my leg.
I'd worry about making a fool of myself.

B ⊘ 5.4 **Listen and find out which of the activities in exercise A Molly's uncle has done. Then compare your ideas with a partner.**

C **In pairs, decide if these sentences about Molly's uncle are true or false.**

1 He taught Chloe and Kyle how to do handstands at his home.
2 He stopped ice-skating after an hour because Molly and Kyle were bored.
3 He used to go hang-gliding once a month.
4 He gave up hang-gliding because he badly injured his neck.
5 He's only taken up windsurfing recently.
6 He lives by the sea now.
7 He drinks lemon juice every day because he thinks it's good for him.
8 Kyle admits Molly's uncle can be fun – but only for very short periods of time.

D **Listen again and check if you need to.**

LANGUAGE PATTERNS

Write the sentences in your language. Translate them back into English. Compare your English to the original.

We watched him going round and round for another hour.
He was going on and on about how amazingly healthy it is.
We walked for miles and miles looking for the place.
I've been wanting to do it for ages and ages.
I tried and tried to do it, but I just couldn't.
I just laughed and laughed when I saw it. It was so funny.

E **Discuss these questions with a partner.**

- Does Molly's uncle sound mad to you? Why? / Why not?
- Do you know anyone who's unusual for their age? In what way?
- Do you know anyone who's only OK in small doses? Why?
- Do you know any other things (like lemons) that are supposedly good for your skin / feet / hair / eyesight, etc.? Do you think it's true?

GRAMMAR Present perfect continuous / simple

A Which of the following sentences from this unit:
- a talk about completed actions that happened sometime between the past and now?
- b emphasise that an activity, an intention or a feeling started in the past and continues up to now?

1 I've been meaning to go round and see him.
2 I've been doing it for about six months now.
3 He's always loved sport.
4 I've put on five kilos since January.

B How is each sentence above connected to the present?

> The present perfect continuous shows that something started in the past and is unfinished. It emphasises an activity that is repeated over time – or a feeling / intention that is still going on now.
>
> Some verbs such as *be, belong, exist, know, love*, etc. are hardly ever used in the *-ing* form in the present perfect continuous.
>
> The present perfect simple is used to talk about actions completed before now which have a present result.

C Match the sentence halves.
1 She's been trying to call you all morning,
2 I've been meaning to ask Luis if he could help me,
3 I've been putting off going to the dentist for ages,
4 She's been thinking about dropping out of the course,
5 I've asked my landlord to fix the shower loads of times,
6 I've only met him once before,
7 I've never really fancied going skiing.
8 I've heard that song so many times recently,

a but he still hasn't done it! It's really annoying.
b but I just haven't found the right moment to ask.
c but your phone has been switched off.
d I don't know why. I guess it's not my kind of thing.
e that I'm a bit sick of it.
f as she's been struggling to keep up with the work.
g but he seemed like a really nice guy.
h but it's so painful I guess I should have it looked at.

D Discuss why do you think 1–4 use the present perfect continuous while 5–8 use the present perfect simple?

▶ Need help? Read the grammar reference on page 143.

E Complete these sentences so that they are true for you. Then tell your sentences to a partner and explain them.
1 I've been meaning to ....
2 I've been thinking about taking up ....
3 I've been putting off ....
4 I've always fancied ....
5 I've never really been interested in ....
6 I've never ....

VOCABULARY Lucky escapes

A Discuss which of the problems you think is worse in each case:
1 He had a hairline fracture
  He broke his leg completely.
2 I tore my knee ligaments.
  I sprained my knee.
3 She knocked herself out.
  She banged her head.
4 I twisted my ankle.
  I broke my ankle.
5 She passed out.
  She drowned.
6 He was paralysed from the waist down.
  He was killed.

B Take turns having conversations like this:
A: *Was he OK?*
B: *Well, he had a hairline fracture.*
A: *Oh no! That's awful. Still, it could've been worse, he could've broken his leg completely.*
B: *I suppose.*

SPEAKING

A Choose one of the speaking activities.
Imagine one of the things in *Vocabulary: Lucky escapes* happened to you or someone you know. Tell a partner what happened.
OR
Think of a true situation where you had a problem but things could've been worse. Tell your partner what happened.

"What do you mean 'It could have been worse.'?!"

06 ACCOMMODATION

SPEAKING

A Discuss the advantages and disadvantages of staying in:

a self-catering apartment	a camping van
a tent	a posh hotel
a youth hostel	a bed and breakfast

- Which have you stayed in?
- What's the best / worst place you've ever stayed in? Why?

VOCABULARY Where you stayed

A Decide if the sentences below are about good places or bad places – or if they could be about either.
1 The site was really muddy and everything got filthy.
2 We had some stunning views from our window.
3 The whole place was spotless.
4 The weather was just unbearably hot.
5 It overlooked a building site.
6 The people were incredibly welcoming.
7 The place was a bit of a dump, to be honest.
8 The facilities were incredible.
9 It was in the middle of nowhere.
10 The beaches were deserted.

B How would you describe the places in the pictures on this page?

LISTENING

You are going to hear two conversations about places that people have stayed in.

A ⑤ 6.1 Listen and answer the questions.
1 Where did they stay?
2 In what ways did they have a good time?
3 What problems did they have?

B Listen again and check your answers if you need to.

LANGUAGE PATTERNS

Write the sentences in your language. Translate them back into English. Compare your English to the original.

Considering how cheap the place was, it was fair enough.

Considering how expensive it was, I was disappointed.

The service was really good, considering how busy it was.

It was surprisingly quiet, considering the location.

She did really well, considering she'd never surfed before.

GRAMMAR Modifiers

> Modifiers are words like *a bit, quite, really, completely,* etc. They weaken or strengthen the adjective, adverb, verb or noun that follows.

A **Decide which sentences below are correct and which are wrong. Correct the mistakes.**
1 It was a bit nightmare.
2 We got very soaked
3 It was a bit nice.
4 I'd get quite restless.
5 We stayed in this absolutely amazing place.
6 There were hardly people there.

▶ Need help? Read the grammar reference on page 144.

B **Which modifiers from the box below go with each of the following groups of words?**

a bit	a bit of a	hardly	absolutely	very

1 pain / tourist trap / waste of money / dump
2 anywhere to eat / anything to do / slept
3 brilliant / spotless / disgusting / gorgeous / dead / freezing
4 cut off / noisy / rough / chilly / overwhelming
5 posh / welcoming / friendly / expensive / historic

C **Use some of the words and modifiers above to talk about places you've been to or visited on holiday.**

PRONUNCIATION
Modifiers, stress and meaning

> With *quite, pretty, fairly* etc. we usually stress the adjective, not the modifier: It's quite *easy*; it's fairly *expensive* etc. It shows we basically think it's easy, expensive etc. If we stress *quite, fairly* etc., the meaning changes. It shows it's <u>only a little</u> and not very easy, expensive, etc.

A 🔊 6.2 **Listen to the beginning of five sentences. Decide which of the two options is the best ending for each.**
1 a which was good.
  b but I was expecting it to be nearer.
2 a so we didn't go there much.
  b but there was still enough room to relax in.
3 a I really didn't know what to do!
  b but really exciting and fun as well.
4 a It's very green and it's nice to hire a bike.
  b but there are a few factories, which kind of spoil it.
5 a which was a pleasant surprise.
  b although it was a bit too greasy for my liking.

B **Practise saying sentences 1–5 in two different ways – stress the adjective and then the modifier.**

DEVELOPING CONVERSATIONS
Negative questions

> **Use negative questions to show surprise or opinions.**
>
> *Couldn't you stay* somewhere else?
> *Wasn't that a pain,* having to rely on the bus?
> *Didn't they run* more often than that?

A **Complete the questions with correct negative forms.**
1 A: .... it a bit noisy?
  B: Yeah, really noisy. The bar opposite had music playing full blast all night.
2 A: .... you find it annoying, the way the sand gets everywhere?
  B: Yeah, a bit, but stony beaches are just really uncomfortable. They're no good for sunbathing.
3 A: .... you ever heard of it? It's well known.
  B: Not in Asia, it's not!
4 A: I couldn't go diving. .... you scared?
  B: Not at all. I loved it. I'm thinking of taking it up.
5 A: .... it really uncomfortable, camping?
  B: It can be a bit, yeah, but we've got mattresses and chairs and stuff, so it won't be too bad.

B **Ask negative questions about these sentences using the words in brackets. Then have conversations using your ideas.**
1 We stayed in a big five-star hotel in Cairo. (expensive)
2 Eight of us are going to share a room in a youth hostel. (crowded)
3 The area's quite rough, but the rent is really low. (scary)
4 I had to share a room with my boyfriend's mother. (feel awkward)

CONVERSATION PRACTICE

A **With a new partner, have conversations about places you've stayed in recently. Start by asking *Did you go anywhere in the holidays?* If you haven't been anywhere, use your imagination.**

LISTENING

You are going to hear four conversations about accommodation.

A **Before you listen, discuss these questions in groups:**
1 Have you ever had any problems with:
 • hotels?
 • renting accommodation?
 • sharing a room or a flat / house?
 • any other kinds of accommodation?
2 Explain what happened. Did you manage to sort out the problem? How?

B 🔊 **6.3 Listen to the conversations. Match each one to one of the pictures.**

C **Match two statements to each conversation.**
 a Someone didn't know what was supposed to happen.
 b The place is dirty.
 c There is nothing to change the temperature in the room.
 d Someone is sarcastic at the end of the conversation.
 e The heating system was dangerous.
 f Someone is refusing to pay money.
 g The person's second complaint is stronger than their first.
 h Someone was paid to sort out a problem.

D **Discuss what you would do in each situation. For example:**
 A: What would you do in the first conversation?
 B: I'd ask to see the manager?
 A: How would that help?

NATIVE SPEAKER ENGLISH

Sarcasm
We often say the opposite of what we mean when we want to show anger or be funny. This is called sarcasm.

That's great, that is! (= It's an annoying problem)
Lovely weather! (= It's pouring with rain)
Charming! (= That's a disgusting thing to do)

SPEAKING

A **Read the situations below. With a partner, choose three that you would like to role-play.**
 • The bath in your house has leaked and flooded the house. Your landlord wants you to pay for the damage.
 • Your landlord doesn't want to give your deposit back on the flat.
 • The room in your hotel is too hot and so you complain to the receptionist.
 • You arrive late at a hotel because your flight was delayed – and the receptionist tells you your room has been given to someone else
 • You are staying in a five-star hotel. You need to get up early for an important meeting tomorrow. A rock band is staying downstairs. They are having a huge party. You decide to go and ask them to keep the noise down.
 • You go on holiday with your family. You have to share a room with your brother, who has some disgusting habits. You decide to try and persuade him to change!

B **Decide what roles you are going to take. Before you start, look through the audioscript on page 170 and underline any expressions you think will be useful.**

C **Now role-play the conversations.**

GRAMMAR *have / get* something done

A Look at the sentence from *Listening*. Can you remember what they were talking about? Compare your ideas with a partner.
You were right to have it checked and to get it repaired.

> ***Get / Have*** + object + past participle is a passive construction. It's used when the person who did an action is unknown or unimportant. It emphasises both the object and the person the thing belongs to.

▶ Need help? Read the grammar reference on page 144.

B Work in pairs. How many different ways can you complete each of these sentences?
1 You ought to get .... X-rayed.
2 You should get .... framed.
3 I should get .... dry-cleaned.
4 She's got to have .... removed.
5 I've just had my .... stolen.
6 I need to get .... fixed.
7 We had the house .... last month.
8 I'm going to have my hair ....

C Use the ideas above to talk about things:
a you've had / got done recently
b you need to have / get done.
c you're going to have /get done.
d you'd never have / get done.

VOCABULARY
Understanding idioms

> In *Listening*, you heard these two idioms:
> *You're taking the mickey* and *I'm completely out of pocket.*
>
> An idiom is a group of words that mean something different to the meaning of the individual words. You can sometimes work out the meaning of an idiom from the words and the context. If you look up the idiom in a dictionary, it's usually listed under the entry for the noun.

A Replace the definitions in *italics* with the idioms from Units 1–5 in the box.

> cost an arm and a leg
> make ends meet
> taking the mickey out of
> finding my feet.
> having a whale of a time
> out of pocket
> through rose-coloured glasses
> in small doses

1 Did everybody pay you back after you paid for dinner? I hope you didn't end up *losing money.*
2 Don't get me wrong. I think it's good to be optimistic. I just think that you sometimes look at things *in an over-optimistic way.*
3 We had to bribe the kids with ice cream to get them to leave the playground. They were *really enjoying themselves.*
4 Don't get me wrong. She's great *for very short periods of time.* It's just that after too much of her, I get an overwhelming desire to fall asleep!
5 They must be finding it difficult to *pay for everything they need,* now that she's lost her job.
6 I don't know how they can afford a car like that, considering what they earn. It must have *been very expensive.*
7 They were all *making fun of* me because of my haircut. I didn't find it very funny though.
8 I changed jobs a few months ago. It was really hard to begin with, but I'm slowly *getting used to things.*

B Think of three situations in which you could have used any of these idioms. Tell a partner about them.

READING

You are going to read a series of emails from a marketing manager, Ben, who has moved from Britain to Hong Kong.

A **Look at the pictures of where he is moving from and to. Discuss the questions in pairs.**

- How easy do you think a change like this would be? Why?
- What things do you think he'll have to get used to?
- How would someone find moving the opposite way, from Hong Kong to the UK?
- Which place would you rather live in? Why?

B **Read the first email. How many of the things you thought of does he mention? Are you surprised by his reaction? Why? / Why not?**

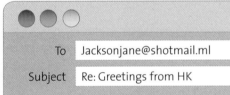

To	Jacksonjane@shotmail.ml
Subject	Re: Greetings from HK

Hi Jane,
Just a quick email to say I've arrived and am slowly finding my feet. It's been an absolutely mad few days. Got off the plane and was immediately hit by the heat – just unbelievably hot and humid. I was picked up at the airport by Tony, who works for the company. He was taking the mickey a bit in the taxi because he said I looked like some little boy just up from the country – and I guess I was – with my mouth hanging open, gazing out of the window. I mean, it's SO different. It's been quite overwhelming, but in a good way.

Anyway, after a couple of days getting over my jet lag and orientating myself a bit, I started at work. Mind you, I can't say I've exactly been slaving away at my desk. I seem to have spent most of my time being taken out for lunch, meeting people and partying! It's been pretty wild. Better get down to some proper work soon or the company will wonder what they're paying me for!

Anyway, they've already sorted out an apartment for me – 15th floor, stunning view – so that's all gone very smoothly. I already know I'm going to love it here.

How're things with you?
Ben

C **Below is Ben's second e-mail – written a few weeks later. Before you read, discuss what changes you might expect to have happened. Then read and find out if you were correct.**

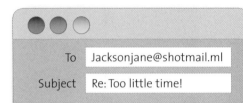

To	Jacksonjane@shotmail.ml
Subject	Re: Too little time!

Hi Jane,
Sorry it's been a while. Things have settled down a bit since I last wrote. In fact, I've been working fairly long hours. People just don't seem to stop here. When I used to travel into London from the country, I thought the pace of life was pretty fast, but here it's completely ridiculous! Then there's the noise – people seem to scream at each other all the time, they have the TV on full blast, and constantly beep their horns in the car. Mind you, I don't know why or what they're shouting, because when I'm in the office, most of the time you can't get a straight answer out of anyone. It's like they're speaking in riddles.

Fortunately, I've hooked up with this guy who joined around the same time as me and we go out and have a moan about things and just generally share our frustrations. Tony calls us The Moaning Twins, but he really is an idiot! To be honest, I'm already thinking of leaving. I honestly can't bear it! I never thought I'd miss home so much! Skype me sometime soon.

D **Discuss these questions in groups.**
- Have you ever been homesick? When? Why?
- What kind of things do you moan about in terms of school, work or family? Who do you moan to / with?
- What kind of things do you think a foreigner might find difficult about your country?

E **Read the next two emails and answer the questions.**

1 How does Ben's attitude change?
2 What things happen to him?
3 Why do you think there's such a big gap between the two emails?
4 How does Ben come across in the emails?
5 Based on what Ben says, do you think you would like to live in Hong Kong? Why / Why not?

To	Jacksonjane@shotmail.ml
Subject	Re: Why go back when you can go forwards?

Hey Jane,

I know I said I was going to be back in England over Easter, but then I thought why would I want to go back to the miserable weather, rubbish food and dull conversation! I decided to cash in my flight and use the money to travel round here a bit. There are some amazing places to visit and I've been onto the Chinese mainland quite a bit. The people are so much more in touch with their culture here – back home, people just aren't interested anymore. It's all reality TV and celebrities.

Have you ever thought of coming out here? There's a lot to be said for it. It's a lot easier. I have all my laundry done through a service in my block; a maid comes and sorts out my flat every day. It's not like the service in England – half-hearted and late! It's really efficient. People seem to take pride in what they do. And as for the food – honestly, I don't know how you lot eat the bland rubbish that gets served up there. Hong Kong is miles better. Anyway, gotta dash – got my Chinese lesson.

Ben

To	Jacksonjane@shotmail.ml
Subject	Re: Surprise, surprise!

Hi Jane,

Hope this address still works for you. I bet this is a bit of a surprise! It's my fault, of course. I realise I've cut myself off a bit. If you're annoyed with me and don't want to know or respond, then fair enough. Anyway, it was just to let you know that I'm going to be over in England soon and it'd be really good to get back in touch – and introduce you to my wife and new son – Huang Fu. See picture attached. Email me.

Ben

F **Match the verbs from the four emails with the words they were used with.**

1	gaze	my flat
2	get over	pride in what they do
3	get down to	out of the window
4	go	very smoothly
5	honk	me
6	sort out	work
7	take	their horns
8	email	my jet lag

LISTENING

You are going to hear an extract from a radio programme about culture shock.

A 🔊 6.4 **Discuss what you understand by culture shock, when you might experience it and what might happen. Then listen and see how similar your ideas are to those you hear.**

B **Listen again and answer the questions.**

1 What two misconceptions about culture shock are mentioned?
2 What is acculturation?
3 What four stages do people go through?
4 What happens in each phase?
5 Why might it be a problem if you don't complete the cycle?

C **Look back at the four emails and find examples of the following things mentioned in the extract.**

1 wonder and joy
2 settling into a routine
3 swinging from one extreme to another
4 looking down on something
5 putting someone down
6 refusing to mix with people
7 getting stuck in a phase

D **Has the extract changed the way you feel about Ben? Why? / Why not?**

SPEAKING

A **Think of a time when you experienced culture shock and had to adapt to new ways of new doing things – maybe in another country, or perhaps when changing schools, starting university, beginning a new job, etc.**

Spend five minutes thinking about what was strange for you, the different feelings you went through, how well you adapted – and any things you just couldn't get used to. Then share your experiences in groups.

In this unit you learn how to:
· talk about weather and natural disasters
· exaggerate
· talk about issues connected to animals
· talk about plants and animals

Grammar
· Narrative tenses
· Participle clauses

Vocabulary
· Weather and natural disasters
· Plants and trees

Reading
· Animal issues

Listening
· Experiences of extreme weather
· Plant life

VOCABULARY
Weather and natural disasters

A **Which of the things in the box below can you see in the pictures?**

a flood	forest fires
an earthquake	a volcano erupting
a famine	a drought
a tsunami	a tornado

B **In pairs, discuss the questions.**
· Have any of these things happened in your country? When? What happened?
· How many people were affected? In what way?
· How well was the problem dealt with?

C **Match the weather expressions in the box to the descriptions / comments in 1–10. You will need to use two words twice.**

cold	fog	heat	mist
rain	snow	a storm	wind

1 I don't know how you slept through it. The thunder was so loud and the lightning was incredible.
2 It's really thick. I wouldn't want to go driving in it while it's like this. Why don't you wait till it's lifted?
3 It was unbearable – and it was so humid I just didn't want to move unless it was to jump into the pool.
4 Honestly, I nearly froze to death. It was unbearable!
5 I got absolutely soaked on the way there. It took me all day to dry out.
6 There was a bit last night when I was coming home, but it melted. It was all gone when I woke up this morning.
7 You usually get a stunning view from up there, apparently. I heard you can even see the sea on a good day, but we could only see for a couple of miles when we were there. It was still nice, though.
8 It's eased off quite a bit. It's only really spitting now. Shall we go to the shops now before it starts pouring again?
9 It's really blowing outside. It almost knocked me off my bike it was so strong.
10 We tried to fly the kite, but there was only a slight breeze. It wasn't enough to keep it in the air for long.

D **Underline any new expressions or collocations in 1–10 above. Compare what you underline with a partner.**

E **In groups, discuss these questions**
· who has experienced the hottest / coldest / wettest / foggiest / windiest weather?
· who has been in the biggest storm?

LISTENING

You are going to hear two people sharing experiences of extreme weather conditions.

A 🔊 7.1 **Listen and answer the questions.**
1   Where were the two people when they experienced extreme weather?
2   What kind of weather did each person experience?
3   How did they feel?
4   What did they do as a result of the weather?

GRAMMAR Narrative tenses

A **In the conversation, the speakers used the tenses below to tell their story. In pairs, discuss:**
  • what the form of each tense is.
  • when these tenses are used.

past simple	past continuous	past perfect

▶ **Need help? Read the grammar reference on page 145.**

Need help? Read the grammar reference on page 145.

B **Complete this summary of the second story from exercise A by putting the verbs in brackets into the correct tense.**
We were in Israel and we [1] .... (visit) this town called Acre. It [2] .... (be) boiling all day and in the evening we [3] .... (take) a walk along the old walls to look at the view across the bay when suddenly we [4] .... (see) this incredible forked lightning. It [5] .... (start) spitting and then just two seconds later, it started pouring down. As we [6] .... (not bring) an umbrella, we just [7] .... (run) to the nearest café we [8] .... (can) find. It can't have been more than a minute, but we got absolutely soaked. I must have emptied like a litre of water out of my shoes.

C **In pairs, re-tell the first story from *Listening*. Then listen again to check your ideas.**

DEVELOPING CONVERSATIONS
Exaggerating

People often exaggerate when they are telling stories – to make things more interesting. They sometimes then modify what they have said. For example:

A: *The hailstones were as big as golf balls.*
B: *Really?*
A: *Maybe I'm exaggerating a bit, but they were pretty big.*

A **Work in pairs. Use the ideas below to have similar exchanges to the example above.**
1   We got absolutely soaked. I must've emptied like a litre of water from my shoe! (wet)
2   There's a terrible drought. It hasn't rained for three years. (long time)
3   She's like twice the size of me. (big)
4   The snow was like two metres deep. (deep)
5   She's like super-intelligent. She speaks something like ten languages fluently. (quite a few)
6   It poured down literally the whole time we were there. (miserable)
7   It was supposed to be the summer, but we were freezing to death. (chilly)
8   Honestly, you couldn't see your hand in front of your face. (foggy)
9   It's brilliant! The best book I've ever read. (good)

B **Practise exaggerating by writing sentences about two or three of the things below:**
  • how hot / cold / wet / windy, etc. the weather is
  • how big / small / dirty / clean, etc. someone's flat is
  • how lazy / hard-working / thin / tall, etc. someone is
  • how posh / dangerous, etc. an area is
  • how good / bad, etc. a film or book is

C **Use your sentences to have similar conversations to the ones you had in exercise A.**

CONVERSATION PRACTICE

A **Think of some extreme weather you have experienced. Take notes on what happened.**

B **Have conversations about your experiences. Your partners should respond by describing similar experiences, saying: *Actually, that reminds me of ... .***

SPEAKING

A Discuss with a partner how far you agree with each of the ideas about animals below.

> The true sign of a civilised country is the way it treats its animals.

> If everyone became vegetarian, we would all be healthier and happier – and it'd be much better for the long-term future of the world.

> The only animals in the world that you really need to be scared of are humans!

> Wearing fur is indefensible!

> Time spent with cats is never wasted.

> Vivisection – carrying out experiments on animals – is morally wrong. It may be true that it helps advance our knowledge, but it also damages the soul, the human spirit.

READING

You are going to read four newspaper articles about animal-related issues.

A The words below come from the articles: two from each. With a partner, discuss which words from the left column could go together with which words from the right – and what kind of story each pair might come from.

intimidation of laboratory staff	maggots
wages are soaring	rightful inheritance
the will is being contested	subsidies
try them for a dare	invaluable insights

B Work in two groups. Group A: read the two articles on the opposite page. Group B: read the articles in File 9 on page 158. Once you finish reading, discuss what you understood with a partner from the same group as you.

C Change partners. Work with a student from the other group. Without looking at your articles, summarise what you read. Share your opinions about each story. Start like this:
A: *Did you see that article in the paper about ...?*
B: *No, what was that?*

D Now read the other two articles. Is there anything your new partner forgot to mention?

E Continue working with your partner from the other group. Decide in which article:
1 a contract was cancelled.
2 business is booming.
3 someone got a nasty surprise.
4 people's privacy has been violated.
5 a long-established tradition has died.
6 a cultural taboo has been broken.
7 there may well be a court case.
8 people are struggling to make ends meet.

F Work in pairs. Discuss these questions.
- Which of the four articles did you find most interesting? Why?
- Have you heard any similar stories to the four you read?
- Have you heard any other stories about animals – or animal-related issues?

GRAMMAR Participle clauses

A Look at the relative clauses that start with the words in *italics* in a and b below. Discuss these questions:
1 Is the verb in each clause active or passive?
2 How could you shorten the start of each clause in bold to make participle clauses? Look back at the articles to check.

a Since adding a range of dishes *which feature* the insects to their menu, Espitas restaurant claims to have been almost constantly fully booked.
b The £18-million centre was intended to allow experiments *which are aimed* at combatting illnesses such as cancer, heart disease and diabetes to be carried out.

▶ Need help? Read the grammar reference on page 145.

B Choose the correct form.
1 the number of animals *abandoning / abandoned* by their owners
2 the number of people *living / lived* together before marriage
3 the number of people *moving / moved* abroad
4 the number of young people *suffering / suffered* from depression
5 the number of people *studying / studied* at university
6 the amount of organic food *selling / sold* last year
7 the amount of money *donating / donated* to charities
8 the amount of food *throwing / thrown* out by the average family

C In pairs, discuss which of the numbers / amounts in exercise B you think have increased and which have gone down over recent years. Explain your ideas.

BULLFIGHTING DYING A SLOW DEATH

Spain's state-run channel Television Espanola has decided to stop showing live bullfights, meaning the only way to now catch the sport is via cable or late-night highlight shows. The news is especially surprising given the station's long history of supporting the sport. Indeed, its very first broadcast back in 1948 was a fight live from Madrid.

However, it is claimed that not only are the rights to show fights now far too expensive, but also that bullfighting is too violent for the many children who could be watching.

The move is just the latest problem for the sport. Bull breeders are finding it increasingly hard to make a profit.

This is partly down to the rising costs of food, but also due to increased competition from the growing number of rich breeders involved in the business mainly as a hobby. Many now only survive thanks to European Union subsidies of around €200 per bull per year.

Live bullfighting is also suffering, with wages for bullfighters soaring and crowds falling. Whilst the sport remains popular with many older Spaniards, the younger generation seems increasingly uninterested. Indeed, in a recent opinion poll, over 70% claimed to have no interest in watching the sport at all.

Animal charity's gain is doctor's loss

A woman who gave up a career as a university lecturer in order to help her parents run their farm was shocked to discover that they had left everything they owned to the RSPCA – the Royal Society for the Prevention of Cruelty to Animals – the main animal-protection charity in the UK.

Dr Christine Gill spent much of the last ten years looking after her ageing parents and working on the farm. However, on his death, her father asked for his entire estate – worth around £1.5 million – to be given to the charity. His will is now being contested as Dr. Gill struggles to win back what she sees as her rightful inheritance.

The RSPCA has said that it hopes the matter can be settled "without the need for legal proceedings." Founded in 1824 (over 60 years before the NSPCC – the National Society for the Prevention of Cruelty to Children), the organization is left over £40 million a year and is one of Britain's biggest charities.

The group has recently come in for criticism for what many see as its involvement in politics after it supported calls for a ban on fox hunting.

VOCABULARY Plants and trees

A Complete 1–10 with the words in the box.

roots	seeds	stems	bushes	herbs	leaves	flower	weeds	oak	palm tree

1 The garden's in a bit of a mess. It's full of .... I think I'll have to spray them to get rid of them.
2 My wife loves sunflower ...., but I just find them really difficult to eat. They're too small and fiddly.
3 I use a lot of .... like basil and coriander in my cooking.
4 There used to be a lovely .... there which I picked dates from, but they cut it down.
5 You can see the plant's diseased. All the .... are curling up and falling off.
6 A: Do you recognise that tree?
   B: It's an .... Apparently, it's like five hundred years old.
7 The vase is a bit small for those flowers. You'll need to cut the .... a bit.
8 It took ages to dig up because the .... went so deep.
9 You can see the effect of global warming. The almond trees never used to .... this early.
10 I heard something moving around in the .... and this fox suddenly shot out of them. I guess we scared it.

B Work in teams. Write down the English names of:
1 as many flowers as you can.
2 as many herbs as you can.
3 as many trees as you can.

You can use a dictionary and organise the team however you like, but you only have three minutes to complete the task.

C In pairs, discuss these questions:
• Do you ever pick or buy flowers? Do you have a favourite flower?
• Which herbs / seeds are generally used in cooking in your country? Are there any you don't like?
• Are you any good at recognising trees?
• Do you know anyone who grows any plants? Which ones?

LANGUAGE PATTERNS

Write the sentences in your language. Translate them back into English. Compare your English to the original.
There used to be a palm tree there which I picked dates from.
It's not something that I'm interested in.
Who's that guy that you were talking to?
One of the women I work with is a keen gardener.
Isn't that the restaurant you told me about?
Have you got something I can carry these things in?

LISTENING

You are going to hear five conversations connected with plants.

A 🔊 **7.2 Listen and match one of the statements in a–f with each conversation. There is one statement you will not use.**

a someone has an illness.
b someone complains about a weed.
c someone realises they're killing something.
d someone goes to a funeral.
e someone was surprised at a hobby.
f someone insulted another person by mistake.

B **In pairs, discuss what you remember about how these expressions were used in each conversation. For example:**

cheer up: *He said he bought some plants to cheer up the flat – they were nice and green and colourful.*

1 cheer up	rot
2 get rid of	native
3 bouquet	awkward
4 lethal	deer
5 gran	settle

C **Listen again and read the audioscript on page 171 to check your ideas.**

PRONUNCIATION Linking

When a consonant sound at the end of a word is followed by a vowel, the words are usually linked together in fast speech:

... they take over the whole place

... they only give them when someone's passed away

When a vowel sound at the end of a word is followed by a vowel, we often add in a consonant /w/ or /j/ sound to join them together.

... so I bought some flowers
/w/
I slept through it
/w/
I took us ages to dry out
/j/

A 🔊 **7.3 Listen and write down the ten sentences you hear.**

B **Which words in each sentence link together? How? Compare your ideas with a partner.**

C **Listen again and practise saying the sentences.**

D **All the verbs in the sentences are from this unit. Can you remember what things the pronouns have replaced in each case? For example:**

They're difficult to get rid of.
→ *'They' refers to some weeds that are invasive.*

SPEAKING

A **In groups, discuss these questions.**
- What kinds of things can kill plants?
- Do you know of any plants or animals that are invasive?
- Which plants and animals have cultural significance in your country? In what ways are they important?
- Have you ever got food from the wild? What? Where from?
- What's the most interesting animal you've seen in the wild? How did you see it?
- Do you know any herbal remedies? What plants / seeds do they use? What do they help to cure?

08 LAW AND ORDER

In this unit you learn how to:
- talk about crimes and what they involve
- add comments and questions
- describe different kinds of punishment
- give opinions about prison life
- talk about the use and abuse of power

Grammar
- Modals + present and past infinitives
- Nouns and prepositions

Vocabulary
- Crimes
- Agreeing and disagreeing

Reading
- Laying down the law

Listening
- Different kinds of crimes
- A radio phone-in programme

SPEAKING

A Work in groups. Discuss these questions.
1 Which crimes are a problem where you live?
2 Do you worry much about crime? Why? / Why not?

VOCABULARY Crimes

A Which of the crimes below can you see in the pictures?

fraud	bribery	blackmail
a murder	a kidnapping	a disappearance
a burglary	identity theft	a bombing
a riot	speeding	a street robbery

B In pairs, test each other.
Student A: describe what happens during some of the crimes above.
Student B: guess the crime.

C Complete 1–9 with the pairs of verbs. You may need to change the order. The first one has been done for you.

stolen – broken into	doing – caught
stabbed – found	grabbed – came up to
held – seized	killed – went off
vanished – came back	set – smashed
~~got hold of – gone~~	

1 I got a phone call from the bank saying I'd *gone* $1000 overdrawn. Someone must've *got hold of* my details somehow and used my card number.
2 I was .... on camera and had to pay a hundred-euro fine. I was only .... about 65!
3 She was .... dead in a park near us. Apparently, she'd been attacked and then .... to death.
4 She went out to the shops and just never .... She just completely ....
5 They made such a mess. They .... shop windows, sprayed graffiti everywhere and .... fire to cars.
6 When we got back, we found the house had been .... Fortunately, they hadn't .... much.
7 I was standing outside the cathedral and this guy .... me and .... my bag and ran off.
8 He was .... when he was working out there. I'm not sure what they're demanding to release him, but he's been .... captive for about a year now.
9 Luckily, there weren't many people around when the device .... so no-one was ...., but it did a lot of damage.

D Work in pairs. Discuss which crimes from exercise A are described in sentences 1–9 above.

E Think of real examples for four of the crimes in 1–9 above. Explain what happened using some of the new vocabulary from this page.

LISTENING

A 🔊 **8.1 Listen to three conversations about crimes and answer the questions for each conversation.**
1   What was the crime?
2   Who was the victim?
3   Who was the criminal?

B **Listen again and answer these questions.**
1   What happened in each case?
2   Do you think the victims brought the crime on themselves in any way?

DEVELOPING CONVERSATIONS
Comments and questions

> When listening to stories, we often make a comment and then follow it with a question.
>
> Oh you're joking! What happened?
> That's terrible! Did it have much in it?

A **Make comments and questions by re-ordering the words. Add exclamation and question marks. For example:**
1   Was dreadful killed That's anyone
    That's dreadful! Was anyone killed?
2   been must've That you awful Were OK
3   anything no valuable they Oh take Did very
4   parents What thinking were dreadful That's the
5   insured a What shame you Were
6   police Did you That's terrible report to the it.
7   did joking they know Do who it You're
8   must It's What awful through his going family be

B **Work in pairs. Using the prompts below, take turns to start conversations. Respond to each prompt with a comment and a question. Continue each conversation for as long as you can, adding extra comments and questions.**
1   I had my camera stolen while I was on holiday.
2   We got caught in the middle of a riot.
3   We had our house broken into last night.
4   I had my bag snatched.
5   Did you hear there's been a bombing in town?
6   Did you read about that guy they kidnapped in Somalia?

GRAMMAR
Modals + present and past infinitives

> Present infinitives are the base form of the verb.
> Past infinitives are formed with *have* + past participle.

A **Match the words in *italics* to the ideas in a–f.**
1   *I should've been* more careful.
2   *They should do* something about kids carrying knives.
3   *It can't have been* very nice
4   *She might've been* involved in some kind of gang
5   *Someone must've seen* it – it was broad daylight.
6   *People could be* just too scared to come forward.
7   *It must be* awful for the parents, losing a child.

a   I imagine someone definitely saw
b   It's possible people are
c   It's possible she was
d   I imagine it definitely is
e   It's a better idea to do
f   I imagine it definitely wasn't
g   It was a better idea to be

▶ Need help? Read the grammar reference on page 146.

B **Work in pairs. Use *should /might / must / can't* + past and present infinitives to give your opinions about the situations below. Comment on causes and the characters' feelings.**
1   A 16-year-old boy has disappeared after having an argument with his parents. He's been gone two days.
2   Your neighbours have been buying a lot of expensive things recently. You've seen a man acting suspiciously outside their house.
3   A small girl is in hospital after being shot at her home. A man is in custody.

CONVERSATION PRACTICE

A **With a new partner, have similar conversations to those in *Listening*. Talk about crimes that happened to people you know or that you have heard about in the news. Your partner should comment and ask questions to keep the conversation going.**

SPEAKING

A **Work in pairs. Discuss these questions:**
1 What punishments do you think people who commit the crimes in *Vocabulary: exercise A* on page 54 usually get in your country?
2 Do you think these punishments are appropriate? Why? / Why not?

Use structures like these:
- *If someone is caught* speed*ing, they should* just get a fine.
- *If someone is guilty of* murder, *they should* get a life sentence.

LISTENING

You are going to hear a phone-in programme about prisons.

A **Look at the pictures from different prisons. What do you think is happening in each?**

B 🔊 **8.2 Listen to the introduction to the programme. Answer the questions.**
1 Which picture does the person talk about?
2 What are the prisoners doing?
3 Has the activity worked?

C **Work in pairs. Discuss these questions.**
1 What are the advantages and disadvantages of each activity or situation in the pictures?
2 Do you know if any of these things happen in prisons in your country?
3 Do you think prisoners have a hard time in prison? Why? / Why not?

D 🔊 **8.3 Now listen to the programme and decide if Gary (the presenter) and the callers Doreen and Nigel think prisoners have a hard time or not.**

E Check you understand the statements in the table below. Then listen to the phone-ins again. Mark a ✓ where someone agrees with a statement and a ✗ where they disagree. If the information is not given, leave the box blank.

	G	D	N
1 The current system isn't working.			
2 The idea of mass dancing is a good one.			
3 Criminals aren't punished enough in prisons.			
4 Life inside prisons is comfortable for most people.			
5 Inmates should do community service while they are in prison.			
6 Prisoners should be made to do hard labour.			
7 Prisons breed criminal behaviour.			
8 More thought needs to be given to ways of preventing further crimes from being committed.			
9 Prisoners need to learn how to use technology.			

F Compare your decisions in pairs. Listen again if you need to.

LANGUAGE PATTERNS

Write the sentences in your language.
Translate them back into English.
Compare your English to the original.
They're like holiday camps, prisons today.
He's a strange man, my uncle.
She looks great for her age, your grandmother.
It's increasingly common nowadays, identity theft.
It isn't much fun, listening to you moan all day.
It must be awful for the parents, losing a child.

VOCABULARY Agreeing and disagreeing

A Look at the audioscript on page 172 and find expressions used to agree and disagree with others' opinions.

B Complete 1–8 with the words in the box.

agree	idea	point	mean
see	complete	way	with

1 Well, that's one .... of looking at things.
2 I agree with you up to a ....
3 I'm .... you on that.
4 I know what you ....
5 I couldn't .... more.
6 That's .... rubbish!
7 I don't really .... it like that myself.
8 That's not a bad ....

C Work in pairs. Discuss these questions
1 Which four of the expressions above show you agree?
2 Which one shows you half-agree?
3 Which three show you disagree?

GRAMMAR
Nouns and prepositional phrases

> **We often add prepositional phrases to nouns to define the nouns more. For example:**
>
> The main *problem with prisons* is that we place too much *emphasis on punishment* and don't pay enough *attention to rehabilitation*.

A In pairs, discuss if you agree / disagree with 1–8. Why?
1 There's never any excuse for *committing crime*.
2 The government has no interest in *improving prisons*.
3 There's no point in *trying to rehabilitate some criminals*.
4 There's no need for *more police*.
5 We don't have a problem with *drugs in our country*.
6 We need a return to *the values of the past*.
7 The quality of life here is *the best in the world*.
8 There's a strong focus on *foreign languages* in our schools.

B Choose four sentences from 1–8 above. Make new sentences by changing the phrases in italics. For example:
There's never any excuse for *dropping litter*.
There's no point in *politics*.

▶ Need help? Read the grammar reference on page 147.

SPEAKING

A Work in groups. You are going to role-play a phone-in programme on the issues of prison and punishment.
Student A: you are the presenter. Look at File 4 on page 156.
Student B: you are a guest. Look at File 6 on page 157.
The other students are callers. They should say what they think.

READING

You are going to read an article about a mother's problems with her teenage son.

A The words in **bold** below all appear in the article. Match the summaries 1–8 to the extracts from the newspaper articles a–h. Look up any words you do not know in the *Vocabulary Builder*.

1 They've **imposed** a **curfew**.
2 He claims he was **tortured**.
3 He was arrested on suspicion of **subversive** activities.
4 His e-mails and phone calls were **monitored**.
5 People are angry about the **confiscation** of personal property.
6 They're opposed to the indefinite **detention** of terror suspects.
7 He was **interrogated** several times.
8 He's under constant **surveillance**.

a The leader of a banned political party was seized by police last night and accused of ploting against the state.

b Mr. Cole's movements are constantly monitored by the police and his house is watched day and night.

c Following a week of rioting, police have warned that anyone caught on the streets of the capital after nine o'clock will be arrested and taken in for questioning.

d Local residents yesterday held a demonstration to protest against the fact that police have seized passports, diaries, computers and even photo albums from their homes.

e The journalist was repeatedly taken into custody and questioned – often for many hours at a time.

f He alleges that he was kept in a top-secret prison for over a year and was repeatedly **subjected to** physical abuse.

g The Popular Democrats have criticised the government's plan to allow those suspected of involvement in terrorist activities to be kept in custody for unlimited periods of time.

h Under new laws, information about Mr. Khan's private conversations and communications are allowed to be used as evidence in court.

B In pairs, discuss what the connection might be between the words in **bold** in exercise A and home life as a teenager.

C Read the article and see if you guessed correctly.

D Discuss these questions in pairs.
1 Why did the writer and her son start arguing?
2 Why does the writer explain what life in a police state is like? What effect does this have on her son?
3 What has she been accused of? What effect does this have on her?
4 What things does she decide she won't allow anymore?
5 What reasons does she give for why her son has turned out the way he has?
6 What's the worst punishment she can think of?
7 Who do you have more sympathy with – the writer or her son? Why?

E Complete the sentences with the correct form of these verbs from the article.

change	storm	turn	get away with	put up with

1 His parents aren't strict enough. He .... murder!
2 He's 31 and still lives at home! I don't know why his parents .... it!
3 He'll have to .... his ways if he wants his relationship to last!
4 She got so angry, she ended up .... out of the room.
5 Sometimes parents have to .... a blind eye. It's better not to know everything your kids are doing.

F Work in pairs. Discuss these questions.
• Do you know anyone who gets away with murder?
• Do you know anyone who needs to change their ways?
• Do you agree with sentence 5? Why? / Why not?

NATIVE SPEAKER ENGLISH

might as well
We often say *might as well* instead of *have no reason not to*.

If he's always going to accuse me of being a dictator, I might as well start acting like one.
This isn't working, is it? We might as well just give up now.
You might as well ask her. You've got nothing to lose.
If your boss treats you like that, you might as well quit.

SPEAKING

A Make a list of six 'household crimes' you can't stand. Tell your partner about them. Explain who does them. Decide on a suitable punishment for each 'crime'.

Laying down the law

The continuing saga of one woman's struggle to lead a normal family life!

"It's like living in a police state, living here", my 15-year-old son screamed as he stormed out of the room. The event that had sparked this explosion of anger had been a simple question about what time he thought he might be back from a party, but apparently, in his eyes, such queries turned me into some kind of evil dictator.

Sadly, this wasn't the first time he'd made his feelings about being asked questions – or being interrogated, as he puts it – clear to me. As he probably knows all too well, his hysterical use of language never fails to annoy me – and yes, before you ask, I have tried discussing it with him. I've pointed out, for instance, that if he really were living in a police state, he'd be under constant surveillance for a start – we'd have CCTV set up in his bedroom and his phone calls, texts and e-mails would be constantly monitored; he'd be stopped and searched on a regular basis and he might well have been arrested by now and perhaps even tortured on suspicion of subversive activities! Of course, none of this makes any difference to him. He is, after all, 15 and I, after all, am his mother!

This latest incident, though, did get me thinking. If he's always going to accuse me of being a dictator, I might as well start acting like one. Maybe then he'll appreciate how soft I've been up till now: from now on, I am going to punish all the 'household crimes' he has been getting away with for so long.

No longer will I tolerate my son stealing the small change from my bedside table; never again will I turn a blind eye as he smuggles girlfriends into the house in the evening; and no more will we put up with him emotionally blackmailing us. I am sick and tired of being told that he wishes he'd never been born when he doesn't get what he wants or that he won't be able to study unless he's allowed to spend a weekend away with his friends!

In fact, now I come to think of it, far from being the poor oppressed victim he claims to be, my son has been allowed to get away with murder. Maybe it's because I vowed never to subject him to the kind of strict discipline my parents subjected me to or simply because I am the product of a fairly liberal age, but I've generally avoided anything approaching rules – and look where it has got me!

From now on, I'll be laying down the law. Any minor offences will be met with appropriate penalties. First, there'll be a curfew, then seven days' detention. Later we may well move onto the confiscation of personal property such as iPods and TVs. Finally, there'll be perhaps the worst kind of torture a 15-year-old can imagine: any girls foolish enough to visit will be dragged into the front room and shown pictures of our darling son as a child. That should surely be enough to make him change his ways!

LEARNER TRAINING

A Look at the views on reading below. Then work in groups and discuss the positive or negative aspects of each approach.

- I read things I'm interested in. I keep a list of new words.
- I'm not into reading. I prefer studying grammar and vocabulary.
- I want to study Business at an English-speaking university, so I read a lot of magazines.
- I like to read simple graded readers and listen to CDs of them at the same time.
- I'm reading a novel by Charles Dickens. It's very hard.
- I read newspapers and find new words and try to use them in my speaking.
- I read graded readers or kids' books below my level, so that I can read quickly and easily. I learn a few new words as well.

GAME

Work in pairs. Student A use *only* the green squares; student B use *only* the yellow squares. Spend 5 minutes looking at your questions and revising the answers. Then take turns tossing a coin: Heads = move one of your squares; Tails = move two of your squares. When you land on a square, your partner looks at the relevant page in the book to check your answers, but *you don't*! If you are right, move forward one space (but don't answer the question until your next turn). If you aren't right, your partner tells you the right answer, and you miss a go. When you've finished the game change colours and play again.

Start	**1** *Native English note* p. 36: if you can say what the *Native English note* was and give an example, throw again.	**2** *Grammar* p. 37: tell your partner about the health and fitness of people you know, using five of the words or expressions.	**3** *Developing conversations* p. 37: your partner will say A's lines. Respond by checking what you heard.	**4** *Grammar* p. 41: tell your partner five things about your last six months using the present perfect simple continuous.
5 **Miss a go!**	**6** *Grammar* p. 42: your partner will say ten different words or phrases from B. You should repeat each one with a modifier.	**7** *Developing conversations* p. 43: your partner will say the statements from exercise B. You should reply with a negative question.	**8** *Native English note* p. 44: if you can say what the *Native English note* was and give an example, throw again.	**9** *Grammar* p. 45: say five sentences using *have / get* something done.
10 *Vocabulary* p. 48: your partner will say the eight words from the box in exercise C. You should say a connected word or expression.	**11** *Native English note* p. 49: if you can say what the *Native English note* was and give an example, throw again.	**12** *Grammar* p. 50: say five statistics using *the number of / the amount of* and a participle clause	**13** *Vocabulary* p. 52: say ten words connected to plants and trees from exercise A.	**14** **Miss a go!**
15 *Vocabulary* p. 54: your partner will read the sentences in exercise C. Can you say eight of the crimes?	**16** *Developing conversations* p. 55: your partner will read 1–6 in exercise B. Respond with a comment and a question.	**17** *Grammar* p. 55: your partner will read situations from exercise B. Give six opinions using *should, might, must* and *can't* at least once.	**18** *Native English note* p. 58: if you can say what the *Native English note* was and give an example, throw again.	**Finish**

For each of the activities below, work in groups of three. Use the *Vocabulary Builder* if you want to.

CONVERSATION PRACTICE

Choose one of the following *Conversation practice* activities.

Sports and interests p. 37
Accommodation p. 43
Nature p. 49
Law and order p. 55

Two of you should do the task. The third person should listen and then give a mark between 1 and 10 for the performance. Explain your decision. Then change roles.

ACT OR DRAW

One person should act or draw as many of these words as you can in three minutes. Your partners should try to guess the words. Do not speak while you are acting or drawing!

out of shape	deserted	shade	a riot
pass out	lightning	fiddle	cliffs
a ligament	knitting	filthy	dive
hysterical	a sprain	gather	a stem
pull over	a lie-in	rot	grab
target	scramble	hail	gaze

QUIZ

Answer as many of the questions as possible.
1 Why might a footballer get **sent off**?
2 What do you do if you **take the mickey** out of someone?
3 Why might you **put off** doing something?
4 Say two things that make a place **welcoming**.
5 When do you suffer from **jetlag**? How do you **get over it**?
6 What helps to **settle your stomach**? What's the problem?
7 Why might someone **storm out** of a room or a meeting?
8 What's the difference between **bribery** and **blackmail**?
9 What happens if a child **vanishes**? What else can **vanish**?
10 Say three things people often have to **put up with**.
11 What's the difference between **fog** and **mist**?
12 What do you associate with **ageing**?
13 Say three things people often **moan about**.
14 Say three ways you could **chill out**.
15 Why might you stay in a **self-catering** apartment?

COLLOCATIONS

Take turns to read out collocation lists from Unit 5–8 of the *Vocabulary Builder*. Where there is a '~', say '*blah*' instead. Your partner should guess as many words as they can.

PRONUNCIATION
Stress in compound nouns

> Compound nouns are formed by joining two nouns together. Many are written as two separate words, some become one word, and others are joined by a hyphen. The main stress is usually on the first word.

A Work in pairs. Decide where you think the main stress in each of the compound nouns below is.

volunteer work	a camping van
a master class	a health hazard
crosswords	a forest fire
racket sports	hailstones
a comic fair	identity theft
a fitness fanatic	a street robbery
a goalkeeper	the death penalty
injury time	community service
rock climbing	a rehabilitation centre

B ♫ R 2.1 Listen and practise saying the words.

C Work in pairs. Take turns to explain each of the compound nouns. Your partner should guess the correct noun.

DICTATION

You are going to hear a short extract from one of the texts you read in 5–8. You will hear it only once.

A ♫ R 2.2 Work in your groups. Listen and take notes on what you hear. You won't have time to write everything.

B Work together to write the whole text.

C Compare what you have written with the audioscript on p. 172.

LISTENING

A ⟳ R 2.3 **Listen to five people talking about things they do in their free time. Match activities a–f to speakers 1–5. There is one activity that you do not need.**

a ... playing football
b ... watching football
c ... knitting
d ... doing DIY
e ... sailing
f ... ballroom dancing

B **Listen again and match items a–f to speakers 1–5. There is one item that you do not need. Which speaker:**

a ... persuaded someone else to do something?
b ... has got fitter because of their hobby?
c ... was in danger and had to be helped?
d ... talked about other people spoiling their day?
e ... is not as good as their partner?
f ... has discovered a hidden talent?

[... / 10]

GRAMMAR

A **Choose the correct word a–c to complete each gap.**

We were having some work done on our house, so we decided to go away for a few days to a town in the South West. We ¹......................... there for years because there are some absolutely stunning beaches. We love it. When we arrived, though, we found that the hotel we usually stay in was full. There ²......................... been a conference or something, because there were a few people walking round with nametags on. Anyway, someone suggested a place a few miles away. It was a ³......................... dump, to be honest, but we didn't have any alternative as it was getting late. We ⁴......................... before we left home. Maybe then we could ⁵......................... somewhere else more decent. Anyway, the following day, we were driving down the coast and we came across a little hotel ⁶......................... the sea. It was ⁷......................... posh – not the kind of place we ⁸......................... stayed normally, but we decided there was no point going back home and so we checked in. We had a fantastic few days, even if it was a bit more expensive than we'd planned.

1 a 've been going   b went   c 've gone
2 a must've   b can't have   c should've
3 a quite   b absolutely   c bit of a
4 a should ring   b would've rung c should've rung
5 a find   b be finding   c have found
6 a overlook   b overlooking   c overlooked
7 a quite   b absolutely   c bit
8 a must've   b should've   c would've

[... / 8]

B **Complete the second sentence using the word in bold, so that it has a similar meaning to the first one.**

1 Someone stole my passport while I was on holiday.
   .... while I was on holiday. **I**
2 I imagine she didn't hear you – she wouldn't ignore you.
   She .... – she wouldn't ignore you. **heard**
3 It's possible that they're waiting for us outside.
   They .... outside. **might**
4 They should ban advertising which targets children.
   Advertising .... should be banned. **aimed**

[... / 4]

C **Complete the witness statement below by putting the verbs into the correct tense.**

On Saturday 14 August, at around 10pm, I ¹......................... (sit) in my living room watching TV with a couple of friends. It was unbearably hot, so we ²......................... (open) all the windows. Suddenly, we heard some loud bangs outside and I ³......................... (look) out of the window to see what was happening. A nearby car ⁴......................... (be) on fire. I realised that someone must have thrown fireworks at it and it ⁵......................... (catch) fire. Just down the street, I ⁶......................... (see) a group of youths acting suspiciously. I went out with a friend to see what they ⁷......................... (do), but they ⁸......................... (run off). I ⁹......................... (chase) after them, but I couldn't keep up and after a few minutes I ¹⁰......................... (must) stop to get my breath back and the kids disappeared.

[... / 10]

PREPOSITIONS

Complete each sentence with the correct preposition in each gap.

1 There's simply no excuse .... being rude.
2 I've no interest at all .... lying around in the sun, getting sunburnt.
3 A lot of people think security cameras are an invasion of privacy, but I don't have a problem .... them.
4 The police should place greater emphasis .... crime prevention.
5 In the past, the police didn't pay enough attention .... domestic violence.
6 We nearly froze .... death watching the match.
7 The wind was so strong, it knocked me .... my bike.
8 Personally, I'm totally opposed .... the death penalty.

[... / 8]

LANGUAGE PATTERNS

Find the five incorrect sentences and correct them.

1 Considering little exercise he does, he's in great shape.
2 She did really well, considering she'd never done it before.
3 He went on and went on about how good it was.
4 It's a stunning view. You can see for miles and miles.
5 Who's that guy you were talking?
6 Gardening is not something I'm interested at all.
7 It's increasingly common nowadays, voluntary work.
8 It was overwhelming, visit India for the first time.

[... / 8]

FORMING WORDS

Complete the sentences with the correct form of the words in bold.

1 They're looking for .... to help out at the festival. **voluntary**
2 I had physiotherapy to regain .... in my arm. **flexible**
3 The police set up an .... zone around the area following the recent riots. **exclude**
4 You should have seen me in the Pilates class. I'm so .... I was doing the opposite to everyone else. **co-ordinate**
5 The law faced a lot of .... when it was introduced. **resist**
6 The amount of racial .... he faced when he played doesn't bear thinking about. **harass**
7 It's no .... to say his room is a health hazard! **exaggerate**
8 The number of tourists visiting the area has fallen .... **drama**

[... / 8]

PHRASAL VERBS

Choose the correct word to complete the phrasal verbs.

1 It's been very chaotic at work, but things have *settled / put* down now.
2 The race has been *put / played* off till tomorrow, due to the thick fog.
3 She *went / passed* out suddenly and was unconscious for about five minutes. It was quite scary.
4 A lot of kids *hang / stay* around on the streets because they haven't got anything else to do.
5 We had to *stay / put* up with a lot of noise because our room overlooked the main road.
6 He's very arrogant. He really *puts / talks* people down when he speaks to them.

[... / 6]

COLLOCATIONS

Match the nouns in the box with the groups of words they go with.

phase	insight	seed	bomb
tent	weed	match	ankle

1 put up the ~ / blew down the ~ / take down the ~
2 have a twisted ~ / sprain your ~ / his ~ ligament
3 an invaluable ~ / provide fresh ~ / lack any ~
4 the ~ was fixed / pull out of the ~ / an exciting ~
5 have three distinct ~s / go through a ~ / enter the final ~
6 get rid of the ~s / dig up a ~ / the ~s are spreading
7 plant a ~ / a ~ went off / a ~ scare
8 a sunflower ~ / plant some ~s / gather the ~s

[... / 8]

▶ **Find this difficult?** Re-read units 5–8 in the *Vocabulary Builder* for more information on collocation.

VOCABULARY

Complete the words in *News in brief*. The first letter(s) are given.

News in brief

Heavy rain has brought an end to widespread forest [1]f.......................... in Germany, but it may now cause [2]fl.......................... . Forecasters say storms with [3]th.......................... and lightning are likely to continue and they don't expect the rain to [4]ea.......................... o.......................... until next week.

Pirates have [5]sei.......................... another ship off the east coast of Africa. Ten crew members are being held [6]ca.......................... and the pirates are demanding $10 million to [7]re.......................... the men and return the ship to its owners, JShipping.

A man has been arrested on [8]su.......................... of murder following the [9]dis.......................... of a 25-year-old woman. The man is being held in [10]de.......................... at Bow Street police station, where he is being questioned.

[... / 10]

[Total ... / 80]

VOCABULARY Working life

A **In pairs, discuss whether the following are good or not – and why. What are the causes and / or results of each thing?**
1   I got promoted.
2   I handed in my notice last week.
3   I got a raise last month.
4   I'm getting on-the-job training.
5   I actually got made redundant last month.
6   I'm slowly getting the hang of everything.
7   I'm struggling to cope, to be honest.
8   My boss is a complete control freak.
9   I'm finding it very rewarding.
10 It's really stimulating. I feel I'm really stretching myself.
11 I'm just finding it really emotionally draining.
12 The work is pretty menial most of the time.

B **Have any of the sentences in exercise A ever been true for you – or for any of your friends / family?**

I ♥ my job

LISTENING

You are going to hear a conversation between two friends – Melissa and Richard – who haven't seen each other recently.

A 🔊 **9.1 Listen to Part 1 and answer these questions.**
1   How is Richard feeling about his job? Why?
2   What does his job mostly seem to involve?
3   What are his plans for the future?
4   What does Melissa say to cheer Richard up?

B **Now listen to Melissa talking about her job in Part 2. What do Richard and Melissa say about the following?**

training	presentation	employee
college	business trip	firm
clients	promotion	

LANGUAGE PATTERNS

Write the sentences in your language. Translate them back into English. Compare your English to the original.
I can't see myself staying there long-term.
I just can't see him getting the job. He's not qualified enough.
What do you see yourself doing in the future? Any idea?
Can you see yourself moving to a different firm?

C **Work in pairs. Discuss these questions:**
1   What advice would you give Richard? Why?
2   Do you know anyone whose job is going really well at the moment? In what way?
3   What do you see yourself doing in five years' time?
4   And what do you see your best friends doing?

GRAMMAR
Conditionals with present tenses

> Use present tenses in *if*-clauses and a variety of result clauses to talk about real / probable events now or in the future.
>
> *If I ask* about doing other stuff, *he* just *tells* me to be patient.
> *It might get* better *if I* just *give* it a bit more time.

A Complete the sentences with the pairs of words.

end up + carry on	fails + come
is + start	do + goes
work out + give	sack + change
happens + get	talk + feel

1 If all else ...., you can always ....
   and work for me!
2 You should .... to your tutor if you
   .... that way.
3 If the situation really .... that bad, why
   don't you .... looking for something else?
4 If things don't .... with your new job,
   .... me a ring.
5 If this merger they're talking about ....,
   I might actually .... a few more
   opportunities.
6 I'm going to .... a Master's in the States
   next year, if all .... well.
7 He said they'll .... me if I don't
   .... my attitude!
8 You'll .... running the company if things
   .... like this.

▶ Need help? Read the grammar reference on page 148.

DEVELOPING CONVERSATIONS
Feelings about the future

> When we answer questions about the future, we use a range of different expressions to show how sure we are that something will happen.
>
> *You're bound to get lots of offers.* (= I'm 95% sure you will.)

A Below are five answers to the question *Do you think you'll get the job?* Choose the correct response in each.
1 *I doubt it. / I'm bound to.* I'm not qualified enough.
2 *Definitely. / I might.* Stranger things have happened!
3 *Probably not / Hopefully not* – but it's worth a try.
4 *Hopefully. / Probably.* I really need the money!
5 *I'm bound to. / I doubt it.* They're desperate for new staff at the moment.

B Discuss the questions in pairs. Answer using the responses above. Then ask similar questions of your own.
1 Do you think you'll ever do a Master's?
2 Do you think you'll ever speak fluent English?
3 Do you think you'll ever become a boss?
4 Do you think you'll ever be self-employed?.
5 Do you think you'll live to be a hundred?

CONVERSATION PRACTICE

You are going to have a similar conversation to the one you heard Melissa and Richard have.

A Work in pairs.
Student A: imagine you are working and your job is going really well. Think of at least three reasons why.
Student B: imagine your job is going badly. Think of at least three reasons why.

B Role-play the conversation. Greet each other and catch up with each other's news. Then ask: *So how're you finding your job? Is it going OK?* Try to use at least two conditional sentences with present tenses each.

LISTENING

You are going to hear a news report about changes in the way a particular job is done.

A **Work in pairs. Look at the pictures below and discuss these questions:**
- What do you think the job is?
- What changes in the way the job is done do you think might be happening?

B 🔊 **9.2 Listen and see if you were right.**

C **Discuss these questions. Then listen again to check.**
1 What are the causes of the changes?
2 Why does Bud Keynes think the changes are bad?

SPEAKING

A **In groups, Discuss these questions:**
- Do paperboys / papergirls exist in your country?
- Are there any jobs that you think only happen in your country?
- Do you agree that it's good for teenagers to be able to do part-time jobs like working as a paperboy?
- Would you deliver papers? Why? / Why not?
- Are there any jobs that people typically do when they are at school or college in your country? Would you do them?
- Can you think of any other jobs where either the people who do them or the way they're done has changed over time?
- What caused the change? Is the change a good thing?

READING

You are going to read a text about five people's first jobs.

A **Read the text on the opposite page and decide who you think had the best first job. Explain and discuss your choices in groups.**

B **Work in pairs. Answer these questions.**
1 Who suffered physically in their job?
2 Who never got a break?
3 Whose job is sometimes misunderstood?
4 Who does fewer hours now?
5 Who behaves differently because of their job?
6 Who received training?
7 Who was bullied?
8 Whose job didn't live up to expectations?
9 Who went to work when they were ill?
10 Whose manager interfered a lot?
11 Who thinks certain people are better at a job?
12 Whose work has been publicly recognised?
13 Who has a better job now?
14 Which two people didn't just earn money for themselves?

C **Find the adjectives and / or verbs that go with these nouns in the text.**

trays	foot	college	cancer	choice
army	benefits	rank	lesson	boss

D **Discuss how far you agree with these statements.**
1 I would never do manual work or a low-paid job.
2 It's good to have a job for life.
3 People should never have to retire.
4 University students should work, not just study.
5 The army is a good career choice.
6 Women are better at some jobs than men.
7 Getting a good job is about who you know, not what you know.

Eduardo, Brazil

I got my first job this summer, working in a bar on a beach in Porto Seguro. It sounded ideal – chill out on the beach, get a suntan and earn some money before going back to university. Big mistake! I started work at two in the afternoon, cleaning the place, and then worked solidly through till five in the morning – re-stocking the bar, rushing from one table to the next, taking orders, carrying **trays**, clearing tables – it was non-stop! It didn't help that my boss was a complete control freak. By the time I got home, I was dead, and slept till one. I never actually set **foot** on the beach! Still, by the end of the summer, I'd saved enough to take my girlfriend on holiday. It was great to have money I'd earned myself and to be able to spend it as I wanted. However, if I work next summer, it won't be near a beach – it's too frustrating seeing what you're missing!

Jock, USA

I got my first job in 1961, when I was straight out of **college**, working in the urban planning department in Michigan – and I'm still basically in the same job! What's great about my job is that you see the physical results of what you do – on my way to work, I actually walk down a road that was named after me. When I reached retirement age, I went part-time, but it never really crossed my mind to quit completely. Time flies when you're doing something you enjoy. I had **cancer** a few years back and I'm not sure I'd have got through it if I hadn't been working. I feel truly blessed.

Eun Suk, South Korea

In the summers, I work at a theme park as a cartoon character. In Korea at that time of year it often gets unbearably hot, even if you're wearing a T-shirt and shorts, so imagine what it's like when you're stuck inside a two-metre rubber costume! Of course, I wouldn't do it if I had the **choice**, but my parents aren't that well-off and I need the money to help them out while I'm studying.

Carla, Chile

I joined the **army** after leaving school because I was a restless person and didn't like 'academic' things. Funnily enough, I've actually spent quite a lot of time in a classroom since I joined, as we get training for things like logistics. It's OK, though – you see the practical **benefits** more than at school, so I don't regret joining at all. And if I wasn't in the army, I would never have gone somewhere like Haiti. I went there as part of a UN humanitarian mission. For sure, people associate the army with war, but nowadays it's more about peacekeeping and helping people involved in conflicts. My area – logistics – is really about solving problems and communication and women are often better than men in those roles, so I'm certainly staying in the army and hopefully I'll achieve a high **rank**.

Simon, UK

My first job was in an office when I was 18. I got the job through a friend of my dad's. It wasn't the best experience, but it did serve as an invaluable **lesson**. If my dad hadn't got me the job, I might've left sooner. I was pushed around a bit and it was annoying how little some others did – they'd just drink coffee and surf the Net all day, but then they'd suck up to the **boss** and get away with it. I'm a manager myself now for a different company and I'm very conscious of being fair to staff at all levels and making sure everyone pulls their weight.

GRAMMAR
Conditionals with past tenses

> Use the past simple (not present tenses) in *if*-clauses to speculate about unreal / unlikely situations in the present / future. Use the past perfect to speculate about past situations.
>
> To talk about the consequences of these 'unreal' conditions, use *would*, *might* or *could* + a present infinitive to refer to the present / future or a past infinitive to refer to the past.

A **Without looking at the text, complete the sentences by putting the verbs into the correct form.**
1 If I .... next summer, it .... near a beach – it's too frustrating. (work, not be)
2 I had cancer a few years back and I'm not sure I .... it if I .... (get through / not work)
3 In Korea at that time of year it often .... unbearably hot, even if you .... a T-shirt and shorts. (get / wear)
4 I .... it if I .... the choice, but my parents aren't that well-off. (not do / have)
5 If I .... in the army, I .... somewhere like Haiti. I went there as part of a UN humanitarian mission. (not be / never go)
6 If my dad .... me the job, I .... sooner. I was pushed around a bit. (get / leave)

B **In pairs, check your answers against the article and explain the use of the different forms.**

C **Write a conditional sentence about each of the situations in 1–5. Then compare with a partner and decide who has the most interesting ideas.**
1 A friend has just handed in his notice.
   If they'd given him a raise, he might've stayed.
2 A friend has just got a great job.
3 A friend got sacked last year and is still unemployed.
4 You're struggling in class and getting low grades.
5 A friend is marrying someone she met on holiday.

D **Think of four events, situations or people that have had an impact on your life. In groups, explain their importance using conditional sentences with past tenses.**

▶ **Need help? Read the grammar reference on page 148.**

LISTENING

A Work in pairs. Discuss these questions:
- What do you think is good about the higher education system in your country? What could be better? Why?
- Have you ever heard of the Bologna Process?
- If you have, what do you know about it?

B ✎ 9.3 **Listen to a presentation about the Bologna Process and take notes.**

C Compare the notes you took with a partner. Whose notes are more useful? Why?

D Decide whether you think these sentences about the presentation are true or false. Listen again to check your ideas.
1 The Bologna Process is influencing education systems in countries outside Europe.
2 There's a new EU initiative forcing football supporters to wear earplugs at matches.
3 Under the old system, you could have ended up getting a degree simply by studying long enough.
4 Under the new system, the way a student performs in exams will not totally decide their final grades.
5 Most European countries are starting to introduce longer degree courses.
6 In several countries, the government now has less control over what happens in universities.
7 Attempts to put the Bologna Process into practice have caused outrage in Greece and France.
8 The UK is happy about the changes.

E Compare your ideas with a partner. Then look at the audioscript on page 173–174 and underline the words or expressions that helped you.

NATIVE SPEAKER ENGLISH

the odds
We often use *the odds* to talk about the chances of things happening.

If you haven't heard of the Bologna Process yet, then the odds are that you soon will.
To be honest, the odds of me getting the job are pretty slim.
The odds of winning the lottery are about a million to one.
What're the odds of that happening?
The odds are in favour of a Brazilian victory. England has no chance!

SPEAKING

A You are going to discuss your opinions about the Bologna Process and the changes it might involve. Think about the implications for the following areas.

methods of teaching	length of degrees
freedom of movement	implementation
national / international politics	staffing
affordability / funding	access to university

B Now discuss your ideas in groups. Try to use some of the agreeing and disagreeing expressions from page 57. For example:

VOCABULARY Starting presentations

> When you give a presentation, it helps if you begin by explaining what you are going to talk about. We use several common verbs and verb phrases to do this.
>
> What I'm going to try and do today is *tell you a bit about* the initiative *before moving on to explore* what it involves *in more detail*.

A **Complete the sentences with the verbs in the boxes.**

1 What I'm going to try and do today is ...

summarise	take	talk	tell

a .... a look at McDonald's recent performance.

b .... you a bit about the history of the video game industry.

c .... to you about the way in which immigration patterns have changed over the last thirty years.

d .... the main reasons for the war on terror, as I see them.

2 I'd like to begin by ...

commenting	giving	outlining	reviewing

e .... you an overview of the way in which gaming has changed and developed since the 1970s

f .... what the literature has to say about the matter

h .... on their sales figures for the last five years

h .... the main trends in the mass movements of people

3 ... and then after that I'll move on to ...

consider	focus	make	highlight

i .... on why these technological developments occurred.

j .... why these movements have happened.

k .... some recommendations about how the company could improve things in the years to come.

l .... some of the problems with most conventional ways of viewing the matter.

B **Make the introductions to four different presentations by choosing the connected sentences from 1, 2 and 3 above. Then take turns reading out each introduction.**

C **Work in pairs. Discuss these questions:**
- Which of the four presentations would you be most / least interested in hearing? Why?
- How much do you know about each of the four topics?

SPEAKING

A **Work in pairs. Discuss these questions:**
1 Have you ever given a presentation in English – or in your own language?
2 What was it about?
3 How long was it?
4 How did it go?

B **Choose one of the topics below. Plan a five-minute presentation on the subject. Use a dictionary to help you prepare if you need to. Make sure you begin by explaining what you are going to be talking about.**
- the history of your town or city
- an important historical event
- the state of the economy in your town/country/ region
- the achievements of someone important
- the work of one particular artist or musician
- the state of the job market for graduates and post-graduates

C **In small groups, take turns to give your presentations. Ask questions after each speaker finishes.**

D **Who gave the best presentation? What made it so good?**

10 SOCIALISING

SPEAKING

A **Check you understand the words and expressions in bold below. Then discuss the questions in groups.**

1 Which of the following do you celebrate? How do you usually celebrate them?

Mother's Day	Easter	New Year	Eid ul Fitr
Valentine's Day	Carnival	May Day	Christmas

2 Are there any other special days that you celebrate? How do you celebrate them?

3 Which of these ways of celebrating your birthday appeal to you? Why?
- having a big **get-together** or party with your family and friends
- going clubbing with a **bunch** of friends
- going to a **cosy** little restaurant with one or two close friends
- going away for a few days
- going on a big shopping **spree**
- just staying in and **pretending** it's not happening
- going to karaoke
- going out for dinner in a really posh restaurant
- having a **theme** party or a **fancy-dress** party

4 How did you celebrate your last birthday?

LISTENING

You are going to hear three friends talking about what to do on Friday.

A 🔊 **10.1 Listen and answer the questions.**

1 Why are they going out to celebrate on Friday this week?
2 What do you hear about these three places?

Equinox	Rico's	Guanabara

3 What time do they agree to meet?

B **Work in pairs. Try to complete the sentences from the conversation. There are two words missing in each space. Listen again to check your answers.**

1 So .... go out and celebrate on Friday, then?
2 I'd be .... that as well. Do you have anywhere ....?
3 I thought that Equinox might ....
4 I .... the music down there – and besides, it's such a ....!
5 Well, personally, I'd .... to get something to eat at some point, if that's .... with you?
6 Rico's is always a ....
7 Yeah, whatever. ....
8 I'm working till 6 and it'd be nice if I could go home first, so could we .... 8?

NATIVE SPEAKER ENGLISH

up for it

We say we are *up for* something if we are keen to do it.

I'll ring a few other people and see if anyone else is up for it.
I'd be up for trying karaoke, if you fancy it.
Is anyone up for a game of basketball later on today?
I'm not really up for going out tonight. I'd rather just stay in.

GRAMMAR The future perfect

> **In *Listening*, you heard this sentence:**
> *By four o'clock Friday, we'll have finished every single one.*
>
> **This is an example of the future perfect. The structure is formed using *will* (or *won't*) + *have* + past participle. It shows an action will end at – or before – a point in the future.**

A **Complete the sentences with the future perfect form of the verbs in the box. You need to use a negative form once.**

| be | finish | forget | graduate | learn | leave | try |

1 It's my grandparents' anniversary next Friday. They .... married for fifty years!
2 Just give him time to calm down. Call him later on in the week. He .... probably .... all about it by then.
3 I'm going to try and persuade her not to resign. I doubt it'll make any difference, but at least I ....
4 Hopefully, by the end of the course, we .... how to deal with all kinds of day-to-day situations in Dutch.
5 It's a shame you're not coming back till next Tuesday. I .... for Greece by then, so I'll miss you.
6 In a couple of years, the kids .... from university, so we'll have a bit more money to spend.
7 My boss is going to go crazy! The deadline for this report is tomorrow, but I .... it by then.

▶ Need help? Read the grammar reference on page 149.

B **Spend three minutes thinking about how the world will be different in thirty years' time. In pairs, share your ideas. Use the future perfect. For example:**
Hopefully, they'll have found a cure for AIDS by then.
I'll have started losing my hair!

DEVELOPING CONVERSATIONS
Arranging to meet

> If someone suggests meeting at an inconvenient time or place, we often suggest an alternative using *Can / Could we make it ...?* and explain why.
> ....
> A: So what time do you want to meet? Seven? Seven thirty?
> B: I'm working till six and it'd be nice if I could go home first, so *could we make it* eight?

A **Complete 1–6 by adding a–f.**
1 A: What time do you want to meet? Is eight OK?
   B: Can we make it a bit later? ...
2 A: When do you want to meet? Would about nine tomorrow night be OK?
   B: Can we make it a bit earlier? ...
3 A: When would you like to meet? Would sometime this week suit you?
   B: Could we make it some other time? ...
4 A: What day's good for you to meet? Is Friday any use?
   B: Could we make it earlier in the week? ...
5 A: Where shall we meet? How about that new café on the other side of the river?
   B: Can we make somewhere more central? ...
6 A: Why don't we meet at Janet's place?
   B: Can we make it somewhere nearer mine? ...

a It's quite awkward to get to, that place.
b I've got a lot on at work at the moment.
c She lives miles away from me.
d My boss has asked me to work late that day.
e It's my girlfriend's birthday that day.
f I need to try and get an early night if I can.

B **Write three possible endings for questions 1 and 2 below. Then work in pairs. Take turns suggesting where / when to meet. Each time, you should reject your partner's suggestions. Suggest alternatives using *Could we make it ...?* and explain why.**
1 What time do you want to meet? Is .... OK?
2 Where shall we meet? Would .... suit you?

CONVERSATION PRACTICE

A **Imagine that your course finishes on Friday. You are going to role-play a conversation similar to the one you heard in *Listening* – arranging to go out and celebrate. Write down three places you would like to go – and why they would be good.**

B **Work in groups of three. Arrange where to go – and where / when to meet. Reject some of your partners' ideas. Explain why and make alternative suggestions. Use as much language from these pages as you can.**

READING

You are going to read an article about some people who made mistakes in different social settings.

A **Before you read, discuss what you think the problem might be in each of these situations – and in the picture on the right.**
1 Someone says, "You must be Tim's wife".
2 Someone complains about their teacher in a cafeteria.
3 A businessperson makes a joke about their company in a speech.

B **Read the article on the opposite page and find out what each of the five problems actually was – and what the result of each one was.**

C **Discuss these questions in pairs.**
1 What do you think 'putting your foot in it' means?
2 Why does the author see Ratner as a victim? Do you agree?
3 In what way are the Dixie Chicks similar to Ratner? Do you have any sympathy with them?
4 Why does the author think it's good that he's not famous?

LANGUAGE PATTERNS

Write the sentences in your language. Translate them back into English. Compare your English to the original.
Even small violations of protocol can become big news.
It was awful! I couldn't even remember his name.
The first time was embarrassing, but this was even worse!
He's a really good cook, but his brother's even better.
I felt really foolish, but even I had to laugh.
Honestly, not even you could do anything that stupid!

"Oh dear, we forgot to invite the Woods.

VOCABULARY Making mistakes

A **Complete the sentences with the pairs of words in the box. You may need to change the order of the words.**

copying – send	crying – realised
live – stupid	politician – clue
pregnant – due	see – meant
foot – surprise	turned up – dressed

1 I asked her when the baby was ...., but she wasn't actually ....! I felt awful afterwards!
2 I asked him how his girlfriend was – and he burst out .... ! I hadn't .... they'd spilt up.
3 I wanted to .... a private email to a friend, but I ended up .... in everyone in the office by accident.
4 On my first day at work, I .... in a suit and tie – and found everyone else .... really casually! I felt so stupid!
5 I pretended I'd lost his passport. It was .... to be a joke, but he didn't .... the funny side of it.
6 I nearly put my .... in it with my brother last week. He's organising a .... party for my birthday – and I forgot I wasn't supposed to know about it.
7 A top .... was asked on a live TV show how much bread costs – and he didn't have a .... !
8 A government minister made a .... joke about the war – without realising he was .... on air.

B **Which of the eight mistakes above do you think is the most serious? Explain your ideas to a partner.**

SPEAKING

A **Work in pairs. Discuss these questions:**
- Can you think of any other famous people who have made mistakes in public?
- Have you ever put your foot in it – or done anything embarrassing in public? When? What happened?
- Has anything caused outrage in the media in your country recently?

WATCH WHAT YOU SAY!

We have probably all had moments when we have said the wrong thing – like at an office party once, when I introduced myself to a woman a colleague was with by saying, 'Oh, you must be Tim's wife. I've heard so much about you!' The woman then turned to Tim and screamed, 'You're married!' before slapping him in the face. Then there was the time at university when I met a friend in a coffee bar after class and immediately started moaning about our tutor, who was called Dr Gray. I was going on and on about how miserable she was – strict, boring, unfriendly – and my friend wasn't really saying much. After a minute or two, she interrupted me and said, 'Um, I think I should introduce you'. She then turned to this other student who I hadn't really noticed up till then and said, 'This is Tracy. Tracy *Gray*'!

Fortunately, the result of putting my foot in it was only an awkward moment and a stony silence. Maybe my friends thought a little less of me, maybe they thought I was an idiot, but no real harm was done. The same is not true for everyone.

Take Gerald Ratner. He was the multimillionaire owner of a chain of shops that sold cheap jewellery. In what was supposed to be a light-hearted speech to some fellow businessmen, he joked about the quality of some of his products. He said some earrings were 'cheaper than a sandwich, but probably wouldn't last as long'. Other products could be sold at such low prices because they were rubbish. Unsurprisingly, when his customers heard about the jokes they didn't see the funny side and the share price of the company crashed. Ratner had to resign as director and shortly afterwards the company was taken over by a rival.

In some ways, Ratner could be seen as the first victim of a globalised, twenty-four-hour news culture. He was in a semi-private meeting with people he was at ease with – you could even call them friends. However, there just happened to be a journalist there and soon his comments were being broadcast around Britain and then the whole world. These days, people in the public eye have to be careful about every single thing they say or do – even when they are miles away from home. The Dixie Chicks, who were the most popular band in America at the time, lost millions of dollars in sales because of a casual remark they made about the US President, George Bush. Whilst on tour in the UK, they said that the Iraq war had made them feel ashamed to come from the same state as the President – Texas. A comment, which would have passed unnoticed in previous times, was heard by their fans back in the States. They saw it as unpatriotic and stopped buying the band's records in protest.

Even small violations of protocol can become big news. For example, the former Australian Prime Minister, Paul Keating, caused outrage in some British papers for putting his arm round the back of the Queen when introducing her. In a similar incident, the actor Richard Gere was threatened with arrest for repeatedly kissing the Indian actress Shilpa Shetty on the cheek at an AIDS awareness rally in India, where such public displays of affection are frowned on. Such incidents can undermine relationships between countries and even destroy business deals and careers. All I can say is that it's just as well I'm not famous!

SPEAKING

A **Work in groups. Discuss how you would feel in the following situations – and what you would say and / or do.**

1 A friend invites you to a party. When you get there, you don't know the host or anyone else – apart from your friend, who spends the evening with someone else.

2 You get bored during a lecture and sneak out. You then meet someone else coming out of the lecture theatre.

3 You get stuck talking to someone who seems OK to begin with, but then turns out to be a complete bore.

4 You go to a friend's house for dinner and are served a special dish – made from something you really don't like.

5 You're in a club or a café and there's a really long queue for the toilet.

6 Someone you don't know interrupts a conversation you're having.

LISTENING

You are going to hear five short conversations.

A 🔊 **10.2 Listen and decide in which situation from *Speaking* each conversation takes place. One situation is not included.**

B **Listen and decide in which conversations you hear the following:**

1 The speaker wasn't exactly helping either, was he?
2 It's gorgeous.
3 It was so stuffy in there.
4 It's just a temporary loss of form.
5 They're so versatile.
6 I'm his fiancée!
7 She's always moaning about it.
8 My flatmate dragged me along.
9 I love your top.
10 They thrashed them!

C **Compare your ideas with a partner. Can you remember what each person was talking about? Listen again to check your ideas.**

D **Work in pairs. Discuss these questions**

1 In Conversation 1, the speaker made an excuse and left. Would you have reacted in the same way?

2 Have you ever been to a party where you hardly knew anyone? What did you do?

3 Have you had any conversations with people you didn't know recently: on public transport? in the street? at parties? in cafés or restaurants?

4 What did you talk about? How did the conversations start?

GRAMMAR Question tags

We often use question tags to ask for agreement or to ask for confirmation of an idea. Question tags are also used in polite requests. Look at these examples from *Listening*.

They have music later on down there, don't they?
It was so stuffy in there, wasn't it?
The speaker wasn't exactly helping either, was he?
You couldn't pass me the salt, could you?

A **How are the tags above formed?**

▶ **Need help? Read the grammar reference on page 149.**

B **Complete these dialogues by adding question tags in the appropriate places.**

1 A: Miserable weather.
   B: Yeah, awful. It's been like this for weeks.
   A: I know. I can't remember when I last saw the sun. Can you?

2 A: You don't remember me.
   B: It's Yuka.
   A: No. It's Naomi.

3 A Excuse me. You haven't got a light.
   B: Yeah. Here you go.
   A: Thanks.
   B: You couldn't lend me a euro.
   A: No, sorry.

4 A: You missed the class on Monday.
   B: There wasn't one. The school was closed for the holiday.
   A: No. Mind you, you didn't miss much. It was quite boring.
   B: Well, to be honest the whole course is a bit disappointing.

5 A: I love that jacket. It's from Zara.
   B: No, I got it from a shop called Monsoon.
   A: Really? You wouldn't happen to know the address.
   B: Sorry. I've forgotten the name of the road. You know where the McDonald's is? Well, it's the next road down on the left.

Our voice goes up when we are asking a genuine question with a question tag – when we are not sure of the answer.

You're not married, are you?

Our voice goes down when we are just making a comment.

C 🔊 10.3 Listen to the dialogues in exercise B and decide whether the voice goes up or down on each tag.

D Work in pairs and practise the five dialogues in exercise B. Make sure your voice goes up or down in the right places.

E Spend three minutes thinking of questions to ask using the patterns below. Then take turns asking your questions. Your voice should go up when you ask. Answer each question any way you want to.

> You couldn't ..., could you?

> You haven't got ..., have you?

> You wouldn't happen to know ..., would you?

F Write four comments about the weather, the news, food or sport. Include question tags. Say your comments to a new partner. Your voice should go down. Your partner can make up a suitable reply.

VOCABULARY Talking about parties

A Use the extra information in 1–8 to guess the meanings of the words in **bold**. Use the *Vocabulary Builder* to help you if you need to.
1 They **set up** a **marquee** in the garden of their house. They had a band playing in there and everything. They must've spent **a fortune** on it.
2 This guy kept trying to **chat me up** and in the end I had to tell him to **get lost**. It was really awkward.
3 I wasn't going to go because I didn't really know **the host** of the party, but my friends said it didn't matter so they **dragged me along**.
4 Nacho got together with Natalia at the party. Apparently they'd **fancied** each other for ages.
5 It got quite wild! The police had to come and **break it up** in the end because it was getting a bit **out of hand**.
6 I felt a bit **left out** because no-one was really talking to me and I hardly knew anyone there.
7 We **threw** a surprise party for my mum's fiftieth. She didn't have a clue! She **burst into tears** when she saw everyone.
8 I felt a bit sorry for her, because hardly anyone **turned up** and she'd prepared loads of food, which all just **went to waste**.

B Have you ever heard of – or been to – any parties where any of the things in exercise A happened? Tell a partner what happened.

SPEAKING

A Imagine you are at a party. You are going to start conversations with some other students about the subjects below. Spend five minutes planning how you will begin each conversation.
1 the weather
2 what they're wearing
3 a queue you're in
4 something you overheard
5 a recent sports game
6 a topic of your choice

B Now start conversations with another student using your ideas. After two minutes, think of a reason to stop – and start a different conversation with a new partner someone else.

In this unit you learn how to:
- describe the features of different kinds of vehicles
- rent a car
- talk about problems with vehicles
- talk about good / bad drivers

Grammar
- Uncountable nouns
- Emphatic structures

Vocabulary
- Problems with vehicles
- Driving

Reading
- Amazing journeys

Listening
- Renting a car
- Reporting problems
- Driving in different countries

SPEAKING

A **Work in pairs. Look at the pictures of different kinds of vehicles. Discuss these questions:**
- Do you know anyone who has any of these vehicles?
- What's good / bad about each kind of vehicle?
- What kind of person would you expect to own each kind?
- Which would you most like to own? Why?

LISTENING 1

You are going to hear a conversation in a car rental office.

A **When renting a car, which of the things below are: (a) really important, (b) quite important and (c) not very important?**

It's automatic	The insurance covers everything
It has GPS	It has a great sound system.
It's fuel-efficient	You get unlimited mileage
It's diesel	There's plenty of room in the boot.

B **Compare your ideas in small groups. Explain your decisions.**

C **⊗ 11.1 Listen to the conversation and answer these questions.**
1 What's the special offer for the week?
2 Does the customer take it? Why? / Why not?
3 What else has he ordered?
4 Does he take the extra insurance?
5 What else do you hear about the car he's renting?

NATIVE SPEAKER ENGLISH

better safe than sorry

We say *(it's) better (to be) safe than sorry* when it's best to act carefully – even if this is difficult/expensive / time-consuming – to avoid problems later.

Well, it's up to you, but it's better to be safe than sorry, isn't it?
The security checks take ages, but it's better safe than sorry.
Go and have a check-up. It's better safe than sorry, isn't it?
You'd best take out travel insurance. Better safe than sorry.

VOCABULARY Problems with vehicles

A **Choose the correct word in *italics*.**

1 We got a flat *tyre / engine* – and there wasn't a spare one in the boot.
2 The *petrol / engine* overheated on the motorway.
3 Someone knocked the *wing / door* mirror off.
4 The *tyres / wheels* are wearing very thin. One of them's almost bald.
5 The *battery / motor* is completely flat.
6 The front *window / windscreen* was cracked.
7 I filled the *tank / engine* with petrol instead of diesel.
8 There's a big *scar / scratch* down one side of the car.
9 There's a big *dent / bump* in the passenger's door
10 The *brakes / breaks* feel a bit weird to me.

B **Which of the things in exercise A have happened to cars you've been in? Tell a partner what happened.**

LISTENING 2

You are going to hear John Farnham – the man who rented the car in *Listening 1* – calling the car rental office.

A 🔊 **11.2 Listen and answer these questions.**

1 What's the problem with the car?
2 How does Mr Farnham feel about the proposed solution?

" Will it take you long to fix it? I have to be home in twenty minutes."

DEVELOPING CONVERSATIONS
Expressing surprise or shock

> When we are surprised, shocked or annoyed by what we are told, we often repeat the information as a question – with strong stress and a higher voice – and add another question or comment.
>
> A: We guarantee they'll be with you within four hours.
> B: *Four hours?* Is that really the best you can do?
>
> A: I'll be able to come and look at your car next Wednesday.
> B: *Next Wednesday?* That's almost a week away!

A **Write responses to each of the sentences below. Repeat surprising information as a question and then add another question or comment.**

1 A: The taxi fare to your hotel will be 100 euros.
  B: ....
2 A: The cheapest ticket we have left is 875 dollars.
  B: ....
3 A: Our flight leaves at five in the morning.
  B: ....
4 A: It's a bit old, but it's a nice car! I could let you have it for fifteen hundred.
  B: ....
5 A: If you just wait at the station, I should be able to get there within an hour or two.
  B: ....
6 A: The contract does state that there's a 50-euro penalty if you return the car more than an hour late.
  B: ....

B **Practise reading the conversations with a partner. Take turns responding to the sentences in exercise A – with a higher voice! Continue each conversation for as long as you can.**

CONVERSATION PRACTICE

A **You are going to role-play a conversation between a car rental firm assistant and a customer.**
Student A: read File 19 on page 162.
Student B: read File 3 on page 156.

B **Look through the audioscript for *Listening 1* on page 175 and underline any expressions you could use. Then role-play the conversation.**

C **Next, role-play a telephone conversation about a problem with the rented car. First, look through the audioscript for *Listening 2* on page 176 and underline any expressions you could use.**
Student A: phone the company and report the problem. Decide if you are happy with B's response.
Student B: deal with the problem however you want to.

READING

You are going to read a blog about three journeys: a 6000-kilometre train journey from Moscow to Beijing; a 4500-kilometre drive across the United States, and an 800-kilometre walk from the south of France to northern Spain.

A Work in pairs. Discuss these questions:
- What do you think the good things about each journey might be?
- What kind of problems might happen on each one?
- Have you ever heard of anybody making any similar journeys?
- Which of the three journeys most appeals to you? Why?

B Read about the three journeys on the opposite page. Answer these questions.
1 Why did each person decide to make their journey?
2 What was good / bad about each one?
3 Was there anything in the three stories that surprised you?
4 Have you changed your mind about which journey most appeals to you?

C Without looking at the stories, complete the sentences.
1 The company I was working for went bankrupt and I got a hundred thousand dollars' .... pay.
2 I know you're upset, but you need to .... things into perspective. I mean, it's not the end of the world!
3 We drove right across the desert – through some incredibly desolate ....
4 It's a remote area – and still very traditional. It's almost .... by the modern world.
5 I've seen that movie so many times that I know most of it by ....
6 I'd rather walk upstairs, if that's OK with you. I get really .... in lifts.
7 A quick .... of advice for you: make sure you take out travel insurance before you set off.
8 The main station must've been incredible once, but over the years it's slowly .... into disrepair.
9 She used to be very religious, but she had a bit of a crisis of .... a few years ago and left her church.

D Now check your answers against the expressions in **bold** in the blog.

E Discuss these questions in small groups.
- What other pilgrimages do people make? Do you know anyone who's ever made one?
- What other famous journeys have you heard of?
- What's the best journey you've ever made? What kind of scenery did you go through?
- Are there any journeys you'd love to make one day?
- Can you think of any famous road movies?

GRAMMAR Uncountable nouns

A Choose the correct form in these sentences about the three journeys. Look back and check if you need to.
1 Artur and Attila didn't do *many researches / much research* before setting off for Chicago.
2 John found some useful *information / informations* about the trans-Siberian railway online.
3 Roisin bought all the *equipments / equipment* she needed for her walk in France.

B Compare your ideas in pairs.

▶ Need help? Read the grammar reference on page 150.

C Complete the sentences with one word in each space.
1 I've just had .... really good news.
2 You travel light! You've got hardly .... luggage with you!
3 I'm really looking forward to this break. I've had so .... time to myself lately!
4 I don't think I'll get the job. I don't have .... experience.
5 I'm not making .... progress at all with my German. If anything, I think I'm getting worse!
6 I couldn't find very .... information about the place on the Internet.
7 Come and sit with us. There's .... of room over here.
8 I spent a great .... of time trying to avoid the people in the tent next to ours!

D Work in pairs. Discuss these questions:
1 Who do you usually talk to when you need advice?
2 Do you usually do much research before going on holiday?
3 How much luggage do you usually take when you go on holiday?
4 How much time do you usually spend packing?
5 Have you had any good / bad news recently?

Artur: Route 66

Growing up in Hungary in the 70s, Route 66 was like a mythical highway. The Rolling Stones' version of the song was very popular back then and I **knew** the lyrics **by heart**. Route 66 represented a dream vision of America: colour, freedom, speed, the romance of the open road. Ever since then, I've wanted to drive it – and last year my dream finally came true.

To celebrate our fiftieth birthdays, I flew to Chicago with an old friend, Attila. We then hired a Cadillac and set off for LA – almost 3000 miles away! We hadn't done much research before we left – and soon discovered that the road is no longer really in use! Its peak years were the 1930s through to the 60s and since then it's **fallen into disrepair**. As a result, much of the journey was quite bumpy; we went through some really out-of-the-way places – and got lost quite a bit as well! We drove through some really **desolate scenery** – mile after mile of farmland – and, of course, we had the occasional row. Spending all that time together meant they were bound to happen! Having said that, though, we ended up better friends than ever.

Strangely, one of the movies they showed on the plane home was the Pixar film, *Cars*, much of which is set along the road!

John: The Trans-Siberian railway

I lost my job in April 2008 and decided to spend my **redundancy pay** travelling overland to Beijing – to watch Team GB compete in the Olympics. I found some useful information online and managed to get a coach to Moscow. From there I booked a ticket on the world's longest stretch of railway – the trans-Siberian. Including a three-day stopover in Irkutsk, the whole trip took almost a fortnight and was truly unforgettable – though not always for the right reasons!

Whilst we did pass through some amazing countryside and meet some remarkable people, being stuck on a train day after day actually **got quite claustrophobic**. I started losing my sense of time after a while – which wasn't helped by the fact that many of the other passengers kept encouraging me to drink with them!

Having said that, Lake Baikal, near Irkutsk, was simply breathtaking: a vast area of incredible natural beauty almost **untouched by the modern world**. By the time we finally reached Beijing, though, I needed a proper holiday! Still, the British team did really well in the Olympics, which made the whole thing worthwhile.

Roisin: The Camino de Santiago

The Camino de Santiago is a pilgrimage route to the cathedral of Santiago de Compostela in northern Spain, where – according to legend – the remains of St. James are buried. Pilgrims have been walking this path for hundreds of years, and I decided to embark on the journey myself a few years ago. My mother had just died and I was experiencing **a crisis of faith**. I decided that walking a few hundred miles would help to **put things into perspective.**

I started in Saint-Jean-Pied-de-Port, in France, where I bought all the equipment I'd need, and set off. The walk took over a month and it was a truly spiritual journey. Although I met many other wonderful pilgrims, I travelled alone as much as possible. That helped to bring me closer to God again. As I walked through the countryside, I slowly came to accept the things that had happened to me over recent years.

A **word of advice**, though, if you're thinking of doing the walk yourself: learn some Spanish first. It'll make life easier! Oh, and buy good walking boots. I ended up with holes in mine – and got terrible blisters as well!

VOCABULARY Driving

A Match the verbs to the words they collocate with.

1	drive	a	your handbrake on
2	flash	b	in the mirror and indicate
3	overtake	c	in the middle lane
4	put	d	your lights
5	look	e	the car in front
6	make	f	a hundred and twenty
7	swerve	g	on your brakes
8	get	h	to avoid another vehicle
9	do	i	points on your licence
10	slam	j	a claim on my insurance

B In pairs, discuss why and / or where you would do the actions in 1–10 above.

LISTENING

You are going to hear two friends talking about driving experiences. Lily is from Britain and Sanjar was born in Iran.

A 🔊 11.3 Listen and answer the questions
1 What laws did Lily break?
2 What's her punishment?
3 How did she feel about driving in Paris, and why?
4 What's driving in Tehran like?

B Listen again and decide if the following statements are true or false.
1 Lily went over the time she'd paid for on the machine.
2 Lily argued with the traffic warden.
3 Lily's not going to appeal against the fine.
4 She was stopped by the police for speeding.
5 Sanjar doesn't think speeding is a problem in Britain.
6 Some other drivers didn't like Lily's driving when she was in France.
7 Sanjar was surprised that pedestrians in Britain weren't more careful.
8 They both agree that drivers are more polite in Britain.

LANGUAGE PATTERNS

Write the sentences in your language. Translate them back into English. Compare your English to the original.
You have to be really careful not to get knocked over.
Be careful not to spill your coffee.
You need to be careful to avoid paying for extras.
You have to be careful where you park.
You have to be careful what you say to him.
Be careful crossing the road.

C Work in pairs. Discuss these questions:
• Do you think driving is getting better or worse in your country? Why?
• Are some cities worse to drive in than others?
• Do you think speed cameras are a good thing? Why? / Why not?
• Is there anything you need to be careful (not) to do in your town / city?

GRAMMAR Emphatic structures

A Look at the pairs of sentences related to the listening and discuss the questions.
• In your language, can both sentences be constructed in the same way as in English?
• Which sentences emphasise how you feel?
• Which sentences have a shorter subject for the verb?

1 a People driving up really close behind you is really horrible.
  b It's really horrible when people drive up close behind you.
2 a The fact that I was given the ticket while I'd gone to look for change for the machine is really infuriating.
  b The thing that really infuriates me is that it happened while I'd gone to look for change for the machine.

> **The following patterns add extra emphasis – especially when talking about feelings or opinions:**
>
> | | | | |
> |---|---|---|---|
> | *What*
 The thing that ... | *verb phrase* | *be* | *that ... .*
 the fact / way that ... .
 the amount of ... . |
>
> *What worries me is the lack of investment in public transport.*
> *The thing that bothers me most is the amount of time and money they waste on stupid projects!*

B Find two further examples of these patterns in the audioscript on page 176.

▶ Need help? Read the grammar reference on page 150.

C Complete the sentences below. Compare your ideas with a partner.
1 What concerns me most about the world today is ... .
2 What I don't like about our city is ... .
3 What annoys me about him is ... .
4 The thing I enjoyed most on my last holiday was ... .
5 It's really embarrassing ... .
6 It's quite sad ... .

D In groups, discuss things that you love or can't stand about travelling – and things that annoy or worry you about it. Talk about cars, planes, trains, etc. in general. Then talk about public transport in your city. Think about the following: cost, reliability, cleanliness, efficiency, etc.

SPEAKING

A Read the questionnaire below and answer the questions for yourself – or for someone you know who drives. Check any words you're not sure of in the *Vocabulary Builder*.

B Work in pairs and discuss the questions. How good a driver does your partner sound?

C Who's the best / worst driver you've ever driven with? Give examples of how they were good / bad.

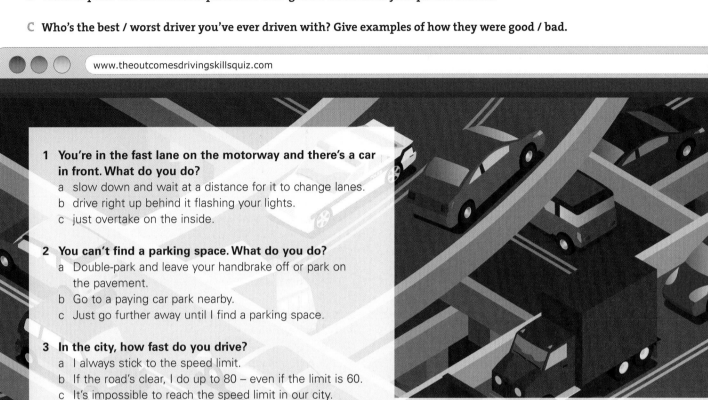

www.theoutcomesdrivingskillsquiz.com

1 **You're in the fast lane on the motorway and there's a car in front. What do you do?**
   a slow down and wait at a distance for it to change lanes.
   b drive right up behind it flashing your lights.
   c just overtake on the inside.

2 **You can't find a parking space. What do you do?**
   a Double-park and leave your handbrake off or park on the pavement.
   b Go to a paying car park nearby.
   c Just go further away until I find a parking space.

3 **In the city, how fast do you drive?**
   a I always stick to the speed limit.
   b If the road's clear, I do up to 80 – even if the limit is 60.
   c It's impossible to reach the speed limit in our city.

4 **If you're trying to turn into a busy road, what do you do?**
   a Patiently wait until there's a clear space for you to move into the traffic without causing cars to slow down.
   b Just shoot out into the traffic – the oncoming cars will slow down.
   c Creep slowly out to encourage someone to let you out.

5 **Which is true for you when turning or changing lanes?**
   a I always look in the mirror and indicate beforehand.
   b I don't always look or indicate, but I generally do.
   c I don't usually use my mirror or signal – I only need to worry about what's in front of me.

6 **Choose any that are true for you.**
   a My car has a few scratches and dents in it.
   b I've never had to make a claim on my insurance.
   c My car is really messy inside.

7 **Choose any that are true for you.**
   a I've never gone through a red light.
   b I once had my car towed away.
   c I've never had any points on my licence.

8 **What annoys me most is ....**
   a when people swerve in and out of the traffic.
   b people driving slowly in the middle lane of the motorway.
   c the way cyclists ignore road signs.

9 **Which concerns you most?**
   a running someone over one day.
   b having my car stolen some day.
   c the price of petrol.

12 HEALTH AND MEDICINE

In this unit you learn how to:
- describe health problems in more detail
- pass on sympathetic messages
- tell jokes
- discuss issues connected to health systems

Grammar
- *supposed to be, should* and *shouldn't*
- Determiners

Vocabulary
- Health problems
- Parts of the body and illnesses

Reading
- Laughter is the best medicine
- Health and sickness jokes

Listening
- Suddenly falling ill
- Medical tourism

SPEAKING

A Look at the picture of the hospital waiting room below. Name as many problems as you can.

B In groups, discuss the order you'd treat the patients if you were the doctor.

VOCABULARY Health problems

A In pairs, match the groups of words in 1–9 with the health problems. Explain the connection between each word in the group and the problem.

the flu	upset stomach	a cold
an allergy	asthma	stress
a broken leg	eczema	an accident

1 itchy / scratch / steroid cream / childhood / stress
2 swell up / rash / sneeze / throw up / nuts
3 fever / sore throat / earache / infection / stiff
4 dizzy spell / faint / high blood pressure / insomnia
5 scratches / bruises / bump / bandages / stitches
6 operation / pin / in plaster / remove / crutches
7 runny nose / sore throat / cough / herbal remedy
8 short of breath / inhaler / tight chest / smoke and fumes
9 a bug / settle / diarrhoea / rough / throw up

B Test each other. Take turns to act or draw words from 1–9 in exercise A. Your partner should say the word.

LISTENING

You are going to hear two telephone conversations.

A 🔊 12.1 Listen and answer these questions.
1 Why are the people phoning?
2 What health problems have the speakers' partners had?

B Listen again and decide if 1–8 are true or false.
Conversation 1
1 Joop's girlfriend, Kattje, is still feeling dizzy.
2 A lot of people have had a virus recently.
3 Kattje has an appointment to see someone in a few days.
4 Michelle gives Joop some advice.
Conversation 2
5 They don't really know what caused Lachlan's problem.
6 They had to call an ambulance.
7 He'll be in hospital for two nights.
8 Nina is annoyed they'll miss the concert.

SPEAKING

A Work in pairs. Discuss these questions:
1 Do you know anyone who:
   - has an allergy? What to? What reaction do they have?
   - has a chronic condition like asthma? How bad is it?
   - has had stress-related health problems?
   - has had a bug recently? What were the symptoms?
   - has ever broken a bone? What happened?
2 Have you ever missed something important or nice because of illness or an accident? What happened?

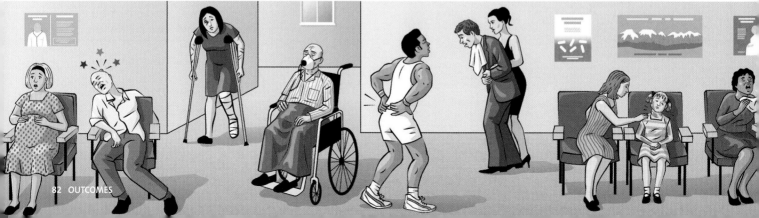

DEVELOPING CONVERSATIONS
Passing on messages

> In the first conversation, Michelle showed sympathy for Joop's girlfriend, Kattje, like this:
>
> *Tell her there's no need to apologise and I understand.*
> *Send her my love and tell her I'm thinking of her.*
>
> It is polite to use imperatives to ask people to pass on messages.

A **Put the words in the correct order to make messages.**
1 best them regards give my
2 me her a hug give from
3 give them my apologies for not coming
4 thinking tell say I'm hi and of them them
5 tell her not love her send worry my and to
6 to tell soon him better it take and get easy
7 himself need there's tell him apologise to look and after no to
8 give tell the baby my them wait and them can't congratulations I to see

B **Are there any messages in exercise A above that you don't like or would feel uncomfortable saying? Why?**

C **In pairs, take turns passing on different messages. Keep going until one of you can't think of anything different. For example:**
A: *Send Ana my love and tell her I'm thinking of her.*
B: *Thanks, I will. Give her my best regards.*
A: *Thanks, I will. Say hi and tell her to look after herself.*
B: *Thanks, I will. etc ... .*

GRAMMAR *Supposed to be -ing and should*

> We can use *be supposed to be -ing* to show things we have arranged to do in the future, but which we now can't or don't want to do.
>
> *We're supposed to be going* away for a few days.
> I know *we're supposed to be going* to the concert tonight.
>
> *Shouldn't* and *should* can show we have a positive feeling or expectation about a probable future event.
>
> *It shouldn't be too late.* (= I don't think it will be too late, which is good.)
> *We should be at yours by lunchtime.* (= I think we will be at yours by lunchtime, which is good.)

A **Complete the sentences with *should, shouldn't* or *be supposed to be -ing* and the verb in brackets.**
1 The doctor's given me some antibiotics, so I .... OK to come back to work soon. (be)
2 I .... a friend later, but I think I'm just going to go home to bed. I feel really rough. (meet)
3 You'll probably feel something when the needle goes in, but it .... too much. (hurt)
4 He .... the operation next week, but he's picked up an infection, so they might need to postpone it. (have)
5 Apparently, it's not a bad break so it .... long to heal. Hopefully, she'll only be on crutches for a few weeks. (take)
6 I .... to a concert tonight, but I've got so much work to do. You don't want to buy my ticket, do you? It .... really good! They're a great band. (go, be)

▶ **Need help? Read the grammar reference on page 151.**

CONVERSATION PRACTICE

You are going to role-play similar phone conversations to the ones in *Listening*. Look at the ideas below. Think about what you might say / ask using language from these pages. Have the conversation. Then swap roles.

Student A	Student B
Explain that a friend / family member is ill, so you can't ...	
	Show concern. Ask more about the problem.
Give some more details.	
	Comment / ask further questions.
Respond.	
	Pass on message and end conversation.

VOCABULARY Parts of the body and illnesses

A Label the picture with the words below.

lung	kidney	skin	rib	knee
liver	chest	brain	hip	elbow
ankle	toe	finger	skull	wrist

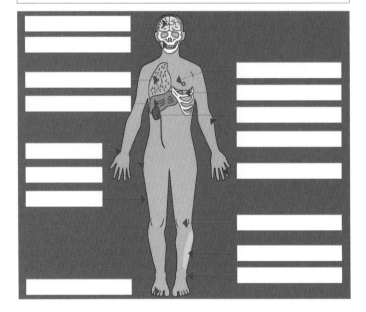

B Look at the diseases and conditions below and discuss the questions in groups.

AIDS	athlete's foot	tuberculosis
diabetes	Alzheimer's	arthritis
a stroke	Parkinson's	hepatitis

1 What part or parts of the body do they affect?
2 Do you know what causes any of them?
3 Can you think of any famous people who have suffered from or died of these things?
4 Can you name five other diseases or conditions?

READING

You are going to read a news article about health and humour.

A Before you read, discuss what effect laughter or a sense of humour might have on health – and in what ways.

B Read the article below and discuss these questions with a partner.
1 Did you learn anything new? What?
2 Did you find anything surprising or unbelievable?
3 Was there anything you didn't understand?

C In groups, discuss whether you find any aspects of the following things funny:

> things you do yourself
> school and teachers
> seeing someone trip over
> Hollywood comedies
> practical jokes played on others
> death

D Read the jokes on the right. Give each a rating of 1 to 5. Put a ? by any you don't understand.

E In groups, compare your ratings. Do you agree? Can anyone explain the jokes you didn't get?

F Complete 1–10 with the correct form of the words in bold from the jokes.
1 She's .... a radical treatment for a rare tropical disease.
2 The test .... positive, so they referred me to a consultant.
3 When he discovered it was ...., he made a will.
4 I had to wait six weeks to get a check-up. It's an ....!
5 TB is contagious and it can be difficult to ....
6 I was on crutches for two months after I .... on my kid's toy and broke my leg.
7 The government has .... permission for several new private hospitals to be built.
8 I was quite irritable the next day because he was .... so loudly that it kept me awake all night.
9 I've been trying to .... him all day, but he won't answer.
10 After he died, the family .... his organs for transplant.

LAUGHTER IS THE BEST MEDICINE

Researchers have found that laughter has important health benefits because it can relieve stress by releasing endorphins – the natural chemicals that help us feel good – and also by reducing levels of stress hormones such as adrenaline. In addition, laughter can help to clean out the lungs and to exercise a large number of muscles and organs in the body. Non-stop laughing for an hour would burn 500 calories – the equivalent of a good run. It is even claimed that laughing can make you live longer. However, for that to happen, Norwegian researcher Sven Svebak says that the outward signs of cheerfulness are less important than a sense of humour. A sense of humour is more of an attitude – an ability to see the funny side of things in all situations. A sense of humour is not genetic, it's something we develop and work on with others. This may be why, Svebak suggests, country people have a better-developed sense of humour than people in the city: they have closer communities.

❶

A salesman was walking along a beach when he came across an old lamp. When he rubbed it, a genie appeared. 'I'll **grant** you three wishes,' announced the genie, 'but for each wish your biggest rival will receive double what you ask for.' The salesman smiled. 'For my first wish, I'd like $100 million.' Instantly, the genie deposited the money in the salesman's bank account and said, 'but your rival now has $200 million.' The salesman then asked for a Ferrari and instantly one appeared. 'Enjoy it,' said the genie. 'Your rival now has two! What is your last wish?' 'Well,' said the salesman, 'I've always wanted to **donate** a kidney for transplant.'

❷

'Doctor, Doctor. I swallowed a bone.'
'Are you choking?'
'No, I really did!'

❸

A woman stormed into an eye hospital one day and started shouting at the receptionist. 'I demand to see the doctor in charge. Someone swapped my wig over while I was **undergoing** surgery to correct my eyesight yesterday. It's an **outrage**!' The receptionist called the surgeon in question. The woman explained. 'I looked in the mirror this morning and my wig was completely different – just cheap and nasty-looking!'
'So what are you complaining about?' replied the surgeon. 'The operation was obviously a complete success!'

❹

'Doctor, Doctor. I **snore** so loudly I keep myself awake.'
'Sleep in another room then!'

❺

'Doctor, how do I stop my nose from running?'
'Stick your foot out and **trip** it over!'

❻

A man ordered a drink in a café. He drank half and poured the rest over the waiter. The waiter grabbed him and asked, 'Why did you do that?'
'I'm so sorry. It's an illness I have. I can't **get rid of** it,' the man explained. 'I'm so ashamed. This is the first time I've been out in weeks.' The waiter suddenly felt sorry for the man. 'Haven't you seen anyone to get treatment?'
'No. It's just too embarrassing'.
'Listen, here's the number of a therapist I know. She's really good. Don't come back here until you've seen her.'
A few months later, the man comes back to the café. He orders a drink, has half of it and he chucks the other half in the waiter's face. 'Hey!' says the waiter. 'I thought I told you not to come back until you'd had some therapy!'
'I have had some! I don't feel ashamed of my condition anymore!

❼

A patient suffering from a strange bug goes to see his doctor. The doctor says, 'The test results have **come back** and I'm afraid I've got some bad news and some really bad news. The bad news is, it's **terminal** – you have just one day to live.'
'Oh my goodness! What could possibly be worse than that?'
'Well, we called yesterday, but we couldn't **get hold of** you.'

PRONUNCIATION
Sound chunking and stress

> When we read out a lot of text – for example, a joke – it's important to think first which words go together in sound chunks (groups) and which words are stressed.

A Read the joke below to yourself. Follow the stress and pauses that are marked. Guess how the joke might end.
A <u>man</u> goes to a <u>doctor</u> // and <u>says</u> // "<u>Doc</u>. // I <u>think</u> there's something <u>wrong</u> with me // <u>Every</u> time I <u>poke</u> myself // it <u>hurts</u>. // <u>Look</u>!" // And he starts <u>poking</u> himself. // He <u>pokes</u> himself in the <u>leg</u>. // "<u>Ouch</u>" // He <u>pokes</u> himself // in the <u>ribs</u> // "<u>Aagh</u>" // He <u>pokes</u> himself // in the <u>head</u> // and he literally <u>screams</u> in agony // "<u>Aaaaagh</u>! // You <u>see</u> what I <u>mean</u>, Doc?// You <u>see</u> how <u>bad</u> it is? // What's <u>happening</u> to me?"// And the <u>doctor</u> replies // "Yes . . .

B Tell a partner the joke with your ending. Whose ending is better?

C ✇ 12.2 Listen to the joke and find out the actual ending.

SPEAKING

A Work in groups of three.
Student A: look at File 10 on page 158.
Student B: look at File 5 on page 157.
Student C: look at File 14 on page 159.

Read the jokes and choose your favourite.

B Spend five minutes working on your favourite joke. Mark the words that are grouped together and the words that are stressed. Practise saying the joke to yourself in a whisper. What actions could you do to emphasise what happens in the joke? Finally, take turns telling your jokes. Use actions if you think they will help.

NATIVE SPEAKER ENGLISH

chuck

Chuck is a common, more informal way of saying *throw*.

He chucks the other half in the waiter's face.
Just chuck your things in the back of the car.
Can you chuck that rubbish in the bin?
He was chucked out of college for bad behaviour.

GRAMMAR Determiners

Determiners are words like *the, no, each, all* and *other* that go before nouns or pronouns to show which things you mean. Some refer only to singular nouns – e.g. *a, each, another, this*; some refer only to plural nouns – e.g. *these, those, few*; some refer to plural countable nouns and to uncountable nouns – e.g. *both ... and, all, some*; and some to all kinds of nouns – e.g. *my, no*.

Determiners don't normally have *of* between them and the noun they refer to: *each person, several hospitals, no doctors*. However, *of* follows when they are used with another determiner: *each of my sisters*. Also, with pronouns, they are usually followed by *of*: *both of them, most of us*, etc.

A Complete the quotes with the words in the box.

a little	all	any	many	more	much	no

1. A hospital is .... place to be sick!
2. So .... people spend their health gaining wealth – and then have to spend their wealth regaining their health!
3. The best medicine in the world is to love your job and to know who .... your enemies are!
4. Confidence and hope do .... good than medicine.
5. Lots of people spend so .... time watching their health that they don't have time to enjoy it!
6. .... doctor will tell you that the most dangerous patient is the one with .... knowledge!

B Which quote do you like best? Why?

▶ Need help? Read the grammar reference on page 151.

C Choose the correct words in italics.

1. *Both / Both of* nurses and doctors are underpaid.
2. There have been *a few / several of* incidents of negligence in hospitals, which have resulted in legal action.
3. *Many / Much* trainee nurses never actually complete their training and many *other / others* nurses leave the profession soon after qualifying.
4. *Most / Each* people get free health care – paid for by the state.
5. *Every / **All*** dental care is private. You have to pay for *any / some* dental work you need done.
6. In many cases, patients have *none / no* choice about how or where they are treated.
7. They're investing *less and less / fewer and fewer* money in health care. *The whole / All of* system is about to collapse.
8. *Every / All* hospital provides the same kind of treatment.
9. Far too *many / much* doctors end up only working in private healthcare.
10. More and more people are looking for *another / other* treatments outside the normal health service.

D Tick the sentences in exercise C that you think are true for your country. Decide why you think the sentences you didn't tick aren't true. Compare your ideas in groups.

LISTENING

You are going to hear a radio programme about the rise of medical tourism.

A Read the Fact File below. Then discuss these questions.
- What surprises you the most? Why?
- Is there anything you don't find surprising? Why?
- Why do you think medical tourism is such a huge growth area?

FACT FILE

- The global medical tourism industry is worth $1 billion a year.

- Around 50 million US residents – over 15% of the population – have no health care or insurance plan at all.

- Every year, hundreds of thousands of US citizens cross the border to Mexico for more affordable hospital treatment.

- India provides perhaps the most hi-tech services. Among other things, it specialises in cancer therapy and heart surgery.

- A hip replacement in Malaysia costs around £2,000, compared to around £10,000 in the UK (if you pay for it privately).

- Last year, more than 50% of all Austrian dental patients were treated in Hungary.

- Singapore attracts a quarter of a million overseas patients a year and ranks among the top six countries in the world for overall health care.

- Thailand is one of the most popular destinations in the world for those seeking cosmetic surgery.

B 🎧 **12.3 Listen to the introduction. Complete these notes.**

Ways globalisation already affects health care:

1 ¹ ....

2 Hospitals outsource record keeping to
   developing countries

3 ² .... also outsourced
   - helps cut costs

Predicted that over ³ ....
Americans and ⁴ ....
Britons will soon be travelling abroad for
treatment.

Mexico, Jordan, ⁵ ....,
⁶ .... and Thailand to be
main beneficiaries

Business expected to reach ⁷ ....
a year sometime soon.

However, questions starting to be asked.

C **Work in groups. Think of three good things and three bad things about medical tourism.**

D **Listen to the rest of the programme. Take notes on any good / bad things about medical tourism they mention.**

E **Decide if a–f apply to Damian, Cindy or Lily. You may choose more than one person. Listen again and check.**
a They have had some kind of treatment.
b They are trying to address the lack of care for those at the bottom of society.
c They believe that some doctors are more interested in money than in their patients.
d They are concerned about the rising number of scams.
e They became frustrated with the health system.
f They mention cutting edge medical techniques.

F **Work in groups. Discuss these questions:**
- Would you ever go abroad for treatment? Why? / Why not? Do you know anyone who has been? How did it go?
- Have you heard any stories about operations going wrong? What happened?
- Have you heard of any scams? How do they work?

LANGUAGE PATTERNS

Write the sentences in your language. Translate them back into English. Compare your English to the original.
Anyone thinking of going abroad for treatment needs to know they are taking a risk.
Anyone planning on coming should send me an email Anyone wanting to do a bungee jump is mad if you ask me.
Anyone going to the concert tonight?
Anyone thinking of taking the IELTS exam in the spring?
Anyone else finding this exercise difficult?

SPEAKING

A **You are going to conduct a class survey about health and medicine. Read the survey sheet below and add four extra things you would like to find out about.**

How many people in the class . . .
1 hate having injections?
2 have a check-up at least once a year?
3 would consider having plastic surgery at some point?
4 know they should really visit a dentist sometime soon?
5 are on a diet at the moment?
6 think health care should be free for everyone?
7 ....
8 ....
9 ....
10 ....

B **Carry out the survey. Ask extra questions to find out more information if you want to. Keep a record of numbers.**

C **Write a short report detailing the findings of your survey. Use some of the expressions in the box.**

Everyone in the class
The vast majority of the class
Approximately half the class
Around a quarter of the group
Several people
Only a few people
Hardly anyone
Nobody in the class

03 REVIEW

LEARNER TRAINING

A Work in groups. Discuss whether vocabulary or grammar is more important. Explain your ideas.

B Look at the statistics about grammar below. Then discuss these questions in small groups.
1 Do any of the statistics surprise you?

2 What might each fact mean for your learning?

- In spoken and written English, around 80% of all verb tenses used are in the present simple or past simple.
- Many grammatical structures, such as the future continuous, are used less than 1% of the time.

- Many words and expressions go with particular grammatical patterns. For example, *make someone redundant* is often used in the passive: *He was made redundant.*

GAME

Work in pairs. Student A use *only* the green squares; student B use *only* the yellow squares. Spend 5 minutes looking at your questions and revising the answers. Then take turns tossing a coin: Heads = move one of your squares; Tails = move two of your squares. When you land on a square, your partner looks at the relevant page in the book to check your answers, but *you don't*! If you are right, move forward one space (but don't answer the question until your next turn). If you aren't right, your partner tells you the right answer, and you miss a go. When you've finished the game change colours and play again.

Start

1 *Vocabulary* p. 64: say four good things and four bad things about a job.

2 *Developing conversations* p. 65: your partner should read the questions 1–5. Give five different short answers.

3 *Grammar* p. 69: your partner will say four situations in exercise C. Say a conditional sentence for each.

4 *Native English note* p. 6 if you can say what the *Native English* note wa and give an example, throw again.

5 *Native English note* p. 70: if you can say what the *Native English* note was and give an example, throw again.

6 **Miss a go!**

7 *Developing conversations* p. 71: your partner says the first questions in 1–6 and you reply *Can we make it ...* + reason.

8 *Grammar* p. 75: your partner will read three of the dialogues, stopping when there should be a tag. You say the tag.

9 *Vocabulary* p. 75: say eight of the words / expressions in bold.

10 *Native English note* p. 76: if you can say what the *Native English* note was and give an example, throw again.

11 **Miss a go!**

12 *Vocabulary* p. 77: say eight problems you could have with a vehicle.

13 *Developing conversations* p. 77: your partner will say 1–6. Show surprise. Add a comment or question.

14 *Grammar* p. 80: say six sentences about transport and travel, starting with *What* or *The thing that.*

15 *Vocabulary* p. 82: your partner will say six medical problems. You say three words connected to each.

16 *Developing conversations* p. 83: pass on six different messages.

17 *Native English note* p. 85: if you can say what the *Native English* note was and give an example, throw again.

18 *Vocabulary* p. 84: say ten parts of the body and four diseases.

Finish

For each of the activities below, work in groups of three. Use the Vocabulary Builder if you want to.

CONVERSATION PRACTICE

Choose one of the following *Conversation practice* activities.
Careers and studying p. 65
Socialising p. 71
Transport and travel p. 77
Health and medicine p. 83

Two of you should do the task. The third person should listen and then give a mark between 1 and 10 for the performance. Explain your decision. Then change roles.

ACT OR DRAW

One person should act or draw as many of these words as you can in three minutes. Your partners should try to guess the words. Do not speak while you are acting or drawing!

gambling	tray	overtake	polish
earplug	sneak	handbrake	frown
overhear	bald	tow away	swerve
crutches	poke	swelling	liver
jewellery	dent	windscreen	sneeze
pavement	slap	pedestrians	itchy

QUIZ

Answer as many of the questions as possible.
1 What happens when a company **restructures**?
2 Think of two **menial** jobs. Are they **stimulating**?
3 Say two different **ranks** in the army.
4 Who might someone **suck up to** at work – and why?
5 How do you feel about something that's an **outrage**?
6 What can be **cosy**? Is it nice?
7 Give two reasons why a politician might **resign**.
8 What do you do if a room is very **stuffy**?
9 What's the difference between **chat** and **chat up**?
10 What happens if a party **gets out of han**d?
11 Say three things which are used as **fuel**.
12 If you're driving, when do you need to **indicate**?
13 Where do you **embark** from?
14 Where do you usually get **blisters**? Why?
15 What kinds of things do you do to **recuperate**?

COLLOCATIONS

Take turns to read out collocation lists from Units 9–12 of the Vocabulary Builder. Where there is a '~', say *'blah'* instead. Your partner should guess as many words as they can.

PRONUNCIATION Word stress

A **Work in pairs. Decide how many syllables each of the adjectives below has – and mark the main stress in each one.**

automatic	pioneering
claustrophobic	remarkable
contagious	rigorous
desolate	spiritual
fraudulent	stimulating
globalised	terminal
infuriating	undervalued
irritable	unpatriotic
menial	versatile

B 🔊 R 3.1 **Listen and practise saying the words.**

C **With your partner, think of at least one thing that each of the adjectives in exercise A can describe.**

D **Spend three minutes memorising the adjectives. Then work with another pair. Group A: close your books. Group B: explain each adjective by saying what it can describe. See how many words Group A can remember. For example:**
B: *Lots of diseases can be this. Bird flu is highly …?*
A: *Oh, OK. Contagious.*
B: *That's right.*

E **When you have finished, change roles. Group B: close your books. Group A: explain the adjectives.**

DICTATION

You are going to hear a short extract from one of the texts you read in 9–12. You will hear it only once.

A 🔊 R 3.2 **Work in your groups. Listen and take notes on what you hear. You won't have time to write everything.**

B **Work together to write the whole text.**

C **Compare what you have written with the audioscript on page 177–178.**

LISTENING

A ⟡R 3.3 **Listen to five people talking. What they say is connected to different celebrations. Match items a–f to speakers 1–5. There is one item that you do not need.**

a ... explaining why they're retiring
b ... explaining their future plans
c ... describing an accident they had
d ... talking about what they do
e ... giving a lecture
f ... warning people of dangers

B **Listen again and match items a–f with speakers 1–5. There is one item that you do not need.**

a ... They're going to be the host of a party.
b ... They couldn't deal with a problem, because of someone else's mistake.
c ... They say people are wrong in their beliefs about celebrations.
d ... They say they partly caused a problem.
e ... They say they made an embarrassing mistake.
f ... They say someone hurt their foot.

[... / 10]

GRAMMAR

A **Complete the conversation with *one* word in each gap. Some answers are negative contractions.**

A: What's the matter?
B: Well, I'm ¹........................... to be going out with some friends for dinner, but I'm not sure I can make it now. I've got so ²........................... work on at the moment.
A: You really can't go?
B: Well, if the boss ³........................... agreed to take on this new order, I might have ⁴........................... able to, but I've already got a deadline for Friday. ⁵........................... really annoys me ⁶........................... that he expects us to do all these things and work overtime for ⁷........................... extra money.
A: I know. He's given you a big workload, ⁸........................... he?
B: You couldn't help me, ⁹........................... you?
A: Not now, but hopefully I'll ¹⁰........................... finished what I need to do by lunchtime, so I could probably give you ¹¹........................... help this afternoon.
B: Really? That'd be great. Anyway I suppose we ¹²........................... stop moaning about it and just carry on, or else we'll never get it finished!

[... / 12]

B **Complete the second sentences using the words in brackets so they have a similar meaning to the first ones.**

1 I don't think we will be home too late.
We .... too late. (should)
2 I've arranged to go out tonight, but I don't feel very well.
.... tonight, but I don't feel very well. (supposed)
3 I find her laugh really annoying!
What really .... the way she laughs. (annoys)
4 He crashed because he was driving too fast.
He would .... so fast. (if)
5 I was offered a job – that's why I'm living here now.
If I hadn't .... living here now. (been)

[... / 5]

LANGUAGE PATTERNS

Find the six incorrect sentences and correct them.

1 I can't see myself to stay there long-term.
2 Be careful to spill your coffee.
3 Be careful to cross the road.
4 What do you see you doing in the future?
5 Anyone else finding this exercise difficult?
6 The first time was bad, even but this was worse!
7 I felt really foolish, but even I had to laugh.
8 Anyone plan on coming should send me an email.

[... / 8]

PREPOSITIONS

Choose the correct preposition.

1 I can't prove anything. It's my word *against / at* theirs.
2 The TV presenter swore *in / on* air and had to apologise.
3 I was ashamed *of / for* their behaviour. It was an outrage.
4 People who are *in / of* the public eye always have to watch what they say.
5 We learned lots of poems *by / for* heart at school. I can still recite some!
6 They lost the court case, but they're appealing *against / at* the decision.
7 I put my foot *in / with* it when I said I'd seen him.
8 There was too much food and most of it went *to / for* waste.
9 They went *on / to* a pilgrimage to Jerusalem.

[... / 9]

COLLOCATIONS

Match the nouns with the groups of words they go with.

effect	fortune	spell	organ	surgery
remark	chest	breath	brake	faith

1 have a knock-on ~ / cause side ~s / a positive ~
2 do ~ transplants / suffer from ~ failure / ~ donors
3 make a ~ / cost a ~ / seek fame and ~
4 undergo ~ / recuperate from ~ / pioneering ~
5 have a dizzy ~ / a hot ~ of weather / a brief ~ in hospital
6 slam on the ~s / put the hand~ on / replace the ~s
7 make a casual ~ / a stupid ~ / his ~s caused outrage
8 have a crisis of ~ / lose ~ / restore your ~
9 be out of ~ / save your ~ / get your ~ back
10 have a tight ~ / get a ~ infection / severe ~ pains

[... / 10]

▶ **Find this difficult? Re-read Units 9–12 in the *Vocabulary Builder* for more information on collocation.**

FORMING WORDS

Complete the sentences with the correct forms of the words in CAPITALS.

1 My dad reached .... age last year, but he decided to carry on working. RETIRE
2 They told me I didn't have the right .... QUALIFY
3 Make sure you take out some travel .... before you go. INSURE
4 I think you've .... me. That's not what I meant at all. UNDERSTAND
5 A campaign group is trying to stop the .... of a new law to censor the Internet. IMPLEMENT
6 The whole area is incredibly beautiful – and because it's so remote, it's still pretty much .... TOUCH
7 They were planning to get married this year, but she broke off the .... for some reason. ENGAGE
8 It used to be a really lovely house, but over recent years, it's fallen into .... REPAIR
9 He lost his job last year – and he's spent most of his .... pay already! REDUNDANT
10 Can you just .... the main points of the talk? SUMMARY

[... / 10]

PHRASAL VERBS

Complete the sentences with the correct form of the phrasal verbs in the box.

live up to	frown on	turn up	break out
freshen up	work out	take out	pass out

1 Do you want to have a rest and then .... before we go out?
2 We were together for about three years, but it didn't .... and we split up.
3 I thought it'd be really good, but unfortunately it didn't .... my expectations.
4 I missed the start of the meeting because I .... late.
5 I'd .... travel insurance if you're going abroad.
6 When he saw all the blood, he just ....
7 Kissing or hugging in public is .... there. It's not really acceptable behaviour in their society.
8 I put this cream on, which made me .... in a rash.

[... / 8]

VOCABULARY

Complete the words in the text. The first letters are given.

I work with kids from deprived backgrounds. It's a very [1]re........................... job, although some have a lot of difficulties, which can make it quite emotionally [2]dr........................... . At the moment, I'm really enjoying it, and last month, I got [3]pr........................... to a new position with more responsibility, so I feel I'm really [4]st........................... myself and getting somewhere. I also got a small [5]ra........................... so I can afford to replace my car now. The kids all laugh at the car I have now because it's covered in dents and [6]sc........................... . They must think I'm a terrible driver, but I've actually never had an accident. The worst that's happened is that I got a flat tyre once. I bought the car second-hand and it's served me well. The problem now is that the engine [7]ov........................... in summer and the [8]wi........................... is cracked, which is a bit dangerous!

[... / 8]

[Total ... /80]

13 LIFE EVENTS

VOCABULARY Life events

A Work in pairs. Think of an example of each of the things below. The examples could be things you have heard about in the news or they could involve people you know. Tell each other what you know about each story.

· a couple getting together
· a couple splitting up
· someone being sacked
· someone dropping out of university
· someone being kicked out of somewhere
· someone changing careers
· someone getting a degree, a Master's or PhD
· someone moving house
· someone passing away
· someone getting killed
· someone being sent to jail
· someone giving birth

B Match the sentences below to events from exercise A.

1 He was convicted of corruption. Apparently, he'd been taking bribes for years.
2 He'd been struggling for a bit and he got offered a job, so he decided not to bother graduating. He's really happy.
3 The baby weighed five kilos. It's no wonder she was in labour for so long.
4 I was told someone had insulted him and he'd then overreacted, so they told him to leave!
5 I heard she'd been having treatment for cancer for over a year, but unfortunately, it continued to spread.
6 He'd been thinking about it for a while, as he was fed up with all the travelling, so he retrained as a counsellor.
7 I think they'd been through a rough patch before and got through it, but this time they decided to call it a day.
8 Apparently, he'd fancied her for ages, but she was seeing someone else, so when they split up, he asked her out.
9 His team had been on a terrible run. They'd only won one game in ten. Then they got knocked out of the cup, so that was it.

C Complete the collocations below with nouns from exercise B. Then translate the complete collocations.

a take ...
b get offered a ...
c be in ...
d ... spreads
e retrain as a ...
f go through a rough ...
g call it a ...
h ask ... out
i be on a terrible ...
j get knocked out of the ...

D Compare your examples from exercise A with a new partner. Explain what led up to each event and what followed. Try to use some of the language from exercises B and C.

GRAMMAR
Past perfect simple and continuous

> Past perfect forms emphasise something that happened before another past event that has already been mentioned.
>
> A: So why did he drop out of the course?
> B: *He'd been struggling* and he just decided *he'd had* enough.

A Look at *Vocabulary* exercise B. Underline five examples of the past perfect simple and circle four examples of the past perfect continuous. In pairs, discuss the differences in the way they are used.

▶ Need help? Read the grammar reference on page 152.

B Think of a response to each of these sentences using the past perfect simple or continuous.
1 So why did your father decide to start running?
2 But how come she didn't have any money?
3 What made them decide to move to Brazil?
4 So what made you decide to become a zoologist?
5 How come he gave up playing basketball?
6 So how come you sold your flat?

LISTENING

You are going to hear two conversations where the speakers gossip about other people.

A 🔊 13.1 Listen and answer the questions for each conversation.
1 Why do they start talking about the other people?
2 What pieces of news surprise one of the speakers?

SPEAKING

A Work in groups. Discuss these questions:
- What are the most popular gossip magazines in your country? Do you ever read them? Why? / Why not?
- Would you ever consider adopting children?
- Can you think of something you heard which changed your opinion of someone? How?
- Do you know anyone who has ever been in a long-distance relationship? How did it work?
- Would you consider moving to a different country for love? If not, why not?

DEVELOPING CONVERSATIONS
Showing uncertainty

> We use lots of different expressions to show we are reporting things that we're not sure are true.
>
> *Apparently*, she's got a really good job there.

A Complete the phrases in the dialogue with one word in each space.
A: Did you hear about Gavin getting married?
B: Yeah. It was a bit sudden, wasn't it?
A As ¹f...................... as I know, they'd only been going out for five weeks!
B: Really? ²A...................... I understand it, they'd actually been at school together.
A: Right. Well, ³f...................... what I've heard, she's a really nice woman and, ⁴a...................... , she's from an incredibly rich family.
B: Really? I was ⁵t...................... they didn't invite many people to the wedding because they couldn't afford it.
A: Well, ⁶a...................... to my friend Justin, she had a falling-out with her father because he didn't really approve.

B You are going to have a conversation like the one in exercise A – about an imaginary man called Bill. Invent 'facts' about where he has moved to, why, what it's like and who he is living with. In pairs, have the conversation using your ideas and the expressions from exercise A. Begin:
A: *Did you hear about Bill moving?*
B: *Yeah. From what I've heard, he's gone to Greece.*

CONVERSATION PRACTICE

A You are going to have similar conversations to the ones you heard in *Listening*. Think about someone you know or a celebrity. Think of some news you heard about them recently.

B Work in pairs. Take turns starting conversations with:
Did you know / hear about X ....?

Try to keep each conversation going for three minutes by asking questions or adding extra bits of information.

SPEAKING

A Work in groups. Discuss these questions:
- Do you argue a lot or do you tend to avoid confrontation?
- When you argue, who do you usually argue with? What about?
- What annoys you most about your friends / family? Why?
- Is there anything you'd like people in your family to stop – or start – doing?

GRAMMAR *be always -ing / wish and would*

> **be always / constantly + -ing** emphasises habits.
> *I'm very argumentative. I'm constantly arguing with people.*
> *He's very charming. He's always complimenting you.*
>
> **I wish + would** shows you want people to behave differently.
> *I wish he would listen more carefully.* (he doesn't usually)
> *I wish she wouldn't smoke inside.* (but she does normally)

A Use *be always / constantly + -ing* or *wish + would* and the follow-up ideas to add to the initial comments in 1–7.

1 She's so sweet, so affectionate.
   give me hugs and kisses
   She's constantly giving me hugs and kisses.
2 He's not a very good listener.
   shut up and let others speak sometimes
3 He's such a bore.
   talk about something else apart from studying
4 Honestly, he's so romantic.
   buy me roses and say he loves me
5 She's so intense about everything.
   lighten up a bit and have a laugh a bit more
6 Don't be so defensive!
   take everything I say as a personal attack.
7 My sister's so bad-tempered and spoilt.
   My dad let her get her own way

▶ Need help? Read the grammar reference on page 152.

B Write two-line comments similar to those in exercise A about these characteristics.

| stubborn | laid-back | disruptive | generous |
| competitive | moody | vain | polite |

C In pairs, tell a partner about:
- Five people you know who should change their habits:
  I (sometimes) wish … would(n't) … .
- Five people you know with characteristics in A or B:
  … is so / such a … . (S)he's always … . / (S)he never…

READING

You are going to read a Wiki page on how to avoid conflicts.

A Read the introduction below. In groups, answer the questions.
1 Could you imagine yourself in any of the situations? Why? / Why not?
2 Which is the most difficult situation to be in?
3 Do you think any of these conflicts could have been avoided? How?
4 How would you try to end the situation if you were involved or were watching?

 www.dealwithconflicts.com

Imagine these situations: a three-year-old has a tantrum while her parents are shopping. She throws herself on the floor, kicking and screaming.

A parent shouts at a teenager 'This place is like a pigsty. I'm constantly clearing up after you and I'm sick of it. I wish you'd put your stuff away just once and stop being such a slob.'

Two lads start fighting after one of them bumps into the other and spills a drink he was carrying.

Two colleagues – a woman, who is relatively new to the company, and a man – have stopped talking to each other after clashing several times. The woman complains that her colleague is stubborn and never accepts any of her ideas. The man says that she is constantly making comments which undermine him in the office, and that she shows no respect.

Conflicts of one kind of another are bound to happen on occasion. However, many can be avoided entirely and when they do happen, we can learn to handle them better so the situation doesn't get out of control. Furthermore, the techniques apply to all conflicts, whether they are with babies and toddlers or between adult colleagues.

B Read the Wiki on the right and match the headings below to each paragraph. There is one extra heading you will not need. In pairs, check your answers and explain your choices.
a Mind your language
b Not getting angry doesn't mean giving in
c Give choices
d Stay calm
e Don't wait to repair the damage
f You need to pay attention to body language
g Remember there are two sides to every story
h Know the flashpoints
i Be flexible

C Find the sentences in the Wiki that have the same meaning as 1–8.

1 If you end up insulting people, the situation won't improve.
2 When you speak to each other again, don't talk about what you said or did before.
3 Another person's body language may show us that we are annoying that person unintentionally.
4 We shouldn't continue to argue just because we want to avoid seeming weak.
5 It's OK to provide rules and defend your beliefs.
6 Don't start shouting.
7 Attempt to delay awkward discussions till less stressful times.
8 When you think about it, different backgrounds can make you think in different and reasonable ways.

D Work in pairs. Discuss these questions:
- Do you agree with all the techniques mentioned?
- Do you think they would work in all the different conflicts in the introduction?
- Could you learn from any of the pieces of advice? In what way?

E In pairs, re-write the Wiki. Remove things you don't agree with – or change them so you do agree. Add at least one new idea of your own.

---

www.dealwithconflicts.com

| SEARCH | ARTICLE | DISCUSS | EDIT | HISTORY | SHARE |

1 You may be in the right. The child might be screaming because you won't buy him chocolate, a colleague might be genuinely setting out to block your ideas. Setting children boundaries or standing up for yourself is sometimes necessary. What's important is to steer through these confrontations calmly and successfully – not to steer clear of them altogether or to simply let others get their way.

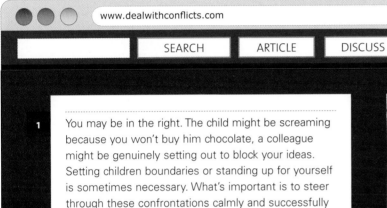

2 Don't raise your voice. If you do, your 'opponent' will also inevitably increase their volume and the discussion will turn into an irrational shouting match.

3 Saying *always* or *never* is likely to immediately make people defensive, while *wishing* someone would do something suggests the idea is an impossibility already! Resorting to personal abuse will then only make matters worse. Instead, try using *sometimes*, or describe your feelings without directly referring to the other person: 'I don't like it when people scream, 'I want' or 'Seeing an untidy room upsets me''.

4 Sometimes it's best to postpone an argument. We all have buttons that certain people know how to push and which are guaranteed to irritate us. It is best to acknowledge this and attempt to step back when you see things coming. In the same way, if you're not a morning person, for example, try to put off sensitive topics of conversation till later on in the day, when you will be naturally less tense.

5 Listen to others. When it comes down to it, differences in gender, generation, character or nationality may produce a different perspective to yours, and one that is equally valid. Is the child asking for chocolate really saying he's tired? Is your colleague in a vulnerable position within the company? Is the underlying message he's giving actually 'I'm worried about redundancy'?

6 Don't get stuck defending an unreasonable position just for the sake of not losing face. Be prepared to accept that you may have been wrong or that there might be some middle ground where you could compromise.

7 Never tackle sensitive or controversial matters over the phone or by email. Remember that gestures and facial expressions can provide warning signs that you're rubbing someone up the wrong way, which may lead you to change your approach to the subject. The way you stand can also send messages.

8 You may occasionally have a falling-out despite your best efforts. The key then is to try and get in touch as quickly as possible rather than letting things drift and making an upsetting incident worse. When you get in touch, don't go over old ground again. Say 'I'm sorry we argued' or 'Can we agree to disagree?' And in return, accept any such offers you receive with good grace and move on.

SPEAKING

A **Put the life events below into the order you think they most usually happen in.**

a engagement
b your funeral
c retirement
d your birth
e wedding
f getting a job
g starting a family
h coming of age
i leaving home
j naming ceremony
k buying or renting a flat / house
l learning to drive

B **In pairs, compare your ideas. Discuss any differences.**

C **In groups, discuss which of the life events in exercise A you think are:**
- the most significant
- the most stressful
- the most joyous
- the most financially draining
- the most emotionally draining

VOCABULARY Birth, marriage and death

A **Read the short text below. Translate the words in bold into your language.**

Our son, Jackson, was born last year. Thankfully, it was quite ¹**a straightforward birth**. My wife ²**went into labour** in the middle of the night and we ³**rushed to the maternity ward** in the local hospital. She was only ⁴**in labour** for six hours. She then took the full year of ⁵**maternity leave** that she was entitled to by law – and now she's ⁶**expecting another baby**. She ⁷**had her first scan** last week and apparently ⁸**it's due** sometime around the middle of May!

B **In pairs, Discuss these questions:**
- Do you know anyone who is pregnant at the moment? When's the baby due?
- Do you know how much maternity / paternity leave people are entitled to in your country?
- What do you think the best age to have kids is? Why?
- Do you know any rituals / ceremonies connected to birth?

C **Decide which of the nouns in the box are connected to weddings and which are connected to funerals.**

mourners	bride	coffin	town hall
cemetery	groom	condolences	reception
best man	grave	ashes	honeymoon

D **Complete the sentences below with nouns from exercise C.**

1 We didn't actually get married in church. We had a civil ceremony in the ....
2 Over 500 .... came to my father's funeral.
3 I was so sorry to hear about Miguel's mother. Please send him my .... when you see him.
4 The actual wedding was only for close friends and family, but about 500 people came to the .... afterwards.
5 I go and visit her .... every Sunday. I like to keep it clean and leave flowers there.
6 We spent our .... in Hawaii. It was perfect!
7 He wasn't buried – he was cremated. His .... were scattered at sea.
8 I'd like to propose a toast to the .... and groom.

E **Work in pairs. Discuss these questions:**
- Have you been to many weddings? Whose? What were they like? Where were they held?
- What's your idea of the perfect wedding / reception / honeymoon?
- Do weddings and funerals vary much in your country? How? Have you heard of any unusual ones?

LISTENING

You are going to hear four people talking about significant life events.

A **You will hear all the groups of words below. With a partner, discuss which life event each group might be connected to – and how.**

1 the second Monday of every January / 20 / many thousands of pounds
2 three to seven days / dawn
3 65 / 60 / 75% / three
4 90 / over 3000 / five blossoms

B 🔊 **13.2 Listen and take notes on the connections.**

C **Listen again and answer the questions about the four extracts.**

1a Where are the coming-of-age ceremonies held?
1b What happens during / after the ceremonies?
2a How have Moroccan weddings changed?
2b What happens after the groom leaves his house?
3a How did Ernesto find being retired to begin with?
3b What are the best things about retirement for him?
4a What was the funeral like?
4b What do the five blossoms represent?

Ernesto Amina Hui Misato

LANGUAGE PATTERNS

Write the sentences in your language. Translate them back into English. Compare your English to the original.

Parties and feasting continue throughout the week.

My kids have ten weeks' holiday throughout the year.

I'm not sure if it's celebrated throughout the world.

The school has recently been redecorated throughout.

Their flat has got these lovely old wooden floors throughout.

It was a tough time, but my family were great throughout.

SPEAKING

A **Work in groups. Discuss these questions:**
- Do you know why your parents gave you your name?
- What are your favourite names for boys / girls? Why?
- How many different ways of marking someone's coming of age can you think of?
- What's the best age to leave home? Why?
- Do you think it's a good idea to have a long engagement before getting married?
- What do you think is good / difficult about retirement?
- Describe a typical funeral in your country. What usually happens?
- Do you want to be buried or cremated? Why?

In this unit you learn how to:
- deal with banks
- apologise and explain problems in formal settings
- use descriptive literary language
- express regrets

Grammar
- Passives
- *wish*

Vocabulary
- Banks and money
- Metaphor

Reading
- The Magic Moneybag (Part 1)

Listening
- Two money-related problems
- The Magic Moneybag (Part 2)
- A debate about the lottery

VOCABULARY Banks and money

A Add the nouns in the box to the groups of words they go with 1–8.

account	currency	loan	money
overdraft	debt	cash	credit

1 withdraw money from my ~ / deposit money in my ~
2 be short of ~ / pay in ~ / a ~ point / ~ flow problems
3 be refused ~ / have a bad ~ rating / offer ~ / buy on ~
4 run up huge ~s / write the ~ off / get into ~ / be in ~
5 strengthen the ~ / the ~ collapsed / a stable ~
6 run out of ~ / be good with ~ / ~ laundering / make good ~
7 ~ sharks / apply for a ~ / pay off my ~ / a student ~
8 go into ~ / an ~ facility / apply for an ~ / my ~ limit

B Work in pairs. Discuss these questions:
- Why might a company have cash flow problems?
- Where might you be offered credit?
- Can you think of any currencies that have collapsed?
- If a person is good / bad with money, what kind of things do they do?
- Why – and how – does money laundering occur?
- What problems might you have if you borrow from a loan shark?

LISTENING

You are going to hear two conversations connected to banks and money.

A 🔊 14.1 Listen and answer the questions for each conversation.
1 What does the first speaker want?
2 What problems does the first speaker encounter?
3 What happens in the end?

B Work in pairs. Try to complete the sentences. Then listen again to check your answers.
1a Do you have some form of .... ?
1b We also need .... of your current address.
1c I just pay a .... amount every month.
1d What we can do is give you a three-month .... period on a current account.
1e This is ...., really, but what choice do I have?
2a That .... be a problem.
2b I'm afraid we're actually completely .... of bolivar.
2c I'll get some dollars just to be on the safe ....
2d What's the .... rate?
2e There's 2% .... on all transactions.

C Work in pairs. Discuss these questions:
- Have you ever opened a bank account? What kind? Who with? Was it easy to do?
- Can you think of four different problems people sometimes have with banks and bank accounts?
- Do you know anyone who has had problems with banks? When? What happened?

NATIVE SPEAKER ENGLISH

after
We often use *after* to mean *trying to find* or *looking for*.

What kind of account were you after?
How much are you after?
Are you after anything in particular?
I'm after a new phone for under three hundred euros.
Did you manage to find what you were after?

DEVELOPING CONVERSATIONS
Apologising and offering explanations

> **In formal settings, we can use these expressions to apologise:**
> *I'm really / terribly / awfully sorry.*
> *I do apologise.*
>
> **When dealing with problems in business situations, it is common for people to apologise and then offer a polite explanation or solution.**
> *I'm awfully sorry, sir, but I'm afraid we're actually completely out of bolivars.*
> *I'm terribly sorry this is taking so long, madam. The computers aren't usually this slow!*

A **Put the words in the correct order to make the kinds of explanations people give after making an apology.**
1 the look at once I'll into matter
2 are the very being today computers slow
3 have some of there been kind must mix-up
4 down at the I'm our moment is afraid system
5 can we absolutely afraid nothing there's I'm do
6 afraid to make decision I'm not authorised I'm that
7 word can see manager do and I'll a with my what I have

B ✎ 14.2 **Listen and check your answers. Practise saying 1–7.**

C **In pairs, take turns saying and responding to the sentences below. When responding, apologise and offer an explanation / solution.**
a Why is it taking so long?
b Why don't you have any record of my deposit?
c My driving licence should be sufficient identification, shouldn't it?
d The cash point outside has eaten my card.
e I keep forgetting my PIN number. Can I change it?
f I've just had my statement. Why am I being charged every time I withdraw money from my local cash point?

GRAMMAR Passives

A **Look at the two sentences from *Listening* below and discuss these questions in pairs.**
1 How is the passive formed in each case?
2 Why is the passive used in each case?

> The thirty pounds will be refunded.

> It looks as if it's all been bought.

▶ **Need help? Read the grammar reference on page 153.**

B **Complete the sentences with the correct passive form of the verbs in brackets.**
1 The computer's very slow this morning, I'm afraid. The system .... at the moment. (update)
2 I pay all my bills by standing order, so the money .... automatically at the end of every month. (send)
3 It would appear that your overdraft limit .... repeatedly .... over recent weeks. (exceed)
4 I spoke to someone yesterday and they told me the money .... already .... (transfer)
5 My credit card .... three times yesterday and I'd like to know why. (reject)
6 We can't accept this cheque, I'm afraid. Look. It .... yet. (not / sign)
7 It's not my fault! Up until last week, all my correspondence from the bank .... to the wrong address. (forward)
8 According to our records, the letter .... to you on the 28th of last month. (send)
9 We have all your details and you .... as soon as a decision .... (contact, make)

CONVERSATION PRACTICE

Work in pairs. You are going to role-play six short conversations between customers and bank clerks, similar to the ones in *Listening*.

A **Student A:** read File 7 on page 157.
Student B: read File 19 on page 161.

Spend a few minutes preparing what to say. Use as much language from these pages as possible.

B **Role-play the conversations. Take turns being the customer and the bank clerk. Sort out the problems that arise.**

SPEAKING

A **Read the traditional Chinese sayings connected to money below. Decide what you think each one means – and how far you agree.**
1 Be careful what you wish for.
2 A long march starts with the very first step.
3 An ambitious horse will never return to its old stable.
4 When you have only two pennies left in the world, buy a loaf of bread with one, and a flower with the other.
5 Without rice, even the cleverest housewife cannot cook.
6 A single tree makes no forest; one string makes no music.
7 Giving your child a skill is better than giving them a thousand pieces of gold.
8 A bird can only sit on one branch; a mouse can't drink more water than flows in a river.
9 An inch of time is worth an inch of gold, but it is hard to buy one inch of time with one inch of gold.

B **Discuss your ideas with a partner. Do you know any similar sayings to 1–9 above?**

READING

You are going to read a Chinese folktale about attitudes to work and wealth.

A **Read the first part of the tale on the opposite page. Then answer the questions in pairs.**
1 Why do you think the bundles of wood were taken up to the heavens?
2 Why do you think the old man refused to let the woodcutter take the moneybag he wanted?
3 What problems / opportunities did the magic moneybag bring?
4 How do you think the story will end?

B 🔊 **14.3 Now listen to the end of the story. In pairs, compare what was similar to and what was different from your predictions.**

C **Replace the words in *italics* with the more descriptive literary synonyms used in the first part of the tale.**
1 The husband *realised* something strange was going on.
2 An enormous rope *came down* from the sky.
3 *Looking* out of the bundle of wood, the woodcutter saw an old man.
4 The old man *laughed*.
5 The young man was *shown* into a magnificent palace.
6 The golden walls were *shining* in the sunlight.
7 The first bag the woodcutter grabbed was *full of* precious things.
8 *Holding* onto the enormous rope, the woodcutter was lowered to the ground.

D **Work in groups. Discuss these questions:**
- Which of the following topics do you think the story deals with? In what way?

| poverty | honesty | greed | fame and fortune |
| justice | death | dignity | fear |

- What values do you think the story expresses? Do you agree with these values?
- Do you know any similar stories – or any other folktales – connected to money?

GRAMMAR *wish*

A **Look at these sentences and complete the rule.**
I wish we didn't have to, but we are penniless
How I wish I'd never opened that bag.

> After *wish*, we use .... to refer to current situations that can't be changed and .... to talk about regrets about past situations.

B **Choose the correct form in the sentences below.**
1 Obviously, I wish *I hadn't taken out / didn't take out* the loan with them, but at the time I really needed the cash.
2 I really wish *I hadn't had to / didn't have to* do this, but I've got no choice.
3 I wish *I'd stuck / I stuck* with my old job.
4 I wish *he'd been better / he was better* with money. Then we might be able to afford to buy a house in the future.
5 I wish *I could've paid / could pay* you, I really do, but I'm still waiting for people to pay me back what they owe me.
6 I wish *you'd said / you said* something. I might not have made such a fool of myself!
7 I wish there *had been / was something* I could say to make you feel better, but I know there isn't.
8 I sometimes wish *I'd never started / I never started*. It's turning out to be a bit of a nightmare.

C **Discuss what actually happened – or what the situation now is for 1–8 above.**

▶ **Need help? Read the grammar reference on page 153.**

D **Play a game of *'Be careful what you wish for.'* Think of five wishes each. Take turns saying a wish. Your partner should say how the wish goes / went wrong.**
A: *I wish I was a millionaire.*
B: *Your wish is granted, but now you'll get married to someone who's only interested in your money. They'll divorce you and the legal fees leave you penniless.*

The Magic Moneybag

There once was a poor young couple who lived in a tiny hut. They survived by chopping and selling wood. One day, they placed a big bundle of wood in their courtyard, to take to market next day. The other bundle they kept in the kitchen for their own use. When they woke the following day, the bundle in the courtyard had mysteriously disappeared. There was nothing to do but sell the one they'd been keeping for themselves.

That same day, they chopped another two bundles of firewood. They left one in the courtyard again and kept the other. The following morning, the bundle in the courtyard had vanished again. The same thing happened on the third and fourth days as well, and the husband sensed something strange was going on.

On the fifth day, he hid himself inside a bundle in the courtyard. At midnight, an enormous rope descended from the sky, attached itself to the bundle and lifted it up to the heavens, with the woodcutter still inside it.

They came to a halt on a cloud and, peering out, the woodcutter saw an old man with long, grey hair. As he was untying the bundle, the old man found the woodcutter inside and asked, 'Other people only cut one bundle of firewood a day. Why do you cut two?'

The woodcutter replied, 'I wish we didn't have to, but we're penniless. One's for our own use and the other we sell – to buy rice with.'

The old man chuckled. 'I know you lead a frugal life,' he said. 'I'll give you a present. Take it with you and it'll provide you with a living.'

The young man was then ushered into a magnificent palace, its golden walls glistening in the sunlight. He was taken to a room full of moneybags and told to choose whichever he wanted.

The woodcutter grabbed the largest moneybag, which was crammed with precious things. At this moment, the old man's face became stern. 'No! I'm sorry. Not that one. I'll give you an empty one. Take one piece of silver out of it every day – and no more.' The woodcutter reluctantly agreed. He took the empty bag and, clinging onto the enormous rope, was lowered to the ground.

Once home, he told his wife the story. She was ecstatic. From then on, they'd open the moneybag every morning and a lump of silver would roll out. They started saving up.

Time passed slowly. One day, the husband suggested buying an ox, but his wife disagreed. Later, he suggested buying some land, but his wife didn't agree to that either. More time went by, and the wife proposed building a little thatched cottage. The husband was desperate to spend the money and said, 'As we've got so much, why don't we build a big mansion?' The wife couldn't dissuade her husband and reluctantly went along with the idea.

SPEAKING

A Work in pairs. Discuss these questions:

1 Do you know anyone who has invested money in anything? What?
2 Do you know anyone who has won any money? How?
3 Do you earn money? Are you happy with what you make?
4 How do you feel about getting into debt?
5 How good with money are you? In what way?

VOCABULARY Metaphor

Many words and expressions such as those connected to money are used with a metaphorical meaning. Sometimes the metaphorical meaning is more common.

He's invested a lot of money in stocks and shares. (literal)
I've invested a lot of time and effort in the project. (metaphorical)

A Complete each pair of sentences with one of the words in the box. You may need to change the form.

bet	gamble	lottery	stake
earn	jackpot	odds	waste

1 a He doesn't .... much. He's still a junior in the firm.
  b After all that hard work, I think we've .... a break.
2 a I wish we hadn't bought it. It was a .... of money!
  b I wouldn't .... your breath. You'll never persuade him to change his mind.
3 a He .... £50 on a horse to win, but it came second.
  b I .... it was nice to have a break after all that work.
4 a I don't ...., especially at casinos. I'm not lucky.
  b A recent report has warned that people are .... with their lives by buying cheap medication online.
5 a He's the clear favourite to win at .... of 2 to 1.
  b She recovered from the illness against all ....
6 a I won £10 on the .... I got three numbers out of six.
  b Finding a decent restaurant there is a bit of a ....
7 a There's a rollover on the lottery because no-one won last week. The .... is something like €30 million now.
  b He hit the .... when he got that job. It's great.
8 a We sometimes play poker for money, but only for a very small .... each – one cent – and you can only raise it to ten!
  b It's important voters understand the issues because there's a lot at .... – people's jobs and their future security!

B In your language, can the same word be used in each pair of sentences for 1–8 above?

LISTENING

You are going to hear two speakers present their arguments in a debate. The debate is *'Lotteries should be banned'.*

A Read the Fact File and discuss anything you found interesting or surprising with a partner.

- Are there lotteries in your country?
- What do you know about them?

- The first lottery occurred in China about 200BC. The Great Wall of China may have been partly funded by it.
- Winners of Dutch lotteries in the 17th century received paintings.
- The word lottery comes from the Dutch word *loterij*.
- Lotteries were banned in the United States between 1890 and the mid 1960s.
- The biggest jackpot win ever was $390 million.
- The hardest lottery to win is the Italian *SuperEnalotto* – with odds of over 622 million to one.
- 28p of every pound spent on the lottery in the UK goes to 'good causes'. These include charities, preserving British heritage, funding Olympic athletes, and subsidising theatre and the arts.

B Work in groups. Before you listen to the first speaker, list reasons someone might give for banning a lottery. Which group can think of the most reasons?

C ⏵14.4 Listen to part 1 (Zak) and see if any of the reasons you thought of are mentioned.

D Explain the points Zak was making when he mentioned:

1 promising to give people €2.6m in the next quarter of a million years
2 the focus of the marketing of lotteries
3 subsidising opera and Olympic sportsmen
4 only having to choose six numbers to get rich
5 dreaming of a mansion and a Ferrari
6 the story of John from Sydney

E Listen again and check your ideas. Then discuss the following questions:

1 What mark out of ten would you give Zak's speech? Why?
2 Do you agree with his points? Why? / Why not?
3 What counterarguments do you think Stacy will give?

F Listen to Part 2 and take notes on Stacy's reply to Zak.

G Compare your notes in pairs and then in groups. Finally, compare what you understood with the audioscript of Stacy's arguments on page 180.

H In groups, discuss the following:
1 What mark you would give Stacy?
2 Who do you think won the debate? Why?
3 Do you think any of the points they made were: irrelevant / clever / stupid / confusing?

LANGUAGE PATTERNS

Write the sentences in your language. Translate them back into English. Compare your English to the original.

Not only do lotteries damage society in this way, they also bring pain to individuals.

It not only causes pain to the gambler, but also hurts their family and friends.

They not only gave him food, they gave him money as well.

Not only does it support a good cause, but it'll be fun too.

Not only has the policy failed, it's wasted millions of dollars.

PRONUNCIATION Numbers

In the debate, you heard the following numbers:
I'll give you $2.6 million
Nine out of ten gambling addicts start with lotteries.

You can also say these numbers as:
Two million six hundred thousand dollars
Nine tenths of gambling addicts

A **Can you think of two different ways to say each of these numbers?**
a 3,700,000
b 1,500
c 0.02
d 2/3
e 40%
f −10°

B 🔊 14.5 **Listen and repeat the numbers you hear.**

C 🔊 14.6 **Listen and write down the numbers you hear in the six statistics. Then compare your answers in pairs. Can you remember the complete statistics?**

D **Are there any statistics you find surprising – or don't believe? Why?**

SPEAKING

You are going to have a debate similar to the one you heard between Zak and Stacy.

A **Work in small groups. Decide which of the topics below you want to debate – or propose your own topic.**
a 'Money is the root of all evil.' Discuss.
b 'The best things in life are free.' Discuss.
c 'The world would be a better place without banks.' Discuss.
d 'Everyone should have to vote.' Discuss.
e 'Debating should be part of everyone's schooling.' Discuss.

B **Divide your group into two teams. One team should defend the statement in the topic you have chosen; the other team should counter it. Prepare your arguments. Look back at the debate you heard for techniques and expressions you want to use.**

C **Each team should nominate a speaker. Now have your debate in front of another group. That group will give you marks out of ten and decide the winner. Your group will then do the same for them.**

15 FOOD

VOCABULARY Food and cooking

A **Look at the pictures in File 23 on page 163 and discuss these questions:**
1 Are there any foods you've never tried?
2 Are there any you didn't know in English?
3 Are any of them difficult to buy where you live?
4 Which five of these foods do you like the most?
5 Are there any you can't stand? Why not?
6 Are there any foods you love that aren't pictured?

B **In groups, put as many of the things as possible on page 163 into the categories below – without looking at the pictures. Which group can remember the most words?**

fruits / nuts:	
fish / seafood:	
vegetables / salads:	
pulses / beans:	
herbs / spices:	

C **Complete the sentences with the words in the box.**

almonds	chocolate	courgette	parsley	mixture
chickpeas	coconut	grapefruit	peaches	trout

1 **Peel** the .... and **remove** the stones.
2 **Steam** the .... When it's ready, the flesh should come away from the bones easily.
3 **Soak** the .... overnight in water and then **boil** them for two hours.
4 **Melt** the .... and mix in the raisins.
5 **Squeeze** some .... juice over the salad.
6 **Slice** the .... and **fry** the slices till they are slightly brown on each side.
7 **Crush** the .... and **sprinkle** some on top of the cake.
8 **Chop** some .... and sprinkle it onto the soup.
9 Add the .... milk. Bring it to the boil and then leave for about 30 minutes, but **stir** it occasionally.
10 **Blend** the whole .... until it's smooth.

D **In pairs, take turns to act or draw the words in bold in exercise C. Your partner should guess the words.**

LISTENING

You are going to hear a conversation where a woman comments on a dish and asks how it's made.

A 🔊 **15.1 Listen and answer the questions:**
1 What does the dish contain? (Listen carefully!)
2 What kind of dish is it? How do you know?

B **Discuss with a partner what you remember about how the dish was made. Then listen again and take notes.**

C **Compare your notes in groups.**

D **Discuss these questions:**
- Do you like the sound of the recipe? Why? / Why not?
- Do you know anyone who has a special diet or who avoids certain foods like salt? What do they have to eat or avoid? Why?
- Are you any good at cooking? Do you know anyone else who is? What are your / their best dishes?

NATIVE SPEAKER ENGLISH

dead easy
We use *dead* before some adjectives to mean *very*.

Oh, it's dead easy.
It was dead quiet. You couldn't hear a thing.
I'm dead sure it was him. I'd recognise him anywhere.
It was dead boring. We left halfway through.
We were just dead tired by the end of the day.

DEVELOPING CONVERSATIONS
Vague language

> We can show something is not exact by adding *-ish* to adjectives or *-y* to nouns. We can also add *kind of* or *sort of* before adjectives and verbs and *like* before nouns.
> *Biggish, but not like the huge ones.*
> *It's a greyish white stick. It gives a kind of citrusy flavour.*
> *It looks sort of like a spring onion.*
>
> With quantities, we use words such as *roughly / about / or so*.
> *Use roughly a cupful.*
> *Leave it to boil for fifteen minutes or so.*

A **Make the sentences less exact by adding the forms in brackets in the correct place.**

1 You bake it in the oven for twenty minutes. (roughly)
2 I generally sprinkle some herbs on top and two teaspoons of crushed pistachios. (about)
3 If you add a squeeze of orange, it gives it a sweet finish, which is really nice. (kind of)
4 The colour put me off at first. It was green blue, but it tasted great. (kind of / -ish)
5 It has an odd oil texture and a weird egg smell. (-y / -y)
6 You need a large pan, because you add two litres of fish stock. (-ish / or so)
7 If it's a small chicken and isn't stuffed, then it should only take 40 minutes to roast. (-ish / or so)
8 It's a potato, but it's rounder and it's got purple skin and the flesh is orange. (like / -ish / kind of)

B **Work in pairs. Using vague language, describe different foods for your partner to guess. For example:**
A: It's biggish with a yellowish skin, very juicy flesh and a kind of lemony flavour. It's quite bitter.
B: Is it a grapefruit?

GRAMMAR Linking words

> You have learnt a number of words in this book – especially in the *Writing* sections – that make the relationship between two ideas in a sentence or between two sentences clear. For example, order and time (*and, until, once, when, then, while, during* etc.), result and reason / purpose (*as, so, to*), contrast (*although, however*) and condition (*if / in case / provided*).

A **Choose the correct words to complete the recipe.**

First you chop some onions [1]*and / after* put them in some oil and fry them. Actually, you should heat the oil a bit beforehand and [2]*when / then* you put the onion in, it should sizzle. [3]*Then / After* you need to turn the heat down, [4]*as / so* you want the onion to cook slowly [5]*then / so* it becomes nice and sweet. I also like to add some garlic, [6]*although / however* I know most people don't. Anyway, [7]*while / during* the onion's cooking, peel about four big potatoes and cut them into little pieces – quite small, [8]*otherwise / unless* they'll take ages to cook. [9]*Once / Afterwards* the onion has started to turn brown, add the potatoes and continue to cook everything [10]*until / when* the potato is soft. The onion won't burn [11]*provided / unless* you mix it in with the potato and stir the mixture now and then. Break about eight eggs into a bowl and whisk them with a touch of milk. Spoon the cooked mixture into the whisked eggs – without any of the oil [12]*if / in case* you can avoid it – and mix it all together. You then pour away the oil in the pan – apart from about a spoonful – and heat it up again so it's very hot. [13]*When / Then* pour the egg and potato into the pan and after about a minute, turn it down low and let it cook [14]*for / during* about ten minutes. You then need to get a big plate or flat lid to put on top of the omelette [15]*for / to* turn it over and cook the other side.

▶ **Need help? Read the grammar reference on page 154.**

CONVERSATION PRACTICE

A **In pairs, choose a dish that you would both like to eat from File 22 on page 165. Then discuss how you think you would make it.**

B **Change partners and form new pairs. Have conversations similar to the ones in *Listening*. Start by saying *Mmm! This is delicious! What's in it?* Ask questions about the taste and about how to make the dish. Check details when you're not sure about ingredients or what to do.**

READING

You are going to read an article called *Con-fusion food*. It starts with the British writer seeing someone complaining in a restaurant in Italy.

A Look at the words from the article below. They all feature in the rest of the story. In pairs, try to guess what happens next in the restaurant – and what the author then goes on to talk about.

fish	cockroaches	make a scene	food fraud
cheaper	police squad	law	pizza
certificates	globalisation	trademark	mayonnaise

B Now read the article and find out if you were right.

C Work in pairs. Explain what the article said, using the words in exercise A.

> Many newspaper and magazine articles mix facts and opinions. Opinions are often marked by words like *seems, think, probably*, etc. When reading, be careful not to over-generalise from what is said or to confuse your own opinions with what is actually stated.

D Decide if 1–10 are facts or opinions. Compare your ideas in pairs and discuss how you reached your decisions.

1 The author's mother didn't like her husband to complain in restaurants.
2 The customer in the restaurant wasn't very good at distinguishing between different kinds of fish.
3 Food fraud is quite common in British fish and chip shops.
4 Italians worry about food standards and authenticity more than British people.
5 The Italian government has introduced measures for the quality control of pizzas.
6 Most Italian, Thai and Japanese people think globalisation is destroying their cultures.
7 Japanese food suddenly became very popular around the world.
8 The certification schemes won't stop combinations of food styles.
9 Dried pasta didn't originate in Italy.
10 It's irritating if someone or something is given the wrong name.

E In pairs, complete the collocations with the words in **bold** from the article. Then discuss what you think each word means. Check your ideas in the *Vocabulary Builder*.

1 an ~ of interest / an ~ of activity / an ~ in the use of …
2 an argument ~ / my eczema's ~ / trouble ~
3 a ~ feature film / a ~ crisis / ~ AIDS / a ~ war
4 ~ something under his breath / ~ to himself / ~ 'Sorry'
5 ~ the bill / ~ the argument / ~ the claim out of court
6 ~ certificates / ~ a passport / ~ a warning to the public
7 ~ differences / a ~ change / a ~ scent
8 a ~ of foreign … /a ~ of criticism / the ~ of public opinion
9 ~ standards / ~ workers' rights / ~ the law

VOCABULARY Prefixes

> In the article, the author's father was often dissatisfied with his food because it was *semi*-cooked or *over*-done. Prefixes like *dis-, semi-* and *over-* add meanings to a root word.

A Complete the definitions in 1–12 with the prefixes.

dis	mis	non	over	pro	semi
ex	multi	out	pre	re	super

1 **many** – as in ....-cultural or ....-lingual
2 **no longer** – as in ....-soldier or ....-president
3 **wrongly** – as in ....manage a situation or ....inform the public
4 **more or better than** – as in ....perform a competitor or ....grow your clothes
5 **too much** – as in ....stay your welcome or ....do it
6 **not** – as in ....-stick pan or ....-existent
7 **opposite** – as in ....obey an order or ....qualified
8 **before** – as in ....-war –or ....-heat the oven
9 **again** – as in ....play a game or ....read a book
10 **partly** – as in ....-professional or ....-conscious
11 **in favour of** – as in ....-GM food or ....-democracy campaigner
12 **extremely** – as in ....-fit or a ....-posh hotel

B In pairs, challenge each other to think of another example for each prefix. Your partner should put their word into a sentence. For example:
A: pre-
B: I buy a lot of pre-cooked meals.

SPEAKING

A Imagine you and some friends are in a restaurant. In groups, discuss what would you do in these situations.

1 None of you speaks the local language, which the menu is written in.
2 You asked for your steak to be cooked rare, but when it arrives, it's well done.
3 The dish you chose isn't quite what you expected. You don't particularly like it.
4 The bill comes and it's quite expensive. You only had a main meal, but everyone else had starters and dessert as well.
5 You discover you can't pay by card and you don't have any cash on you.
6 A service charge is not included on the bill.

CON-FUSION FOOD

We were just **settling** the bill when an argument **flared up** between a waiter and another customer. It was clear that something was wrong with the fish. From where I was sitting, there was nothing obviously wrong – no hair being pulled out or cockroaches running from the plate – but the customer was waving his arms around and poking the fish. Personally, I found it kind of shocking. I remember that whenever my dad was dissatisfied with food in a restaurant, he'd usually just **mutter** something under his breath – and my mother would then hiss, 'Harry, don't make a scene'. As a result, he'd carry on eating his semi-cooked pie or tough over-done steak, and leave without saying anything – except perhaps thank you! In this case, our man hadn't simply caused a scene, he had created a **full-blown** feature film: not only had the chef appeared, but what appeared to be a kind of policeman had also arrived and the two were proceeding to inspect the fish. Not wishing to stare, we left – with the slight concern that we may have been poisoned!

But no, according to an Italian friend I spoke to, it was probably just a case of mistaken identity – or food fraud, depending whose side you are on. The

customer had probably ordered a certain fish, but believed he was being served a cheaper variety. Apparently, it's not uncommon for this kind of thing to happen in Britain either. A study once found that 10% of chip shops in Britain selling 'cod and chips' were actually serving haddock or pollack. The difference with Italy is that this customer obviously noticed, whereas the British don't – or else they simply don't want to make a fuss!

The Italians, it seems, take such things rather more seriously. For example, they've trained a police squad of twenty officers as tasters to help combat producers of fake extra virgin olive oil. They can not only distinguish between olive oil which has been mixed with cheap substitutes such as sunflower oil, but they can also taste **subtle** differences between those oils produced in Italy and ones originating from abroad. Italy has also passed a law which establishes the official ingredients, method, shape and size of pizza (the dough, which has to use natural yeast, must be worked and shaped with the hands and then baked on the floor of a wood-fired oven. Only Italian plum tomatoes can be used and it can be no more than 14 inches (35 cm) in diameter and 1/3 centimetre thick in the

centre). The government has an agency to **issue** certificates of authenticity to restaurants home and abroad, following a rigorous inspection to check they **uphold** standards.

The Italians are not the only ones trying to protect their culinary heritage against globalisation. The Thai government has also developed a 'Thai select' trademark, which aims to promote Thai food overseas, while the Japanese have done something similar. They had become concerned that the **explosion** of interest in Japanese food around the world was leading to untrained chefs serving an odd fusion of Asian foods rather than genuine Japanese cuisine.

Is any of this likely to stop this **tide** of foreign fusions? Probably not, as all nations participate at one time or another: the Japanese now love to spread mayonnaise on their pizzas and, depending who you believe, dried pasta originated in either China or Syria. Still, maybe that's not the point. In the end, it's simply annoying if someone calls you Bob when your name is Jim or says you're Spanish when you're Brazilian. These certification schemes are just polite reminders not to confuse 'kind of Italian' or 'Japanese-ish food' with the real thing.

VOCABULARY Food in the news

A Complete the newspaper headlines with the words in the boxes.

staple	advertising	poisoning	GM	production

a Food .... faces challenge from climate change

b Consumers urged not to stockpile .... foods

c .... food should replace organic products, claims expert

d Death toll rises to 24 following outbreak of food ....

e Call for ban on fast food ....

hygiene	allergies	supplies	waste	shortages

f Fear of nut and other food .... 'creating hysteria'

g Food .... now exceeds £10 million a year

h Government to buy land overseas in bid to secure food ....

i Poor food .... accusations prove to be a dirty lie

j Huge numbers facing food ....

B Underline any new collocations in a–j above. Compare what you underline with a partner.

C Work in pairs. Discuss the following.
- Explain in your own words what you think happens in each of the ten newspaper stories above.
- Which stories would you be interested in reading? Why?

LISTENING

You are going to hear four pieces of news about food.

A 🔊 15.2 Listen and match each news story with one of the headlines from *Vocabulary* exercise A.

B Compare your ideas in pairs and discuss how you made your decisions.

C Listen again and answer the questions about the four stories.
1. a How did Mr Gunning trick the restaurants into giving him free meals?
   b What do you learn about his trial?
2. a What does Sir David King think is responsible for food shortages in Africa?
   b How does his attitude towards GM foods differ from that of the EU?
3. a What is CHOICE – and what do they want?
   b Why is Scandinavia mentioned?
4. a How much food is being wasted in the UK?
   b In what way does wasted food 'cost consumers three times over'?

LANGUAGE PATTERNS

Write the sentences in your language. Translate them back into English. Compare your English to the original.

Wouter Gunning had been eating out on a regular basis.
He pleaded not guilty on the basis of temporary insanity.
The accusations have no basis in fact.
The menu is changed on a weekly basis.
The card was rejected on the basis of insufficient funds.
Seating is allocated on a first-come, first-served basis.

D Work in pairs. Discuss these questions:
- Do you know any similar stories to the four you heard? What do they involve?
- What do you know about GM food? How do you feel about it? Why?
- What other reasons might there be for food shortages in Africa?
- Do you think it'd be a good idea to ban fast-food advertising? Why? / Why not?
- Do you think you / your family waste much food? What kind? Why?

GRAMMAR Reporting verbs

> When we report what people said, we often just summarise their main ideas. There are lots of verbs that do this (*accuse*, *claim*, *urge*, etc.). The patterns that follow these verbs vary.
>
> A leading scientist will *blame* the food crises in Africa *on* the rise of organic farming in economically developed countries. In today's speech, he'll *suggest that* genetically modified crops could help Africa.

A Choose the correct verb.

1 Sir David King has *threatened / criticised* what he sees as anti-scientific farming policies and has *urged / demanded* governments to change their policy on GM crops.

2 The government has *announced / informed* a series of measures designed to tackle the growing food crisis.

3 CHOICE *claims / persuades* fast-food advertising is linked to obesity and is *calling for / declaring* a total ban.

4 Doctors are *warning / announcing* that children are eating too much of everything and are *convincing / encouraging* parents to pay more attention to their kids' diets.

5 A major fast food chain has *confessed / confirmed* to using wheat and dairy products to flavour its french fries.

6 The restaurant has been *accused / blamed* of cheating staff out of tips and overtime pay – accusations they strongly *admit / deny*.

7 The company has moved to *reassure / promise* consumers about the quality and safety of its bottled water.

8 I *suggested / offered* to pay half the bill, but he *invited / insisted* on paying for everything.

B Work in pairs. Compare your ideas and explain your decisions.

▶ Need help? Read the grammar reference on page 154.

C Complete these sentences by putting the verbs in brackets into the correct form. You may also need to add prepositions.

1 Given the cod shortage, fish and chip restaurants are now encouraging customers .... alternatives. (try)

2 A celebrity chef has confessed .... recipes from one of his main rivals. (steal)

3 It was terrible, but at least the owner came and apologised .... us wait so long. (make)

4 The government has been accused .... enough to tackle the problem. (not / do)

5 A new campaign is being launched today, urging people .... food. (not / waste)

6 Whenever we go out for dinner, my dad always insists .... steak so rare it comes dripping with blood. (order)

D Work in groups. Discuss these questions:
Can you think of anything . . .
- ... people are currently being urged to do – or not do?
- ... anyone famous has been accused of doing recently?
- ... anyone famous has been criticised for recently?
- ... anyone famous has admitted doing recently?

SPEAKING

A Imagine you are going to make a 'podcast'. With a partner, think of a food-related news story. This could be one of the stories from *Vocabulary*, exercise A – or it could be a different story that you have heard.

B Prepare a short broadcast about your story. Try to use as much language from these pages as possible.

C Present your 'podcast' to another pair. Who told the most interesting story?

16 BUSINESS

In this unit you learn how to:
- explain why you are phoning
- be more polite in business contexts
- pronounce email addresses and websites
- talk about markets, companies and products more fluently

Grammar
- The future continuous
- Expressing necessity and ability

Vocabulary
- Reasons for phoning
- Building up a business
- Business collocations

Reading
- Ten characteristics of successful people
- The green tourism guru

Listening
- I'm just phoning to ...
- Dream and Achieve

SPEAKING

A **Work in groups. Discuss these questions:**
- How often do you make phone calls in English? Who to?
- What was the last call you made in English?
- What did you say? How did it go?
- What kind of calls do you think you might have to make in English in the future? Think about work, holidays, etc.

VOCABULARY Reasons for phoning

A **Match the sentence starters to the sentence endings.**
1   I'm phoning to chase up
2   I'm just phoning to remind you
3   I'm phoning to try to arrange
4   I'm just phoning to pass on
5   I'm just phoning to check

a   an overdue payment on your account with us.
b   stock levels in the warehouse.
c   that you have an appointment with Mr Tanaka at 3.
d   my thanks to you and your team.
e   a suitable time and place for the next meeting.

6   I'm just calling to let you know
7   I'm just calling to enquire
8   I'm just calling to confirm
9   I'm just calling to apologise for
10 I'm just calling to see

f   losing my temper earlier.
g   I won't be able to make the meeting tomorrow.
h   whether you're taking on any staff at the moment.
i   about the vegetarian options on your menu.
j   a booking for three nights next week.

B **Work in pairs. Discuss who you think is calling whom in each of the sentences in exercise A – and why they made each call.**

C **Now think of one other possible ending for each of the sentence starters in exercise A.**
I'm phoning to chase up an order I placed last month.

LISTENING

You are going to hear two business-related conversations.

A **16.1 Listen to the first conversation. Answer the questions.**
1   Why is Ian calling Claudia?
2   What does he suggest?
3   How does Claudia respond?
4   What arrangements do they end up making?

B **16.2 Now listen to the second conversation. Complete the note below as you do so.**

Order No.:

Date placed:

Client's name:

Email address:

Action:

C **Compare your notes in pairs. Listen again to check your ideas if you need to.**

DEVELOPING CONVERSATIONS
Using *would* to be polite

Would can make sentences sound more polite and less direct. For example, *Tuesday would be good for me* sounds more polite than *Tuesday is good for me.*

A Look at the audioscript on p. 181. Find two examples in each conversation where *would* is used to be polite.

B Rewrite the sentences using *would* and the words in brackets so that they sound softer and more polite.
1 Is Friday good for you? (at all)
2 Can you make the 29th? (able / at all)
3 Do you have the address there? (happen)
4 Can you just spell the street name? (mind)
5 Do you want to come with us? (wondering / like)
6 Can you email me over the details? (possible)
7 Any day next week is good for me. (suit)
8 If it's OK with you, I don't want to. (mind / rather)

C Work in small groups. Arrange a time and place for a meeting. Each student should reject at least two suggestions. Use polite expressions including *would*.

PRONUNCIATION
Email addresses and websites

A Work in pairs. How do you say the symbols in the box?

1 @	2 /	3 _	4 .	5 -

B 16.3 Listen and check your ideas

C 16.4 Now listen and write down the email addresses and websites you hear. Compare your ideas with a partner.

D Swap email addresses with other students. Then work in groups. Recommend five websites each. Give the addresses and explain why you like them.

GRAMMAR The future continuous

The future continuous is formed using *will be / be going to be* + a verb in the *-ing* form. It is often used to talk about something we have already arranged to do in the future, but that we now see as the background to another more recently decided event.

I'll / I'm going to be visiting Spain for the trade fair (=already arranged) *so I could fit in a day with you then.* (=event just decided now)

A Complete the sentences by adding the verbs from the box in the future continuous form.

go out	open	talk	take	take on	work

1 I .... the overnight train,
2 I .... late tonight, I'm afraid,
3 We .... new staff over Christmas,
4 I .... to the Cairo office later on today,
5 We .... a new flagship store in Tokyo soon,
6 Your order .... today by special delivery,

B Now match the sentence endings below to 1–6 above.
a so I should get into Sofia around nine.
b so I'll try and chase up the projected sales figures.
c so I won't be able to make the dinner.
d so that'll boost our profile quite a bit.
e so it should be with you first thing tomorrow.
f so it's worth contacting us again nearer the time.

▶ Need help? Read the grammar reference on page 155.

CONVERSATION PRACTICE

A Work in pairs. You are going to role-play four business-related conversations. Together, choose four of the sentences from *Vocabulary*, exercise A. You will begin each conversation with one of these sentences.

B Decide which roles each of you will take in each of the four conversations.

C Role-play the conversations. Use as much language from these pages as possible.

VOCABULARY Building up a business

A Complete the story with the words in the box.

| competition | set up | loss | profit | ploughed |
| broke even | raised | floated | bid | turnover |

About ten years ago, my brother and I decided we'd had enough of working for other people and that it was time to ¹............................ our own company. We had some savings and with the help of the bank, we ²............................ the rest of the capital we needed. For the first few years, we ran at a ³............................, but eventually we ⁴............................ and before too long we were making a healthy ⁵............................ . We ⁶............................ all the money back into the business and expanded quite quickly. Next, we ⁷............................ the company on the stock exchange, but then the economy went into recession and we starting facing some very stiff ⁸............................ . We were the subject of a hostile takeover ⁹............................ and only survived by merging with a rival firm. It's been a tough ten years, but we're still here! We now have an annual ¹⁰............................ of over three million dollars.

B Compare your answers in pairs. Then discuss these questions.
- Do you know anyone who runs their own business? What kind of business is it? How long has it been going?
- Do you know how it's doing?
- Would you like to run your own business?
- What kind of businesses are doing well at the moment? What kind are struggling?
- What do you think are the biggest problems that small business face in your country?

READING

You are going to read about the traits of successful people.

A Read the article on the right. Give yourself a score of 1, 2 or 3 for each characteristic, depending on the degree to which each describes you. (1 = this doesn't sound like me, 3 = this is me!)

B Add up your score (out of 30). Compare your scores in pairs. Explain your decisions. Then discuss these questions:
- Do you agree with the definitions of success in the article? Why? / Why not?
- Are there any other characteristics – or habits – that you would expect successful people to have?
- What does success mean to you personally in terms of your own life?

C Can you remember the nouns that the words below were used with in the article? Read it again to check your ideas.

push themselves to the ....
set high ....
have a wide .... of friends
maintain ....
be on the .... for new ideas
accept .... for your actions
stay one .... ahead of the crowd
maintain your ....
act on ....
seize an ....

TEN CHARACTERISTICS OF SUCCESSFUL PEOPLE

1 They work incredibly hard and push themselves to the limit. They set high standards and put in the hours needed to meet them.

2 They were high achievers at school and are always keen to learn more. They are inquisitive, read widely and are interested in everything around them.

3 They're social animals. They have a wide circle of friends and acquaintances and are always networking. They are good listeners and work hard at maintaining relationships.

4 They're perfectionists. They are never content to sit back and relax. They're always focused on improving themselves and their performance.

5 They display a healthy degree of impatience. They want results – and they want them now! They tend not to perform well in bureaucracies.

6 They're creative and they innovate. They're constantly on the lookout for new ideas, new opportunities and for faster, better solutions.

7 They don't waste time moaning or looking for people to blame. They learn from their mistakes and move on. They accept responsibility for their actions.

8 They're keen observers. They notice new trends, observe changes and keep notes. They keep one eye firmly on the future and try hard to stay one step ahead of the crowd.

9 They tend not to get stressed. They are patient and well-balanced – and maintain their cool and their sense of humour under pressure.

10 They often act before having the full picture. Successful people respond immediately – and act on impulse. If they see an opportunity, they seize it.

D Now read the biography of a famous entrepreneur – Jan Telensky. As you read, consider the significance to his story of each of the places / things below.

an underground lake	England
Poprad	menial jobs
Prague	a delicatessen
school	evening classes
property	a secretarial training institute

E Work in pairs. Decide how the places / things in exercise D are connected. Then discuss these questions:

1 Which of the ten characteristics of successful people do you see evidence of in Jan Telensky's story? In what ways?

2 Are there any other characteristics that he seems to possess?

3 What do you feel has been the single biggest factor behind his success? Why?

SPEAKING

A Work in groups. Discuss these questions:
- Who are the most famous entrepreneurs in your country / in the world?
- Do you know how they achieved their success?
- Do you know of any wealthy people who have spent money in a socially responsible or environmentally friendly way?
- Can you think of any wealthy people who have spent money in ways you disapprove of?

THE GREEN TOURISM GURU

Situated at the foot of the Tatra Mountains, the Slovakian town of Poprad is home to AquaCity – a luxury spa and leisure complex recently voted the world's greenest resort. By exploiting the geothermal properties of a nearby underground lake, the resort is able to provide renewable energy for the whole area. Perhaps the only thing more remarkable than AquaCity itself is the man behind it, Jan Telensky.

Telesnky was born in Prague in 1948, and his parents instilled a strict work ethic into him from an early age. Because of his family background, his teachers at school told him he would only ever be good for blue-collar work. He, however, had other ideas.

Initially, he trained as a locksmith, a job he excelled at, and tried to better himself by taking a series of evening classes, studying Maths, Russian, Physics and Biology.

In 1969, he moved to England. At first, his lack of English presented numerous problems. Despite this, he was determined to succeed. During a string of menial jobs, he improved his linguistic skills and saved enough to buy a delicatessen. Telensky then built the business up and eventually sold it on for £200,000.

The profit was ploughed into a new venture – property – and before too long, he had built up a substantial portfolio. He quickly became restless again, though, and took a part-time job at a secretarial training institute. He climbed the corporate ladder and became UK sales manager, before raising sufficient capital to set up a rival company. This was soon doing so well that in 1989 he put his former employers out of business, buying them for a sum of around £75,000!

He then returned to his native country and established a plastic recycling business, whilst continuing to expand his operations both at home and abroad. Telensky now employs over 1,500 people, with an annual turnover of £70 million.

He married in 1998, and his wife, Alena, originated from Poprad! As a result, he came to love the area – and this led directly to his newest and most incredible venture!

SPEAKING

A **Read the short extract below. Then discuss the questions.**

Dragon's Den is a popular reality TV programme in the UK. Each week, would-be entrepreneurs who want to set up their own businesses present their plans to a panel of five successful business people, with the aim of persuading the five to invest a certain amount of their own money in exchange for a stake in any new company the entrepreneurs are then able to start. After the entrepreneurs have pitched their ideas, they are then subjected to questioning from the panel, as a result of which, each of the business people either offers to give the money the entrepreneur has asked for or declares that they are not interested. There is no negotiation on the amount that is invested, but the entrepreneurs and business people can negotiate what percentage of the new company the business people will end up owning.

1 Does a programme like *Dragon's Den* exist in your country? Is it a programme you would watch? Why? / Why not?
2 Discuss other reality TV shows you know in the following areas. What do they involve? Do you like any of them? Why? / Why not?
   - business
   - living with a group of other people
   - survival or dealing with difficult situations
   - music or dance
   - romance or meeting people

LISTENING

You are going to hear a radio report about a reality TV programme in Afghanistan.

A **Before you listen, work in groups. Discuss what you know about Afghanistan.**

B 🔊 **16.5 Now listen and answer these questions.**
1 What is the programme?
2 Why is it important there?
3 What is different about the programme compared to its British equivalent?

C **Listen again and decide if the following statements are true or false. Then compare your answers with a partner.**
1 The show was originally devised in Britain.
2 The Afghan economy has not been sustaining itself.
3 Most people in Afghanistan work for the state.
4 More people need to learn about aspects of business.
5 Faisulhaq Moshkani has an electricity company.
6 His company is unique in Afghanistan.
7 There are two reality TV shows on Afghan TV.
8 In Afghanistan, women weren't allowed to have paid jobs in the past.

D **In groups, discuss these questions:**
1 Did anything surprise you about the report? What?
2 Do you agree that reality TV is 'overwhelmingly positive'? Why? / Why not?
3 Which programmes on TV in your country are educational? Do you watch them? Why? / Why not?

Remember that words collocate in lots of different ways. It is good to try to notice these combinations in any texts you read. You will do this in exercise E below.

E **Look at the audioscript on page 182. Match the collocations in bold to these combinations. Then find one more example of each different kind of collocation.**
1 adjective + noun   5 noun + noun
2 verb + noun   6 noun + of + noun
3 adverb + verb   7 phrasal verb + noun
4 adverb + adjective   8 prepositional phrase

NATIVE SPEAKER ENGLISH

let alone

We use *let alone* to emphasise that something is impossible – because something else is already difficult.

She wouldn't have been able to work, let alone run a business.
I couldn't even walk, let alone run.
A: *Can we take Jochem and his sisters with us?*
B: *No way! There's hardly enough room for us, let alone three more.*

GRAMMAR
Expressing necessity and ability

> *Must* and *can* appear only in the present tense and don't have infinitive or *-ing* forms. We use forms of *have to* or *be able to*.
>
> ··
>
> It's a risk more investors are going to ~~must~~ have to take.
> It'll soon ~~can~~ be able to produce its own plastic.
>
> To show something makes another thing possible, we can use *enable somebody to do something, allow somebody to do something* or *let somebody do something.*
>
> ··
>
> To show something creates an obligation, we can use *force somebody to do something / make somebody do something.*
>
> ··
>
> The software allows you to create a personalised doll.
> The prize has enabled him to build a mini-hydroelectric plant.
> High fuel costs forced him to close down the plant.

A Use appropriate language from the box above to replace the incorrect uses in italics in 1–8 below.

1 The device allows you to share files without you *must* rely on a computer.
2 If the loan is approved, it will *can us* buy more stock and take advantage of the interest we've generated.
3 The negative feedback that we got *must us* look at the design again.
4 This deal means I'll finally *can* give up my day job and focus entirely on the business.
5 We *can* keep ahead of our competitors over the last few years by developing new products.
6 We were forced to cut costs *for can us* compete.
7 Thanks to all the effort everyone put in, in the end we *can* fulfil all our orders before Christmas. Well done!
8 If we'd done more market research before launching the first model, we would not *must* redesign it so soon.

B Tell a partner about things:
- you haven't been able to do recently.
- you're glad you won't have to do in the future.
- you used to be able to do, but can't anymore.
- everyone should have to do.
- you'd like to not have to do.
- you'd love to be able to do.
- a little more money would enable you to do.
- a lot more money would allow you to do.
- getting a particular qualification would enable you to do.
- which you have to force yourself to do.

▶ **Need help? Read the grammar reference on page 155.**

VOCABULARY Business collocations

A Decide which word from the box completes each set of collocations.

area	business	company	market
order	product	sales	stock

1 the target ~ / exploit a gap in the ~ / break into the American ~ / it's a niche ~ / the ~'s saturated / the ~'s worth $3billion / do a lot of ~ research
2 be in ~ / be out of ~ / check ~ levels / buy new ~
3 fulfil ~s / be flooded with ~s / keep up with new ~s / chase up an ~ / receive a big ~
4 boost ~ / ~ have shot up / ~ have plunged / add to our ~ team / improve ~ and marketing
5 develop a ~ line / launch the ~ / a revolutionary new ~ / the ~ is aimed at teenagers / a large range of ~s / market the ~
6 branch out into other ~s / it's a specialist ~ / it's a growth ~ / it's an ~ of concern / the ~ manager
7 expand the ~ / build up the ~ / plough money back into the ~ / put them out of ~ / it's a risky ~
8 set up the ~ / head of the ~ / take over the ~ / float the ~ on the stock exchange / have a controlling stake in the ~

B Underline any collocations above that are new for you. Then compare what you have underlined with a partner and discuss what you think the collocations mean.

C Discuss which of the collocations in exercise A you think have already been in this unit.

SPEAKING

A Work in groups of four. Form two pairs: Pair A and B.
Pair A: look at the list of products and services in File 13 on page 159.
Pair B: look at the list of products and services in File 18 on page 161.

B You are going to try and persuade the other pair to invest in your products. With your partner, spend five minutes discussing what you are going to say and what language from *Vocabulary* and *Grammar* you could use.

C Take it in turns for each pair to pitch one of their products / services to the other pair. See how many deals you can make.

04 REVIEW

LEARNER TRAINING

A Read the text about listening skills. In groups, discuss how true you think it is. Give examples from your experience.

When native speakers have problems understanding what people say, it's often because they weren't listening. In other words, they didn't hear or remember what was said because they weren't paying attention. As a non-native speaker, one of the problems you might have is that you listen, but either can't hear all the words, or don't understand them. Another problem could be that you focus on trying to understand one part of a conversation and then you miss what comes next!

B Work in groups. Discuss how you feel about each of these ways of improving your ability to hear / listen in English.

- Learn lists of as many new words as you can.
- Read – and listen to what you're reading at the same time
- Do pronunciation exercises.
- Listen to the radio / watch TV in English.

GAME

Work in pairs. Student A use *only* the green squares; student B use *only* the yellow squares. Spend 5 minutes looking at your questions and revising the answers. Then take turns tossing a coin: Heads = move one of your squares; Tails = move two of your squares. When you land on a square, your partner looks at the relevant page in the book to check your answers, but *you don't*! If you are right, move forward one space (but don't answer the question until your next turn). If you aren't right, your partner tells you the right answer, and you miss a go. When you've finished the game change colours and play again.

Start	**1** *Grammar* p. 93: your partner will ask you five questions from exercise B. Answer each one using the past perfect simple or continuous.	**2** *Developing conversations* p. 93: say four things about famous people that you've heard, but aren't sure are true. Use different expressions.	**3** *Grammar* p. 94: your partner will say five statements from exercise B. Agree by saying *I know* + a comment with *wish* or *be always -ing*.	**4** *Vocabulary* p. 96: say five words connected funerals and five word connected to wedding
5 *Vocabulary* p. 98: your partner will say six words from the box. Can you remember two collocations for each word?	**6** *Native English note* p. 98: if you can say what the *Native English* note was and give an example, throw again.	**7** *Developing conversations* p. 99: your partner will say a-f in exercise C. You should apologise and offer a solution or explanation.	**8** *Grammar* p. 100: say three things you wish about your current situation and three things you wish about the past.	**9** **Miss a go!**
10 *Vocabulary* p. 104. explain how to make a dish, using eight different cooking verbs.	**11** *Native English note* p. 104: if you can say what the *Native English* note was and give an example, throw again.	**12** **Miss a go!**	**13** *Vocabulary* p. 106: say eight prefixes and give an example of a word containing each one.	**14** *Grammar* p. 109: give example sentences for *encourage, confess, apologise, accuse* and *urge*, using the pattern in exercise C.
15 *Developing conversations* p. 111: your partner will say 1–8 in exercise B. Give the polite versions using *would*.	**16** *Native English note* p. 114: if you can say what the *Native English* note was and give an example, throw again.	**17** *Grammar* p. 115: give three examples of *be able to* in different tenses and three with *have to* in different tenses.	**18** *Vocabulary* p. 115: your partner will say six words from the box. Can you remember two collocations for each word?	**Finish**

For each of the activities below, work in groups of three. Use the Vocabulary Builder if you want to.

CONVERSATION PRACTICE

Choose one of the following *Conversation practice* activities.

Life events p. 93
Banks and money p. 99
Food p. 105
Business p. 111

Two of you should do the task. The third person should listen and then give a mark between 1 and 10 for the performance. Explain your decision. Then change roles.

ACT OR DRAW

One person should act or draw as many of these words as you can in three minutes. Your partners should try to guess the words. Do not speak while you are acting or drawing!

glance	a feast	rope	vain
gestures	a coffin	crush	steam
a ladder	inspect	slice	scan
sprinkle	an oven	bury	cling
exceed	an inch	dawn	halt
withdraw	a lump	plead	a lid

VOCABULARY

Answer as many of the questions as possible.

1 What's the difference between **drop out** and **kick out**?
2 Why might you give someone a **bribe**?
3 What might a child do if they are **affectionate**?
4 When do you get **ashes**? What do you do with them?
5 Where would you find a **ward**? Say three kinds of ward.
6 What happens if you go into **overdraft**?
7 Who might **launder** money and why?
8 If a chance is **remote**, are **the odds** high or low?
9 Say three things that people can be **driven** by.
10 Say three things you **remove** from food before eating.
11 What do you do if you **make a scene** or a **fuss**?
12 Say two things that can be **full-blown**.
13 What can you **stockpile** and why might you do it?
14 Why would you need to **chase up** a payment?
15 What's the difference between **turnover** and **profit**?

COLLOCATIONS

Take turns to read out collocation lists from Units 13–16 of the *Vocabulary Builder*. Where there is a '~', say *'blah'* instead. Your partner should guess as many words as they can.

PRONUNCIATION
The same or different?

A Work in pairs. Decide if the underlined sounds in each of the pairs of words are pronounced in the same way or differently.

1 br<u>a</u>nch / <u>pa</u>ss away
2 c<u>ou</u>nsellor / m<u>our</u>ners
3 v<u>e</u>to / y<u>ea</u>st
4 n<u>i</u>che / h<u>y</u>giene
5 portf<u>o</u>lio / s<u>oa</u>k
6 st<u>a</u>ke / w<u>a</u>ste
7 w<u>ar</u>d / p<u>a</u>tch
8 <u>u</u>sher / r<u>ou</u>gh
9 f<u>u</u>ss / f<u>u</u>sion
10 host<u>i</u>le / br<u>i</u>de
11 fl<u>oa</u>t / r<u>o</u>pe
12 <u>au</u>thentic / d<u>aw</u>n
13 gr<u>a</u>ve / gl<u>a</u>nce
14 m<u>or</u>tgage / l<u>au</u>nder
15 al<u>er</u>t / entrepren<u>eur</u>
16 comm<u>u</u>te / text<u>u</u>re
17 <u>o</u>ven / t<u>o</u>ll
18 withdr<u>aw</u> / res<u>or</u>t to

B ⟳ R 4.1 Listen and see if you were right. Practise saying the words

DICTATION

You are going to hear a short extract from one of the texts you read in 13–16. You will hear it only once.

A ⟳ R 4.2 Work in your groups. Listen and take notes on what you hear. You won't have time to write everything.

B Work together to write the whole text.

C Compare what you have written with the audioscript on page 183.

LISTENING

A **R 4.3 Listen to five people talking about marriage and weddings. Match the items a–f to speakers 1–5. There is one item that you do not need.**

a ... a counsellor
b ... a government inspector
c ... a newly-wed
d ... a business presentation
e ... an advert for a bank
f ... an advert for a website

B **Listen again and match items a–f with speakers 1–5. There is one item that you do not need. Who talks about:**

a ... their financial plans?
b ... the death of someone they know?
c ... the fact that they've been making a lot of money?
d ... how they don't let other people change their mind?
e ... having less chance of success using traditional ways?
f ... how compromise is usually successful?

[... / 10]

GRAMMAR

A **Complete the second sentences using the words in bold so they have a similar meaning to the first one.**

1 They're still servicing my car.
I can't give you a lift because my car ....
still

2 They are going to build a new school in the area.
A new school .... in the area. **built**

3 What annoys me is the fact that he smokes in the house.
I really .... in the house. **wish**

4 They told us it would be a really good idea if we went.
They really .... **urged**

5 I got married young. At times, I think it was a mistake.
I sometimes wish .... so young. **got**

6 In the end, they said they had had taken the money.
They finally .... money. **confessed**

7 We were able to expand because of the grant.
The grant .... our business. **us**

8 The dish didn't turn out right, even though I followed the recipe carefully.
............................, the dish didn't turn out right. **despite**

9 They had a big row while we were having dinner.
.... a big row. **during**

10 With us, you can get a good wage even though you finish early.
With us, you can earn a good salary without .... long hours. **work**

[... / 10]

B **Decide which six items in *italics* are incorrect. Correct them.**

1 I*'ll be arriving* very late, so I'll just get a room at the hotel by the airport.

2 I sometimes wish I *speak* English better, but I don't have the time to study and improve.

3 We expect the company to increase turnover, *provided* there's a recession.

4 I couldn't cash the cheque because it *hadn't signed*.

5 Luckily, Grace *remembered* me to get the tickets this morning. Otherwise, I would've completely forgotten.

6 My salary *pays* directly into my bank account.

7 My parents always made me *to eat* my vegetables.

8 He was arrested for corruption. Apparently, he*'d been taking* bribes for ages.

[... / 8]

LANGUAGE PATTERNS

Complete the sentences with *one* word in each gap.

1 .... the recession getting worse, now is not a good time to move.

2 The festival goes on .... the month of June.

3 Not only .... he work hard, but he gets on with everyone too.

4 She not only does all the housework, but she has a full-time job as ....

5 He pleaded not guilty on .... basis of insanity.

6 It went bankrupt, with 300 jobs .... lost in the process.

7 You need to change the filter on a .... basis.

8 It was a tough time, but my family supported me ....

[... / 8]

PREPOSITIONS

Choose the correct preposition.

1 The Korean team beat Spain – *for / against* all odds.

2 The street was crammed *of / with* people celebrating.

3 They'd been *of / on* a bad run of ten games without a win.

4 The manager blamed the referee *for / on* the defeat.

5 I bet £10 *on / for* them to win – and I won £1000!

6 I'm not generally very good *at / with* money.

7 Most of the time, I seem to be *at / in* debt.

8 He was convicted *for / of* burglary.

9 I'd never resort *to / with* stealing, no matter how poor I was.

10 My dad always insisted *on / in* leaving really early, so we always had to hang around in the airport for hours!

[... / 10]

FORMING WORDS

Complete the sentences with the correct forms of the words in CAPITALS.

1 We had a .... meeting to try and resolve the dispute, but the union walked out. LENGTH
2 They gets so .... that it's difficult to talk to them. DEFEND
3 The dispute has attracted a lot of negative .... PUBLIC
4 The union agreed to reopen .... NEGOTIATE
5 We finally reached an agreement that satisfied both sides and that will .... the company going forward. STRONG
6 I'm afraid I can't .... this transaction. AUTHORITY
7 It's important to address the underlying causes of .... behaviour, not just the addiction itself. ADDICT
8 The government is doing its best to fight .... CORRUPT
9 The strike causes a lot of .... to our services. DISRUPT
10 It was an overreaction caused by .... fears. RATIONAL

[... / 10]

PHRASAL VERBS

Complete the sentences with the correct forms of the phrasal verbs in the box.

flick through	pass on	take over	knock out
move on	put off	fall out	write off

1 I didn't read it cover to cover. I just .... it.
2 The competition was too stiff and we got .... in the second round.
3 They .... over something stupid and they haven't been speaking to each other for about six months.
4 In the end, the banks had to .... the debt because they knew they would never get the money back.
5 I think we've dealt with this issue now. Can we .... to the next item on the agenda?
6 My mum had an accident, so we .... our wedding until she'd recovered.
7 Our company's going to be .... by one of our rivals. There's not much we can do about it.
8 Can you .... my condolences to the family? It must be awful for them.

[... / 8]

COLLOCATIONS

Match the nouns with the groups of words they go with.

transaction	grave	company	voice
boundary	leave	ground	cash

1 set up a ~ / expand a ~ / float a ~ / the ~ went bankrupt
2 find some middle ~ / go over old ~ / cover a lot of ~
3 improve ~ flow / be short of ~ / go to the ~ machine
4 visit the ~ / lay flowers at the ~ / dig a ~ / a mass ~
5 set clear ~s / establish a ~ / cross a ~ / have no ~s
6 raise your ~ / lose your ~ / put on a silly ~ / a deep ~
7 charge commission on ~s / a business ~ / a financial ~
8 be on maternity ~ / ask for paternity ~ / annual ~

[... / 8]

▶ **Find this difficult? Re-read units 13–16 in the *Vocabulary Builder* for more information on collocation.**

VOCABULARY

Complete the words in the news article. The first letters are given.

Business 'failure' has the last laugh
An entrepreneur who failed to persuade anyone to invest money in his business on the programme *The Dragon's Den* has made a £200,000 [1]pr.......................... Shaun Pulfrey developed his product, which is a special brush for long and difficult hair, for 15 years before meeting the 'dragons'. He felt there was a huge [2]g.......................... . in the market for his revolutionary product, but the businesspeople on the show [3]re.......................... his idea. Sean then took out another [4]mo.......................... on his home to raise the money to [5]lau.......................... the Tangle Teezer ® on the open market. The brush was originally [6]ai.......................... at professional hairdressers, but Internet sales to individuals have taken off, and Sean expects to have a [7]tu.......................... of £1.5 million next year. If the investors on *The Dragon's Den* had taken a 15% [8]st.......................... in the company, as Sean had requested, they would have got their money back in two years and would be set to make a fortune.

[... / 8]

[Total ... /80]

01 WRITING GIVING ADVICE

SPEAKING

Work in groups. Discuss these questions.

- What do you think of your country's capital city?
- What would you recommend seeing there? Why?
- Are there any things you'd tell people to avoid? Why?
- Have you visited any other capital cities? When? Why? What were they like?

GRAMMAR Advice and recommendations

There are lots of ways to give advice. Look at the different ways of answering the question: *What would you recommend seeing there?*

I'd go to Montmartre (*if I were you*).
You should take a boat trip down the river.
You're best staying in an area called Vosstaniya.
You could take a tour round the mountains (*if you wanted*).
You're better off taking the train. (= it's preferable)

. . . .

We often use the structures above with an *if*-clause + present tense - or another expression that refers to a general topic.

If you want to relax, you should take a boat trip down the river.
In terms of accommodation, you're best staying in an area called Vosstaniya.

A **Complete these sentences with advice for someone who is going to visit the area you are in now. Use a variety of structures.**

1 If you've never been here before, ...
2 If you're into art or history, ...
3 If you like shopping, ...
4 If you want to go swimming, ...
5 If you want to escape the tourists,
   ....
6 As far as nightlife is concerned, ...
7 When it comes to getting round the city,
   ....
8 In terms of places to stay, ...

B **Compare your sentences with a partner. Do you agree with each other's advice?**

WRITING

A friend of a friend has written to Harriet for advice about where to stay and what to do in London. You are going to read her reply.

A **Read the email below and decide which of the pieces of advice you'd follow and which you'd ignore? Explain your decisions to a partner.**

The email is written as one long text. When we write, it helps the reader if we divide the text into paragraphs that deal with different subjects. In letters and emails, a paragraph may sometimes be only one sentence. We mark a separate paragraph by leaving a line space.

B **In pairs, divide the email into six paragraphs. Mark the beginning and end of each paragraph with /. <u>Underline</u> expressions that start the paragraphs and / or show a new subject is being introduced.**

| To | cceline@shotmail.fr |
| Subject | Re: London |

Hi Celine,
Anna mentioned you might write. I'll actually be away, so you could use my flat, if you wanted. You'd be doing me a favour, as you could feed my cats. It IS in the suburbs, though – quite a long way from the city centre. As far as places to see are concerned, the Tower of London is well worth visiting, although it is a bit pricey. All the museums are free, though. If you want to escape the crowds, I'd recommend Hampstead Heath. It's a beautiful park and you get stunning views across London on a clear day. You could even swim in the ponds if you're brave enough. While you're here, the Thames Festival will be on. It's mainly held on the South Bank. There are workshops, live music, firework displays, parades – all sorts of things. Check out the website: http://www.thamesfestival.org/. Apart from the festival, there's a huge choice of entertainment. When it comes to nightlife, I'd buy *Time Off* magazine, if I were you. Otherwise, you'll miss out on all London has to offer. Generally, I'd steer clear of the clubs in Leicester Square as they can be a bit of a tourist trap. You're better off going to Old Street – I think it's a bit trendier. In terms of eating out, Brick Lane's good for curry. If you'd like traditional fish and chips, try here: http://www.timeoff.com/london/restaurants/reviews/9382.html. It's a bit in the middle of nowhere, but it's great. Other than that, lots of pubs do decent food. Anyway, if there's anything else you need, let me know.

Harriet

VOCABULARY Describing places

A Work in pairs. Discuss what problems – or what good things – there might be in:

a tourist trap	the suburbs
a rough area	a high-rise building
a posh area	a street market
a lively area	an up-and-coming area

KEY WORDS FOR WRITING Otherwise, other than, apart from

We use *otherwise* to show that something bad will occur if you don't do the thing you just mentioned:
I'd buy Time Off magazine if I were you. Otherwise, you'll miss out on all London has to offer.

You can also use *otherwise* or *other than / apart from that* to mean *in addition (to that) / not including* things you just mentioned.
... it's great. Other than that / Apart from that / Otherwise, lots of pubs do decent food.

You can use *apart from* and *other than* to join two parts of a sentence, but you can't use *otherwise*.
Apart from / other than / ~~otherwise~~ the festival, there's a huge choice in entertainment.

A Decide if one or both options are correct. Cross out the incorrect ones.

1 There's quite a lot of street crime, so don't leave anything valuable on café tables. *Otherwise, / Apart from that*, they might get stolen.
2 There's a small museum in the town, but *apart / other* from that, there's nothing worth seeing.
3 *Otherwise / Other than* the main sights, I can't really suggest anything.
4 There are several hotels in town which aren't too expensive. *Otherwise / apart from*, there's a nice campsite on the outskirts, if you have a tent.
5 *Apart from / Other than* walking, you're best taking taxis as they're not much more expensive than buses.
6 I'd put on plenty of sun cream even if you're not going to sunbathe, *otherwise, / other than that*, you'll get sunburnt.
7 The Chinese restaurant in Havana Road is OK. *Otherwise / Other than that*, there are a couple of decent pizzerias.

PRACTICE

A Work in a pairs or groups. Each pair / group should choose a different city or area in their country which they know fairly well. Imagine someone has written to you about where to stay, what to do there, etc. Make a list of all the points you might make.

B Write your email. Make sure you divide the email into paragraphs as you did in *Writing*, exercise B. Use some of the expressions to introduce new subjects and the advice structures.

SPEAKING

A **Work in groups. Discuss these questions.**

1 What things have you bought over the Internet?
2 Have you ever had any problems with online transactions? What happened? Did you sort it out?
3 Have you ever rung a customer help line? What was the service like?

WRITING

A **Read the letter of complaint below – without filling in the gaps. Answer the questions from *Speaking* for the writer of the letter.**

Dear Sir / Madam,

[1]........................ my telephone conversation today (15th September), I am writing to complain about the digital camera I bought from your website on 18th July this year and the service I have received.

When I ordered the camera, I was informed that delivery would take two weeks, but in [2]........................, it took over a month, arriving too late for me to take it on holiday. I sent a number of emails prior to my holiday, but they were never answered.

When I finally received the camera, it was not exactly [3]........................ advertised. According [4]........................ your website, it supposedly had 100 GB of memory. However, it stated on the packaging that this was only with a memory card, sold separately. I rang to complain, but I [5]........................ told that I should have looked more carefully and was then directed to details on the website.

The main advert is misleading, especially if customers must follow three different links to find the full information on a product. To make [6]........................ worse, when I called your helpline, it took me half an hour to get through and when I [7]........................, the three-minute conversation cost me five pounds and I was told I would still have to write if I wanted to take the matter [8]........................ .

As compensation for the lateness of delivery and the lack of clarity on the website [9]........................ the camera's specifications, I feel that I should be sent the missing memory card free of [10]........................ .

Yours faithfully,

Jamila Benitez

B **Complete the gaps in the letter in exercise A with the words in the box.**

charge	following	further	was	as
fact	regarding	matters	did	to

C **Underline** any phrases that you could use in any letter where you are writing to complain.

D **Work in pairs. Discuss these questions.**
• Do you think the complaint is fair?
• Do you think the company will agree to the compensation? Why? / Why not?

KEY WORDS FOR WRITING According to

We can show sources of information using *according to*.
According to your website, the camera had 80GB of memory.

In letters of complaint, we often contrast this with the reality of the situation using *however* or *but*.
However, it was stated on the packaging that this was only with a memory card, which was sold separately.

A **Complete 1–6 with *according to* plus a noun from the box.**

my brother	the forecast	consumer laws
the flyer	the opposition	your brochure

1 It's going to brighten up by the weekend, ..., so we're still planning to go for a picnic.
2 ...., the government is doing everything wrong, but they're not offering any solutions either.
3 .... this guy gave me, there's a special night at a club in town tonight. Entrance is free before 10.
4 ...., the hotel is in easy reach of the beach.
5 I did warn him that it wasn't a good place to go, but then ...., I know nothing!
6 ...., the company cannot legally charge your credit card until they have sent out the goods.

B **Complete the sentences below with your own ideas.**
1 According to my dad, ...
2 According to the government, ...
3 According to your website, you provide a fast, efficient service. However, ...
4 According to your publicity, your staff are highly professional, but in reality ....

GRAMMAR Passives and reporting

A Look back at the letter and find the ways these written and spoken comments were reported.

1 Your delivery will take two weeks.
2 You should have looked more carefully. The information is on the website.
3 If you want to take the matter further, I'm afraid you'll have to put it in writing.

> In letters of complaint, we often use verbs in the passive form, because we don't know the person who made the comment – or we don't see them as really responsible for the problem we are complaining about.

B Use the correct passive form of the verbs in **bold** to write second sentences that report the first sentences. You will need to add other words.

1 FareAir is sorry to announce that flight 203 has been delayed for five hours.
We were informed that the flight had been delayed by five hours only minutes before we were due to board. **inform**
2 If you're not satisfied, we'll give you your money back.
I .... full refund if I was not satisfied. **promise**
3 Postage and packaging are included.
It .... your website that postage and packaging were included in the cost. **state**
4 Speak to the manager about it.
My husband .... speak to the manager. **tell**
5 We can only replace it. We can't give you a refund.
I .... a replacement. They wouldn't refund the money. **offer**
6 Please could you arrive at the station 30 minutes before departure?
Everyone .... at the station 30 minutes before departure. **ask**
7 The advert said the price was all-inclusive.
It .... being all-inclusive. **advertise**

PRACTICE

A Look at the advert below. In pairs, make a list of things that could go wrong. Then compare your ideas in groups of four. Who had the longest list? Who has the funniest problem?

B Choose two or three of the problems from your list and write a letter of complaint about them. Make sure you write in paragraphs and make clear what you want the company to do (offer compensation, apologise etc.). Include as much language as you can from these pages.

GIFTS MAPPED OUT

Looking for a gift which will provide memories and entertainment? Why not get a personalised jigsaw puzzle based on a special place? Use the location finder on our website and we'll create a puzzle of the map or photo of the area. Alternatively, you can send us a digital photo of whatever you like. Puzzles come in three sizes – 150, 250 or 500 pieces – and are packaged in a durable presentation tin.

We also have a range of gift cards which you can add your own messages to. Orders normally take two weeks. Guaranteed delivery for Christmas on orders received before December 15th.
See our website at
www.giftsmappedout.com

SPEAKING

A **Work in groups. Discuss the following.**
- Have you ever belonged to any organisations such as a club or society?
- What's good about being in a club? Are there any disadvantages?
- What do you think people do when they meet in the organisations below? Explain why you would – or wouldn't – join each one.

a drama club	a history society
an athletics club	a debating society
a cycling club	Boy Scouts / Girl Guides
a reading club	a green activist group
a gastronomic club	a political party

WRITING A leaflet / poster

You are going to read a leaflet / poster that aims to persuade people to join a club.

A **Read the leaflet on the right and put the paragraphs in the correct order according to the following:**
1 Grab people's attention and say the name of club.
2 Explain more about the sport / club and what it does.
3 Persuade a wider group of people – if they have doubts.
4 Add a further reason.
5 Factual information about where / when, etc.
6 Final slogan or encouragement.

B **Work in pairs. Discuss these questions.**
- Would you be interested in joining? Why? / Why not?
- Who do you know that might be interested?

VOCABULARY
Intensifying adjectives and adverbs

In these kinds of leaflets, we often add adverbs that mean *extremely* to adjectives.
It's a *fantastically easy* sport.

We also use adjectives with nouns to emphasise that something is good.
It's all about running, passing and having *great fun*!

A **Match 1–4 with a–d and then 5–8 with e–h.**

1	an incredibly wide / huge	a	enjoyable
2	a passionate / huge	b	range of abilities
3	hugely / tremendously	c	organised
4	superbly / really well	d	interest
5	tremendous / great	e	cheap
6	a really warm / enthusiastic	f	welcome
7	absolutely / endlessly	g	fun
8	ridiculously / amazingly	h	fascinating

B **Give six opinions using words from 1–8. For example:**
I think cycling is tremendously enjoyable.
The festival in my town is superbly organised.

Wanted! Touch rugby players

a Our club runs friendly games, training sessions and league matches three nights a week (Mon, Wed and Fri) from 7 till 9 at the sports centre fields. Sessions cost £2.

b Most of our teams are mixed, so it's not just for men. Nor do you have to be especially athletic or co-ordinated, because there are teams for all levels. There are also lots of substitutions during the game, so if you're out of breath, you can always rest and chat to the others on the bench.

c Come along! You'll find a warm welcome and enjoy a fantastic game.

KEY WORDS FOR WRITING
whenever, wherever, however etc.

> We add *-ever* to question words to mean *'It doesn't matter when / where / how …'* etc.
>
> *It's a sport you can play whenever or wherever you like.*

A Complete the sentences by adding the correct words ending in *-ever*.

1 You can drop into our offices .... you like.
2 .... good you are, you'll find a group to suit you.
3 We'll get you into shape, ... your fitness level.
4 .... you live, you'll find a branch near you.
5 Why not bring a friend? .... joins before the end of August will receive free membership for six months.
6 You can pay .... you like, with the exception of *American Instant* credit cards.
7 .... preconceptions you have about chess players, they're probably wrong!
8 .... you are, and .... your age, this is the sport for you.

---

d Feeling out of shape? Bored of working out in the gym? Looking for a sport with a great social vibe? Look no further: TOUCH RUGBY is the thing for you.

---

e And once you've learned how to play, it's something you can play whenever or wherever you like because it needs no special equipment other than a ball.

---

f Touch rugby is rugby, but with all the tackling, kicking and rough stuff taken out. You have to pass the ball backwards to your teammates as you run and try to put the ball down behind the opposing team's goal line. The defenders stop you by lightly touching your body, at which point you stop and roll the ball to another player. After every six touches, the ball is given to the opposing team. It's a fantastically easy sport and remember, all it involves is a light touch, so there's no risk of injury. It's all about running, passing and having great fun!

GRAMMAR Ellipsis

A Read the explanation box and decide what words have been left out in each of the examples in *italics*.

> Ellipsis is when you leave out words – generally, grammar words such as subject pronouns or auxiliary verbs. You do this:
> - for reasons of style or emphasis.
>   *Feeling out of shape?*
> - to avoid repetition.
>   *…. you can always rest and chat*
> - simply to be shorter / quicker, as in notes or emails.
>   *Gone to lunch. Back at 2. Andrew*
>
> When we leave out words, it should still be clear who or what the subject of the verb is - and what tense it should be.

B Cross out as many words as you can in 1–6 without changing the meaning or making things unclear.

1 Are you planning to work abroad? This is your chance!
2 Do you worry about speaking in public? Do you get nervous in front of an audience or do you forget your words? Our course could help.
3 Have you never been to a gym before? We'll show you how the gym machines work and we'll give you support when you're training.
4 We are having a really great time. We wish you were here and we hope everything is fine with you. Karen.
5 Sara rang. She said she can't come this evening, but she will be at the meeting tomorrow.
6 I had to go out and I won't be back till 8. There's some dinner in the oven. I love you.

C In pairs, compare what you deleted. Is the subject and tense of each verb still clear?

PRACTICE

You are going to write a similar leaflet / poster to the one you read.

A In pairs, decide on a sport, activity or other kind of organisation you want people to join. Then discuss what you would put in each of the paragraphs, using the ideas from *Writing*, exercise A.

B Write the leaflet / poster. Add a design / illustration if you like.

VOCABULARY
Describing disasters

A Read 1–6 below and decide what kind of natural disaster each one is describing.

1 It was absolutely **terrifying**. Half the buildings in the street **collapsed** and I could hear people trapped beneath the **debris** screaming for help.

2 The ground floor was completely under water and all our stuff was **ruined**. We were **stranded** on the roof for hours until they **rescued** us.

3 It **spread** very rapidly. Luckily, they managed to **evacuate** our town shortly before the whole place **went up in flames**.

4 It was **triggered** by a massive underwater earthquake. By the time they hit the coast, the **waves** were thirty feet high. All the villages near the beach were completely **destroyed**.

5 There'd been increasingly strong **tremors** for weeks and then it erupted one evening. All the villagers had to **flee** the area to escape the streams of **lava**.

6 It destroyed everything in its **path**. Our neighbour's house was completely **flattened**. We were incredibly lucky that we only had our roof **blown off**.

B Use the extra information in sentences 1–6 above to guess the meanings of the words in **bold**. Translate the sentences into your language.

C Cover exercise A above. See how much of each description you can remember. Use the words below to help you.

1 terrifying – collapsed – debris – help
2 water – ruined – stranded – rescued
3 spread – evacuate – before – flames
4 triggered – hit – waves – destroyed
5 tremors – erupted – flee – lava
6 path – flattened – lucky – blown off

D Compare what you remember with a partner. Then look back at exercise A and check your ideas.

WRITING A travel blog story

You are going to read a short story from a travel blog. The story is about a natural disaster.

A Read the story below and answer these questions.

1 Where was the writer when the disaster struck?
2 What happened?
3 How did he feel?
4 How did the locals react? What explanation did the writer give?

B Complete the gaps using the words in the box.

active	blocked	breeze	cleared
delayed	journey	minor	slopes

C Work in groups. Discuss these questions.
- Have you heard about any volcanic eruptions in the news over the last year?
- Have you heard about other natural disasters? Where? When? What happened?

AN EXPLOSIVE TRIP!

So we finally made it to Bali! As I write, I am sitting on a hotel balcony overlooking the beach, enjoying the early evening [1].......................... Bet you wish you were here, eh?

The [2].......................... across Java was fairly eventful – and took a few days longer than we were expecting. Believe it or not, what [3].......................... things was getting caught up in a volcanic eruption!

One of the things we'd been really looking forward to doing was climbing Mount Semeru, the highest mountain on the island. It's an [4].......................... volcano, so to be on the safe side, we found a local guide, Kencur, who knows the mountain really well. At two in the morning, we set off up the [5].......................... in total darkness.

The first indication that something was up was a series of tremors, like a [6].......................... earthquake. This was followed by a loud rumbling noise, like thunder, that came up from the ground as we were walking. At this point, Kencur stopped and suggested we return to our hostel. Shortly afterwards, the volcano erupted, leaving the main road out of town completely [7].......................... by rocks and lava. We were stranded in our hostel until the roads were [8].......................... – three days later! It was pretty scary, unlike anything I've ever experienced before, but what really struck me was how relaxed about everything all the locals were. I guess they've seen it all before.

Mount Semeru from a distance

KEY WORDS FOR WRITING *like, unlike*

We often use *like* to show one thing is similar to another.
The first indication that something was up was *a series of tremors, like a minor earthquake.* This was followed by *a loud rumbling noise, like thunder.*

To show one thing is different to another, we use *unlike*.
It was pretty scary, unlike anything I've ever experienced before.

A Match 1–8 with a–h to make complete sentences.
1 Siberia was a really unique place,
2 The festival was a great success,
3 I could hear trees creaking and breaking
4 Thankfully, this volcano is dormant,
5 The hailstones smashed against our windscreen
6 The mist settled over the village
7 It's unbearably humid here,
8 The rain poured down for days,

a like matchsticks as the winds came through.
b unlike anywhere I'd ever been before.
c unlike last year, when it rained non-stop.
d like an endless waterfall from the skies!
e unlike back home, where it's more dry heat.
f like a blanket of cloud.
g unlike most others in the area, which are active.
h like bullets from a machine gun!

B Complete the sentences below with a partner. Then compare your ideas with another pair. Who has the funniest, the most original or the most interesting ideas?
1 Suddenly, there was a huge bang, like ....
2 It was so cold that my hands were like ....
3 He had a face like .... and a voice like
   ....
4 .... was unlike anything I'd ever seen before.
5 .... was unlike anything I'd ever heard before
6 .... was unlike anything I'd tasted before.

C Work in groups. Make comparisons between your country and other countries using *like* and *unlike*.

PRACTICE

A Choose one of the topics below and write a story of around 250 words about it.
1 A natural disaster
2 Extreme weather
3 A crime

SPEAKING

A **Work in pairs. Discuss these questions.**

- Have you ever written a personal statement? When? What for? What kind of things did you put in it? Were you pleased with it?
- How important is it to be honest when writing personal statements?
- Do you think it's OK to be funny when writing personal statements? Why? / Why not?

WRITING

Niran is applying to do an MBA (a Master's Degree in Business Administration) at the University of Sydney in Australia.

A **Look at the notes he made before writing his personal statement. Then discuss these questions in pairs.**

- What would you expect to read in each section?
- What other areas could he include?
- What do you think is the best order to put all this information in?

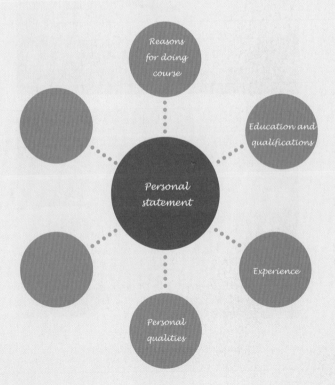

B **Complete Niran's personal statement below with the words in the box.**

active interest	transferable skills
invaluable insight	competitive edge
valuable contribution	solid grounding

I am applying for this course because I would like to broaden my understanding of the world of business and apply the theoretical and practical knowledge I have acquired to date. Furthermore, I feel an MBA will give me a ¹........................... in the job market.

As a teenager, I often accompanied my uncle to his office, where I gained an ²........................... into how businesses are run. It was at this point that I decided to pursue a career in this field. My subsequent degree in Business Studies and Accountancy has given me a ³........................... in core business skills.

I am currently doing a part-time English course in order to improve my language skills. In addition to this, I have almost completed an on-line computing diploma.

At present, I'm doing an internship for a media company. This experience has given me the opportunity to put into practice much of what I learned on my degree course. Despite having been at the company for only a short period of time, I still believe I have acquired a set of ⁴........................... that I can apply to any business environment.

I am a positive, hard-working person who enjoys challenges. I believe I could make a ⁵........................... to the course because I am up-to-date with what is happening in the business world and also take an ⁶........................... in current affairs.

SPEAKING

A **Work in groups. Discuss these questions.**

- What do you think is good about Niran's personal statement?
- Is there anything you would change or add? Why?
- Look at the list of transferable skills below. Which do you think you have? Give examples of when / how you have used them.
- Are there any skills you'd like to develop further?

computer skills	problem-solving skills
people skills	organisational skills
language skills	time-management skills
leadership skills	negotiating skills

VOCABULARY Describing yourself

In the personal statement, Niran gives a description of his character. Note that he doesn't just use an adjective. He also adds a comment to exemplify or clarify the description.

I am a positive, hard-working person who enjoys challenges.

A **Match the descriptions 1–5 to the follow-up comments a–e.**

1 I'm a very ambitious person
2 I am very passionate about my studies
3 I am a highly sociable kind of person
4 I'm very punctual
5 I can be very demanding

a and am determined to be a success in my field.
b and have a wide circle of friends.
c as I expect the best of people around me.
d and really love the subject.
e as I am always on time and never miss a deadline.

B **Now match 6–10 to f–j .**

6   I am a very positive person
7   I am a very conscientious worker,
8   I am quite a creative person
9   I am quite a well-rounded person
10 I can be quite a stubborn person,

f who takes pride in doing things well.
g and excel at finding innovative solutions to problems.
h who finds it hard to see other people's points of view.
i and have a wide range of interests.
j who always tries to look on the bright side.

C **Choose the five adjectives from exercises A and B that you think best describe you. Explain your choices to a partner. Do they agree with your description of yourself?**

KEY WORDS FOR WRITING
Adding information

There are several different linking words you can use to add information. Some link two sentences together and are more commonly used after full stops; others are more often used to link clauses within a sentence.

A **Look at the pairs of linking words in *italics*. For each pair, decide if both choices are possible or if only one is. Cross out any incorrect linking words.**

1 I believe I am well qualified for the course. *In addition, / As well*, I have already gained considerable work experience in the field.
2 I speak fluent English and German. *Additionally, / In addition*, I speak very good French and basic Spanish.
3 I have read widely in the literature of the field and have relevant practical experience *too / as well*.
4 I am very keen on sport. I am a keen cyclist and play tennis regularly. *What's more, / In addition to*, I have been studying karate for the last six years.
5 *In addition to / As well as* being determined and ambitious, I am *also / furthermore* highly organised.
6 I spent a year studying Graphic Design in Canada. *Additionally, / In addition to this*, I have taught myself how to use specialist software such as InDesign and I *also / as well* have excellent Web design skills.

B **Compare your ideas with a partner.**

PRACTICE

A **Decide on a course of study or job you would like to apply for. You are going to write your own personal statement of around 250 words. You will need to give information about:**
- your past and present education
- your work experience
- your skills and abilities

B **Plan the content of each of your paragraphs. Use the model statement on the opposite page to help you.**

C **Write the statement.**

WRITING

You are going to read a report about public transport and car use.

A Read the introduction to the report and a list of the main findings. Then discuss these questions in pairs.

1 What do you think the statistics would be if the report was about your city / area?
2 Considering the aim of the council, which of the statistics do you think is good news and which is bad? Why?
3 What action would you recommend to the council?

Introduction

The survey resulting in this report was conducted with people in the Northsea area. It aimed to find out how people travelled and the reasons for their choices, with a view to the council developing policies to discourage car use.

Main findings

- 75% use the car as their main regular form of transport.
- In the previous month, four out of five people had used some alternative – train, bus, bike, motorbike, or (electric) taxi.
- 90% said they would be willing to use alternative transport to the car.
- 83% of journeys by public transport were by bus.
- Only one tenth of those surveyed felt public transport provision was good or very good.
- The main reasons cited for not using public transport were cost and inconvenience.

B Read the summary of the findings and fill in the gaps with the words from the box.

respondents	widely	mentioned	rated
minority	examples	interviewed	long
majority	factor	favourably	vast

Summary of findings

While the findings of the survey showed that cars remain the main form of transport, there was still some hope in the high numbers of people willing to change. Only a small ¹........................... felt they would continue to use their car, no matter what.

Most ²........................... had used buses, and the ³........................... said they would use them more often if they were cheaper and more convenient. ⁴........................... of inconvenience that were ⁵........................... on numerous occasions were the lack of timetable information and buses running infrequently and failing to connect with other routes.

Even though bus travel actually compares ⁶........................... to car travel, cost-wise, the perception of the ⁷........................... majority of people ⁸........................... was that it was more expensive. Interestingly, those using the train ⁹........................... it highly, **despite** it being more expensive than the bus. This suggests comfort is also a ¹⁰...........................

Recommendations

If the council is to encourage less car use, it clearly needs to develop bus services. It should improve timetabling and make information more ¹¹........................... available, for example through a website. In the short term, a campaign to raise awareness of the relative costs of buses and cars – as well as increasing parking fees in the centre – could help. **However**, to make a real difference, the council needs to invest in new buses in the ¹²........................... term to increase frequency and comfort.

C Work in pairs. Discuss these questions.

1 What extra information is included outside the main findings of the survey?
2 Do you think the summary is a fair summary of the main findings? Why? / Why not?
3 Do you agree with the recommendations?

GRAMMAR *be to*

> **In the report, you read:**
> *If the council is to encourage less car use, it clearly needs to develop bus services.*
>
> *be to* + verb is often used with *if*-clauses to show a desired future result. Negatives are formed as *is not to* or *isn't to*. The main clause shows what must be done first, using *need / must / have to*, etc.
> *We must do something now if the situation is not to deteriorate further.*

A **Write sentences with *if*, *be to* + verb and *need*, etc., using the ideas in 1–6.**

1 the government / win the next election / change their policies now.
2 we / improve our marketing / boost sales.
3 we / reduce crime / increase the number of police.
4 the company / reduce its debts / not go bankrupt.
5 the council / build more cycle lanes / encourage more people to cycle to work.
6 discourage waste / the government / introduce a tax on the amount of rubbish people throw away.

KEY WORDS FOR WRITING
while, despite, however, even though

A **Look at the words in bold in the report. Then discuss these questions in pairs.**

1 Which word contrasts an idea with an idea in the previous sentence?
2 Which three words help to link two parts of a sentence?
3 Which two words could be swapped round?
4 Which word is followed by a noun / *-ing* form?
5 Where are the commas in the sentences with words in bold?

B **Choose the correct words. One or two are correct in each sentence. Cross out any incorrect words.**

1 *While / despite / even though* student numbers fell this year, the school is confident it can grow in the future.
2 Most students were satisfied with their classes, *even though / despite / however* there was a lot of noise from ongoing repair work.
3 The school doesn't have enough resources. *However / while / despite this*, the teachers do an excellent job.
4 Profits were down last year, *despite / however / even though* having more students.

> *Despite this* can be used instead of *however*, and *despite the fact that* can be followed by a clause:
> *Despite the fact that I told him not to, he took the car.*

> *However* can also come in the middle of a sentence.
> *Cars are expensive to run. There are, however, ways to save.*

C **Rewrite the sentences using the words in bold so that your sentences mean the same.**

1 Despite the government investing in buses, most people still prefer to travel by car. **even though**
2 While the cost of air travel to the passengers has been falling, the cost to the environment has increased. **however**
3 Most people rated the service as poor. However, the majority also praised the quality of the food. **while**
4 Things have improved, but we're still struggling. **despite**

PRACTICE

You are going to write a report about improving public healthcare services in your area.

A **Before you write, fill in what you think the statistics are for your area. Then compare with a partner.**

B **Write the report. Write an introduction to explain the survey and purpose. Write a summary and analysis based on the statistics you wrote. Write a conclusion about how things could be improved.**

> **Main findings**
> ....% of people use private instead of public healthcare services.
> ....% visited their local hospital or clinic in the past year.
> ....% of those who saw a doctor required no treatment.
> .... out of ....
> people are currently considered overweight.
> ....% respondents felt public health was good or very good.
> .... tenth(s) of people could get an appointment with their doctor within 48 hours.
> The main reasons for using private healthcare were ...., ... and ....

SPEAKING

Work in groups. Discuss these questions.

- Can you remember the last time you went to a zoo? Who did you go with? What did you see?
- Can you think of three reasons why keeping animals in captivity is a good thing?
- What are the alternatives to zoos?

GRAMMAR Articles

> **Articles are used before nouns. We use *a / an* when we introduce something new.**
> *They've got a huge snake there – and a gorilla!*
> *There is a zoo in my town, but I've never been there.*
>
> **We use *the* when we think the listener knows the specific thing we mean – because they can see it, because they know there's only one or because it's already been mentioned. When we use *the*, we often add a clause to clarify which thing we mean.**
> *Do you know the old zoo near the park? It's a bit depressing!*
>
> **We don't use articles with plurals or uncountable nouns when we talk about them in general, or if they represent the whole of a type/group (e.g. dance music).**
> *Zoos are a thing of the past nowadays, aren't they?*

A **Find the five mistakes and correct them.**

1 The zoos protect endangered animals.
2 When kids visit zoos, they get a chance to see lots of different animals.
3 I saw a TV programme the other day about the zoo in Singapore and it sounds like the amazing place.
4 The zoo in my town is home to the very rare kind of panda. That's the main attraction.
5 The fact that fewer and fewer people are visiting zoos these days does pose the big problem.
6 Without a funding, what will happen to all the animals housed in such institutions?
7 For me, the main issue is whether or not animals should be kept in an unnatural environment.

WRITING

You are going to read an essay in response to this task: "Zoos are not something we need in the 21st century." Discuss.

A **Read the essay. Does the writer agree or disagree with the idea of zoos? How do you know? Do you agree with this point of view?**

B **Complete the gaps with *a, an, the* or nothing.**

C **Work in pairs. Discuss these questions.**
- What is the function of each of the four paragraphs?
- What is the function of each of the three sentences in the opening paragraph?
- In what different ways does the writer introduce ideas they do not agree with?

ZOOS ARE NOT SOMETHING WE NEED IN THE 21ST CENTURY

Over the last twenty years or so, [1]...... fierce debate about zoos has been raging. It is often claimed that [2]...... zoos are [3]...... outdated form of entertainment and should be closed down. However, over recent years, there has been growing appreciation of the work zoos do both in terms of protecting endangered animals and also in terms of public education.

One argument against zoos is that they are cruel. They are seen as being a kind of prison for animals that should supposedly be left in the wild to roam free. It is also believed that zoos somehow legitimize [4]...... idea that it is acceptable to capture animals and to keep them in [5]...... captivity, and that this then encourages all manner of cruelty towards animals in society at large.

Nevertheless, the positive work done by zoos has become increasingly important and is surely sufficient reason for their continued existence. For instance, zoos do a lot to protect [6]...... endangered species. Many have breeding programmes, which are essential if we want these animals to survive. A good example here are orangutans. These animals' natural environment is rapidly being destroyed and, as a result, they are on [7]...... verge of extinction. As such, zoos represent [8]...... final chance of survival for orangutans. Anyone that attacks zoos is, in fact, hastening the demise of these beautiful animals.

If you add to this [9]...... excellent work many zoos do in raising awareness of the problems facing animals in the wild, then you surely have sufficient reasons for supporting [10]...... continued existence of this endangered public institution!

KEY WORDS FOR WRITING Indicating and dismissing weak arguments.

> A common way of structuring an argument is to indicate what we feel are weak arguments first, before we then dismiss them. We use specific words and phrases to indicate that we are doing this.
>
> *It is often claimed that* zoos are an outdated form of entertainment and should now be closed down.
>
> *One argument against* zoos is that they are cruel.

A Can you find three more words or phrases that the essay writer uses to indicate what they see as weak arguments?

B Complete the sentences with the words in the box.

believed	claimed	common
seen	sometimes	supposedly

1 It is .... said that animals in zoos live much longer lives.
2 Zoos are .... enjoyable places to visit.
3 It is widely .... that nature programmes and documentaries will gradually make zoos redundant.
4 It is often .... that zoos perform valuable work by breeding endangered species and then returning them to the wild.
5 Animals are sometimes .... as having no individuality or personality.
6 One .... argument against zoos is that we don't have the right to deprive animals of their freedom.

C Underline the parts of 1–6 above that you can re-use in your own writing.

> When we dismiss weak arguments, we often start the sentence with *However* or a similar word. We then write our own (stronger) ideas as facts, using the present simple. For example:
>
> *One argument against* zoos is that they are cruel. *However, it is also necessary to* consider the cruelty of the wild. Many animals actually live longer, healthier lives in captivity than they would in the wild.

D Work in pairs. Think of ways to explain why each of the arguments in exercise B are felt to be weak. Begin each sentence with *However*.

E Compare the sentences you've written with another group. Do you agree with them? Why? / Why not?

PRACTICE

You are going to write an essay arguing your point of view in response to one of the following titles:
- "Lotteries cause great harm to society and should be banned." Discuss.
- "Criminals need education, not prison." Discuss.
- "Professional sport causes more pain than pleasure." Discuss.
- "Staying at home for your holiday is better than travelling somewhere." Discuss.

A Work in pairs. Choose one of the titles. Discuss possible reasons why people might agree or disagree with the statement above, and then discuss your own opinions.

B Plan the content of each of your paragraphs. Use the model essay on the opposite page to help you.

C Write your essay. Use as much language from these pages as you can.

WRITING

You are going to read an email enquiring about language courses in Manchester.

A **Read the email and answer these questions.**
1 Why does Kathrin address the person she is writing to as *Ms*?
2 Which language does Kathrin want to study?
3 Does she have any previous experience of the language?
4 What expectations does she have of the course?
5 What five things does she ask about?
6 Why does she end with *Yours sincerely* – instead of using a different ending?

To	pennylee99@chinacentre.org
Subject	Re: Courses at the China Centre

Dear Ms Lee,

I am writing to **enquire** about the Mandarin courses **currently** offered by the China Centre.

I am planning to take a Mandarin Chinese course at elementary level sometime early next year, preferably for a period of between three and five weeks. I have studied Mandarin before, but only at beginner level, and **would be looking to** review much of what I **previously** studied.

As such, **I would be most grateful** if you could send me information about what courses you will be offering between January and June next year, and also let me know the prices of these courses. **Furthermore**, I would appreciate it if you could let me know what kind of **excursions** and cultural activities your centre offers. I would also like to know whether or not it is possible to invite friends along on the excursions.

Finally, **I wonder if it would be possible for you to forward me** any information you might have about accommodation in the Manchester area, as I would like to stay locally while studying.

I look forward to hearing from you soon,

Yours sincerely,

Kathrin Jacobson

VOCABULARY
Formal and informal language

> The degree of formality that we use when writing to people depends on who we are writing to, how well we know them, and why we are writing. Generally speaking, more formal writing involves longer, more complex sentences, more multi-syllable words of Latin origin, fewer phrasal verbs, fewer contractions (*I've, You're*, etc.) and fewer abbreviations.

A **The email you read is quite formal. Match the more informal expressions below to the words or expressions in bold in the email with similar meanings.**

can you send me	ask	on top of that
at the moment	before	hope to hear
it'd be great	trips	want to

B **Choose the more formal options in each of the sentences below.**
1 *Cheers / Thank you* for bringing this *matter / stuff* to my attention.
2 *We are looking to / We want to* expand our team and currently have *jobs / vacancies* available.
3 *We are sorry / We regret* to *tell / inform* you that the item you *asked for / requested* is no longer in stock.
4 *If you need / Should you require* any *more help / further* assistance, please do not *hesitate / wait* to ask.
5 I *trust / hope* that this will not *be / prove* too much of *a pain / an inconvenience*.
6 *Is there any chance you could / I wonder if it would be possible for you to* provide me with copies of your *newest / most recent* catalogue?
7 *In the event of any delay / If your goods are going to be late*, we will *contact you / let you know ASAP / as soon as possible*.
8 If you are in any way *unhappy / dissatisfied* with the goods you *buy / purchase*, we *would / will* be more than happy to *offer you / provide you with* a full refund.
9 I *believe / reckon* that there are *plenty / a number of* ways in which this problem could be *sorted out / rectified*.
10 While I *appreciate / understand* the problems your company is having, I would still like to *ascertain / find out* when I might expect to *receive / get* my refund.

C Complete this more informal email by putting one word from exercise A or B into each gap.

To j.arkwright@arkwright.com

Subject Re: A favour

Hi Josh,
¹............................ this finds you well. Not sure if you're in the office at the moment or if you're away on one of your overseas ²............................, but I just wanted to write and ask a couple of favours.

First off, can you ³............................ me the sales figures for the last six months? Mike has ⁴............................ me to go through them ahead of the big sales meeting in Greece next month.

On ⁵............................ of that, I also need about a thousand copies of the new brochure sent over asap. It'd be ⁶............................ if you could courier them, actually, if it's not too much of a ⁷.............................

One last thing. Is there any ⁸............................ you could double-check the hotel bookings for Athens and ⁹............................ me know if there are any problems? Oh, and can you ¹⁰............................ out what time our flights get in and ¹¹............................ out transport to the hotel for us all?

¹²............................ for all your help on this.

Best,
Ella

PRACTICE

You are going to write two emails: one more formal, one less formal, using language from these pages.

A You are going to write a formal email to a company that offers special events for groups. In pairs, discuss which of the activities below you think would best encourage team-building skills among your group. Explain your choice.
- corporate sword-fighting
- mountain climbing challenge
- creating a giant work of art
- ballroom dancing classes
- cooking a special dinner
- a quiz competition
- sailing a large yacht

B Write the email to the company asking about the activity you most like the sound of. Ask:
- which day the activity is available on
- what time it starts / finishes
- how much it costs (and if there are any discounts)
- if you can have a brochure
- if there are any age limits
- how you can book

C Write an informal email to a colleague who works with you. Tell them about the day you have chosen. Ask them to invite everyone in the office, and to tell you as soon as possible if anyone can't make it. Ask them to organise transport for the day – and to send a schedule to everyone.

01 ART AND ENTERTAINMENT

TALKING ABOUT HABITS

To talk about present habits, we mainly use:

Present simple
I hardly ever *go out* these days.
As a rule, I *don't watch* much TV.

tend to + verb
I *tend to stay in* during the week.
I *don't tend to read* much. (or I *tend not to read* much).

We also use this structure. It's more emphatic than the present simple.

will / won't
I'll usually *listen to* music for a while before I go to bed.
I *won't* normally *get up* until 11 or 12 on a Sunday.

Present continuous
The present continuous emphasises that something happens all the time and is often annoying.
He's always *watching* TV! He hardly does anything else!

Past simple
Use the past simple to talk about past habits.
I *did* it every day for ten years, but then I *gave up*.

Don't use the past continuous to talk about past habits.
I ~~was going~~ *went swimming* a lot when I was younger.

used to + verb
I *used to eat out* a lot, but I can't afford to these days.
I *never used to read* much when I was a kid.

Don't say *use to* or *used to* to talk about habits in the present. Say *usually / normally* + verb.
I ~~use to~~ *usually go out* with friends on a Friday.

would
Would is often used to talk about past habits. We usually introduce the past habit with *used to* or the past simple and then add details with *would*.
We used to go to the beach a lot in summer. Sometimes we'*d make* a bonfire, and we'*d stay up* all night telling jokes.

Frequency expressions
These frequency expressions are often used in connection with habits:

more than	before / I used to / I should / you
not as much as	I'd like to / I used to / I should / you
(= less than)	
whenever	I can / I get the chance
	(= every time I can)

all the time (= always / a lot)
(not) as a rule (= (not) usually / normally)
on the whole (= generally)
by and large (= generally)
now and again / once in a while (= occasionally)
hardly ever (= almost never)

Exercise 1
Find the six sentences that contain mistakes with the structures and expressions about habits. Correct them.

1   I'm tend to stay in on Friday nights, as I'm generally too tired to do anything much.
2   I use to go and see films when they come out at the cinema because I prefer to see them on the big screen.
3   I used to eat chocolate whenever I got the chance. I'd probably have at least a bar a day, but I've gone off it now.
4   I don't see her as much as I used, because we're both so busy.
5   He'll always disappear when I want him to do some housework.
6   I not used to do any sport at all, so I do a lot more now than before.
7   I tend not to eat out much, but I go for a Chinese again and now.
8   When I lived in New York, I was going running in Central Park every day.

Exercise 2
Rewrite the sentences using the prompts in brackets (without changing the form of the words).

1   I tend to only listen to classical music.
.... only listen to classical music. (rule)
2   I did like them, but I've gone off them a bit.
I don't like them .... (used)
3   He hardly ever does any exercise.
He .... do much exercise. (tend)
4   We used to constantly fight when we were kids.
We used to .... when we were kids. (time)
5   I'll go to the theatre, just not very often.
I'll go to the theatre .... , but I don't go every week or anything. (while)
6   They never turn the TV off in their house.
They .... in their house. (watching)
7   He was really fit. He went cycling 50 km every day.
He was really fit. .... cycle 50 km every day. (would)
8   On the whole, I only eat food from my country.
.... foreign food. (hardly)

Glossary

gone off: if you go off a band, a programme or some kind of food, you stop liking it
come out: when a film / DVD is first released or a book is first published, it comes out
go for a Chinese: if you go for a Chinese, an Indian or an Italian, you go to eat that kind of food

ADJECTIVES AND ADVERBS

Adjectives

Adjectives tend to go before a noun.
The film had a really *uplifting* ending.
It's quite *dull* music, if you ask me.

Adjectives go after 'linking' verbs.
The painting *looks* quite *sombre*.
This song *is* so *catchy*.
She *went red* with embarrassment.

The following verbs can be followed by an adjective on its own: *be, become, get, go, feel, grow, keep, look, remain, seem, smell, stay, sound, taste* and *turn*.

Adverbs

Most adverbs are formed by adding -*ly* to the adjective, but some adverbs have the same form as the adjective. For example: *alive, fast, hard, late, later*.

Note that the adverbs *hardly* and *lately* have completely different meanings to the adjectives *hard* and *late*.
I *hardly* know him. (= not really)
I haven't been to the cinema *lately*. (= recently)

Add adverbs immediately before the main verb to show frequency or how you did something.
They're *always* shouting at each other.
I *hardly ever* go out these days.
She *angrily* denied she was involved in the scandal.

We also add adverbs after a verb to show how we did something or to show when the action happens.
He was looking at me *strangely*.
I went to this great exhibition *yesterday*.
I'm going there *later*.

Don't use an adverb after a linking verb to modify the subject. Use an adjective.
She *looks* ~~amazingly~~ *amazing*.
You *sound* ~~terribly~~ *terrible*. Are you feeling ~~badly~~ *bad*?

We can use an adverb at the start of a sentence or clause to give an opinion about the whole sentence.
Fortunately, no-one was injured in the accident.
I meant to be here earlier, but, *stupidly*, I got half-way here before I realised I'd left your address at home.
Funnily enough, I never went up the Eiffel Tower, despite living in Paris for ten years!

Adverbs go before adjectives.
His writing is *absolutely* impossible to read.
It was a *strangely* moving film.

Adverbs can come before other adverbs.
The traffic was moving *really slowly*.

Exercise 1
Complete 1–8 with the adjectives in the box, changing them into adverbs if necessary.

interesting	hard	frequent
beautiful	funny	occasional
later	disturbing	catchy
recent		

1 You can buy a season ticket for the museum if you're going to be a .... visitor. It works out a lot cheaper.
2 I don't do much exercise, except for .... going swimming.
3 I've been working really .... to improve my English and I feel I'm making progress at last.
4 Seven in the morning's a bit early. Can't we get a .... train?
5 .... enough, I was just thinking about calling you when you rang.
6 If we want the book to sell, we need a .... title to ensure that people remember it.
7 A .... report has found that kids are being exposed to .... high levels of violence in films and video games.
8 .... , this is one of only two portraits he ever painted, but as you can see it's .... done – a real masterpiece.

Exercise 2
Put the adverbs in brackets into the correct place.
1 I download films from the Internet. (never)
2 I've seen him all day. (hardly)
3 He reacted badly to the news. (fairly)
4 I'm going fishing in the week. (later)
5 To be honest, I haven't even picked up a book. (lately)
6 The car was completely destroyed, but he escaped without a scratch. (amazingly)
7 The special effects are amazing – just realistic. (incredibly)
8 They got married in 2005, but he died after. (sadly, soon)

Exercise 3
Make collocations with adjectives and adverbs from this unit. Look in the *Vocabulary Builder* if you need help.

1	a heated	a	after
2	loosely	b	meaning
3	a symbolic	c	treated
4	ended	d	exactly the same
5	shortly	e	discussion
6	an uplifting	g	ending
7	almost	h	out of control
8	badly	i	tragically
9	totally	j	based on a true story

02 SIGHTSEEING

NON-DEFINING RELATIVE CLAUSES

Non-defining relative clauses allow us to add extra, non-essential information about a noun to a sentence. They do not identify which noun we are talking about in the same way as defining relative clauses do. They are often added as a separate clause at the end of a sentence – and they are preceded by a comma.

To add extra details about a thing, use *which*. Note that you cannot use *that*, *those* or *them* in this kind of clause.

We did the guided tour, ~~that~~ *which* cost us about ten pounds each.
Back in 2002, a fire damaged 15 buildings in the area, five of ~~them~~ *which* were damaged beyond repair!

Which can also be used to add a comment on the whole clause that comes before it.
I spent a week hiking in the jungle, *which was amazing.*

In addition, it is common to use *most of which, many of which, some of which, a few of which, none of which*, etc.
The people back then lived in houses carved into the rock, *many of which* are still used today.
The guidebook listed about a hundred restaurants they recommended, *none of which* we actually went to!

To add extra information about times, we can use *by which time / point, during which time, at which point*, etc.
We didn't go for dinner until about ten, *by which time* I was absolutely starving!
(= I was already starving at ten o'clock)

Then they told us our tickets weren't valid for the museum, *at which point* I just totally lost my temper!
(= I lost my temper when they told me this)

To add extra details about what happens at or inside a building, place, country, etc , use *where*.
I spent a month hitchhiking round Spain, *where* I actually met my wife!
That's the old royal palace, *where* the last king lived.

To add extra details about a person, use *who*.
Leyla has a cousin in Bucharest, *who* very kindly let us stay with him.
I met this amazing guy called Dirk, *who* had once been a famous tennis player.

Non-defining relative clauses can also appear in the middle of sentences. They are separated from the main body of the sentence by commas. This is much more common in written English than spoken.
Perth, *which was once the capital of the country*, is today a relatively small town of approximately fifty thousand.
Padangbai, *where we caught the ferry over to Lombok*, was nothing special – just a sleepy fishing village.

Exercise 1
Complete the sentences with the words in the box.

by which time	who	some of which
at which point	which	none of which
during which time	where	every single one of which

1 The statue was erected by Sukarno, ... was our first president after we gained independence.
2 Next stop for us is Yekaterinburg, ... the last tsar was executed.
3 They had about ten TVs in the restaurant, ... was on at full blast! We could hardly hear ourselves talk!
4 We didn't get into town until after ten, ... all the hotels were already booked for the night.
5 The museum houses a remarkable collection of books, ... date back as far as the tenth century.
6 Margie and the kids spent a few hours shopping, ... I stayed in and updated our travel blog.
7 After lunch, we went to check out the castle, ... was very grand.
8 We strolled along Rue St-Paul until lunchtime, ... we decided to try out one of the local bistros.
9 The guidebooks, ... I actually never bothered to read at all, were soon conveniently 'lost'!

Exercise 2
Rewrite each of the pairs of sentences below as one sentence.
1 We saw Big Ben, Buckingham Palace, Tower Bridge and the London Eye. They were all amazing.
....
2 There were loads of recommendations on the Web. Most of them were really helpful.
....
3 We stayed out dancing until two in the morning. I was completely exhausted by then!
....
4 We spent a week in Bolivia. The election was on while we were there.
....
5 We spent two days in Bergen and then drove down to Stavanger. My girlfriend has family in Bergen.
....
6 Chen's grandfather still lives at home with the rest of the family. His grandfather is 97.
....

Glossary

erect: if you erect something like a statue or a bridge, you build it
execute: if someone is executed, they are killed as a punishment – often for crimes they have committed
check out: if you check a place out, you visit it to see what it's like

THE FUTURE

There is no one future tense in English. A variety of different forms are used. For certain meanings, we prefer one particular form. However, in many cases, more than one form can be used with little or no change of meaning.

Present simple

Use the present simple after time words like *when, after, before*, etc. – or to talk about times of future events that have been fixed by other people or by organisations.
When you hear any news, call me.
When does the meeting *start* tomorrow?
My train *doesn't leave* till nine, so I'll have dinner *before I go*.

NOTE: *My train isn't leaving till nine / My train isn't going to leave till nine* are also both possible and don't change the meaning.

Present continuous

Use the present continuous (NOT *the present simple*) for activities you have arranged to do in the (near or foreseeable) future.
~~I meet~~ I*'m meeting* a friend later.
We*'re returning* to the UK in three years' time.

NOTE: in the examples above, you could also use *be going to* + base form

These verbs are often used with the present continuous to refer to the future: *look forward to, dread, hope, expect, think of, plan* and *intend*.

Be going to + verb (NOT the present continuous) is generally used for longer-term arrangements. Also use it for plans, intentions and predictions based on previous decisions or experience.
A: What *are you* ~~doing~~ *going to do* when you graduate?
B: I*'m* probably *going to carry on* studying. I've already started looking into different master's courses.
I'm sure they*'re* ~~losing~~ *going to lose* the next election.

You could also use *will* in these examples, but *be going to* + verb is more common.

Use *be going to* + verb (NOT the present simple or *will*) for predictions based on what you can see, feel, etc.
Turn the gas down. The food ~~burns~~ *is going to burn*.
I feel really rough. I think ~~I will~~ I*'m going to be* sick.

Will (NOT the present simple or *be going to* + verb) is generally used for promises, predictions, offers and decisions made at the moment of speaking.
Thanks. ~~We pay you back~~ We*'ll pay you back* tomorrow.
~~I'm going to~~ I*'ll give* you a lift, if you like.
A: What are you doing later?
B: I don't know. I*'ll* probably just stay in.

Use *have got to / have to* to talk about future obligations.

Use *will have to* when at the moment of speaking the obligation appears as a consequence of something else.
I've got to go to a meeting at school this evening. Sorry. I forgot to tell him. I*'ll* just *have to call* him later.

Use *might* (NOT *it is possible* + present tense) to talk about possible predictions, future plans and offers.
I *might go* there if I have time. I'm not sure I will, though.

Use *shall* (NOT *will* or the present simple) in questions with *I* and *we* to ask for suggestions about future plans or make offers
~~Will~~ *Shall I help* you?
~~Do~~ *Shall I come* and pick you up around eight?

Use *be due* to talk about times things should happen.
The bus *is due* (to arrive) in five minutes.
When *is* the baby *due*?

Use *(be) bound to* to talk about things you see as inevitable.
It*'s bound to* be sunny in July. It never rains then.
They*'re bound to* lose. Half their side is injured.

Exercise 1

Complete the sentences using the correct structures in **bold** and the words in brackets.

1 **will / shall**
A: .... we .... a coffee? (get)
B: Good idea. You sit here and I .... and get them. (go)

2 **present continuous / be going to**
A: I .... Mary later. Do you want to come? (meet)
B: No. I've got an exam tomorrow. .... some revision (I / do)

3 **have got to / will / present simple**
A: I .... I'm late for class. It .... in ten minutes. (go, start)
B: OK. Hey, where is it? I .... you a lift. (give)

4 **have got to / will have to / will**
A: That was my dad. He's locked himself out of the house. He wants me to go and let him in. Sorry, we .... another time. (chat)
B: I .... with you. I .... that way anyway. (walk, go)

5 **bound / might / present continuous / will / be going to**
A: We .... to Gardaland tomorrow. (go)
B: But what .... you .... if the weather's bad? The forecast said it .... rain. (do)
A: I don't know. I haven't asked the others yet. We .... probably still .... I think there are quite a few rides that are covered over. (go)
B: I'm sure you .... yourselves anyway. (enjoy)

03 THINGS YOU NEED

if, *so* and *to* for describing purpose

We use *to* + verb to explain the purpose of doing things, why we need something or what something is for. It is also possible to say *in order to* + verb. This is more common in formal writing

I'm just going out *to buy* a few things for the house.
A cable is required (*in order to*) *connect* the device to the computer.

We use *if*-clauses (*If* + noun + verb in present tense) to talk about possible situations in which certain things might be necessary.

This is useful stuff to have *if you need* to remove stains.
Hang it up with a nail *if you can't find* anything else.

Use *so* to show that the second part of the sentence is a potential result of the first. The word *that* can be added after *so*, but doesn't have to be. Notice that *so (that)* is often followed by *can*.

Do you want to borrow a torch *so (that) you can see where you're going* on your way home?
Pass me a cloth *so (that) I can grip the lid* of this jar better.

Exercise 1

Complete the sentences by adding *to*, *if* or *so*.

1 Have you got a dustpan and brush .... I can clean up this mess I've made?
2 I must buy some wire .... hang this up with.
3 .... you want to put those shelves up properly, you'll need a drill.
4 You'll need an adaptor .... you're going to use your laptop in the States.
5 Put some cream on .... protect yourself from the sun.
6 What are those things you wear on your knees .... you do skateboarding?
7 You should put a plaster on your foot .... your shoes don't cut into your skin any more.
8 Can I borrow your stepladder .... I can change the light bulb in the hall?
9 Have you got a clip or something .... keep these papers together?

Exercise 2

Complete the sentences using *if*, *so* or *to* and the ideas in brackets.

1 We need some matches or something .... (light) the stove.
2 Maybe you should wrap some tape round where there's a crack .... (it / not / leak)
3 You'll need wire cutters .... that – not scissors. (you / want / cut)
4 Have you got something I can stand on .... this light bulb? (I / can / change)
5 Can't you just use some string .... it? (tie it together / and / make / a handle / carry)

INDIRECT QUESTIONS

Look at these examples of indirect questions.
When does their sale start?
Would you happen to know when their sale starts?
Where are my keys?
Do you know where my keys are?
Do students get a discount?
Do you have any idea if / whether students get a discount?
Are you free later?
I was wondering whether you were free later?

Note: we usually use past forms after *I was wondering*.

We often start requests with *Do you think ...?* and *could* usually follows.
Do you think you could wrap it for me?
Do you think you could give me a ring if you hear anything?

Indirect statements are made in the same way as indirect questions.
I wonder what they're doing now.
I don't know whether it can be fixed or not.
I don't understand what you're talking about!
I can't remember where I bought it.
I've got no idea what time they close.

Exercise 1

Complete the sentences with one word in each space.

1 Do you .... you could send me a catalogue?
2 I've got no .... where I left my credit cards!
3 I'm not .... which aisle the eggs are in.
4 Do you have any .... if that includes postage?
5 Would you .... to know where I could get it fixed?
6 Do you know .... is in charge?
7 Can you remember .... time Fong wants to meet?
8 Do you know .... there's any sugar anywhere?

Exercise 2

Find the five mistakes and correct them.

1 I wonder you could help me.
2 Do you think I could get a receipt, please?
3 Do you know do they open on Sundays?
4 Can you remember how you paid for the item?
5 Do you know when did they stop selling those lovely silver bags?
6 Would you mind if I asked you where you got it from?
7 Sorry, but do you know which floor the toilets on?
8 I wonder where's the best restaurant.

> ### Glossary
>
> **aisle:** in a supermarket, an aisle is a long narrow space between the rows of shelves
> **postage:** postage is the money you pay for things to be sent through the post

04 SOCIETY

SO / SUCH

So and such are often used to link cause and result. In the part of the sentence describing the cause, use *so* before an adjective, adverb or words like *few, little, much* or *many*. Use *such* before a noun, an adjective plus noun and *a lot of* + noun. You don't have to start the result clause with *that* – especially in spoken English.

It was *so* expensive in Moscow, we couldn't stay there long.

There's *so* much traffic, it's quicker to walk sometimes!

So few people had bought tickets *that* they decided to cancel the event.

The party did *so* badly in the elections *that* their leader resigned afterwards.

It was *such* a surprise *that* I just didn't know what to say!

The ride was *such* a laugh *that* we went on it six times.

There's *such* a lot of rubbish on the streets, it makes me angry.

Remember: *few* and *many* go before plural, countable nouns (*people / families*, etc.) and *much* and *little* go before uncountable nouns (*crime / damage*, etc.).

Exercise 1

A Choose the correct word.
1 Our situation sometimes looks *so / such* bleak
2 He was involved in *so / such* a terrible public scandal
3 The government have lied *so / such* many times
4 Food prices have gone up *so / such* quickly
5 The earthquake caused *so / such* widespread damage
6 *So / such* few women are having babies these days
7 They've got *so / such* poor hospitals
8 There's *so / such* little crime now

B Now match the endings below with 1–8 above.
a there have been riots in the street markets.
b that most kids can't even get basic health care.
c – they're making police officers redundant!
d I've just lost faith in them.
e the government's introduced tax breaks for big families to try and boost the birth rate.
f that it's hard not to feel pessimistic about the future.
g that tens of thousands are feared dead.
h that in the end he was forced to resign.

Exercise 2

Complete the sentences by adding the correct missing adverbs.
1 There's so .... poverty in the world that surely tackling that has to be our main goal.
2 So .... people bothered to vote that the election results are almost meaningless!
3 So .... people turned up to vote in the election, there were long queues at the polls.
4 So .... new jobs have been created that there are actually a lot of posts which are unfilled.
5 So .... research has been done into the problem that it's hard to say what's causing it.

THE ..., THE ... + COMPARATIVES

The basic pattern for showing correlations between different things is:

the + comparative + noun (+ verb), *the* + comparative + noun (+ verb).

Look at these examples:

The more roads there are, *the more* people use their cars.

As a rule, *the better educated* you are, *the more* you can earn.

It seems as if *the harder* I try, *the less* success I have!

Obviously, *the stronger* the economy (is), *the less* unemployment there is and the higher the standard of living.

We also use these short patterns – especially in conversation:

The sooner, the better	The smaller, the better
The bigger, the better	The faster, the better
The simpler, the better	The more, the merrier

Exercise 1

Choose the comparatives that make most logical sense.
1 The more you eat, the *thinner / fatter* you get.
2 Generally speaking, the poorer the country, the *less / more* infrastructure it has.
3 As a rule, the more people there are in higher education, the *weaker / stronger* the economy becomes.
4 If you ask me, the fewer people there are living in poverty, the *fewer / more* conflicts there would be.
5 The more people protest, the *less / greater* the pressure is on the government.
6 When it comes to Internet connections, the *faster / slower* the better
7 A: How do you want your coffee?
   B: The *weaker / stronger*, the better. I need to wake up!
8 A: Do you mind if I join you?
   B: Of course not! The *fewer / more*, the merrier.

Glossary

bleak: if a situation is bleak, it's bad and unlikely to get better.

widespread: if something is widespread, it has happened in a lot of places in a big area

riots: riots are violent protests by angry crowds of people

lost faith: if you lose faith in someone, you stop believing in their ability to do anything good

resign: if you resign, you formally announce that you are leaving your job

05 SPORTS AND INTERESTS

SHOULD(N'T) HAVE, COULD(N'T) HAVE, WOULD(N'T) HAVE

should've / shouldn't have

Use *should've* + past participle when you failed to do something and this produced an undesirable result.
We *should've phoned* you. We forgot. Sorry.
I *should've watched* something else. The film was so boring.

Use *shouldn't have* or *should never have* when you did something, but you think it was a mistake.
You *shouldn't have* hit him. It was wrong of you.
He *should never have* been released from prison.

could've / couldn't have

Add a comment with *could've / couldn't have / could never have / might've / might never have* + past participle to show possible past results.
They *should've done* something. They *could've saved* his life.
They *shouldn't even have tried*. They *could never have beaten* the champions.
He *shouldn't have substituted* the striker. They *might've won*.
I *shouldn't have said* anything. He *might never have found* out.

Note: you sometimes see *could've* on its own where the general topic is clear.
We lost, but we *could've won*. We *could've scored* six goals.
It was a bad crash, but it *could've been* worse. He *could've been* killed.

would've / wouldn't have

Add a comment to *should've* using *would've* + past participle to show a certain past result.
It's your birthday? You *should've said*. I *would've bought* you a present.
She *shouldn't have interfered*. Everything *would've been* fine if she'd just walked away.
I *should've gone* more slowly. I *wouldn't have made* that mistake.

Look at this other common pattern with *would've*:
I *would've been* here earlier, but something came up at work. (which stopped me being early)
We *would've won*, but we had a goal wrongly disallowed.
I *wouldn't have said* anything, but he asked me how you were.

Exercise 1
Choose the correct form.

1 It's his fault. He *should've / would've* dealt with the problem sooner rather than letting it drag on.
2 The fire was my fault. I *shouldn't have / wouldn't have* left the stove on while I was out.
3 It's my own fault. I *should've / would've* warmed up more before I started playing. I *wouldn't have / couldn't have* strained my back if I had.
4 I blame the players. They got knocked out because they *wouldn't have underestimated / underestimated* the opposition. They *should've / would've* taken the game more seriously.
5 It's sad. He *should've / would've* given up smoking. He *might not have / might've* died so young.
6 The game was pretty awful, but I suppose it *would've been / might've been* worse – we *could've / wouldn't have* lost.

Exercise 2
Complete 1–4 with the correct form of *would* and the verb in brackets and 5–8 with the correct form of *could*.

1 I .... here earlier, but the traffic was terrible. (get)
2 She .... to come, but it was impossible. She had so much work. (like)
3 I .... him forgetting normally, but I'd told him twice that it was really important. That's why I was so angry. (mind)
4 I .... him, but he'd invited me to his party, so I felt I had to.! (invite)
5 It could've been worse. He .... his neck. (break)
6 It could've been worse. They .... you when they grabbed your bag. (hurt)
7 It could've been worse. She .... her wallet stolen to. (have)
8 The storm was bad, but it could've been worse. It .... a lot more damage than it did. (do)

Glossary

drag on: if a problem or meeting drags on, it continues for a long time and becomes worse or boring
stove: a stove is another name for a cooker
strained: if you strain a muscle, you hurt it by stretching it too much
get knocked out: if you get knocked out of a competition you lose a game and take no further part

PRESENT PERFECT CONTINUOUS

The present perfect continuous is used to talk about actions, intentions or feelings that started in the past and are still going on now. It emphasises the fact these things happened again and again. It is often used to talk about duration (how long) from the past to now.

How long *has* he *been* study*ing* English? (He's still studying.)
She*'s been* talk*ing* about joining a gym for ages now! (She's still talking about it.)

It is also used to emphasise that an activity or feeling was continuing up until now or until very recently – even if it has now stopped.

I*'ve been* wait*ing* for you for the last hour! What happened?
The sun's here at last! It feels like it*'s been* rain*ing* for days!

The following verbs are rarely used in the continuous form: *be, believe, belong, cost, exist, fancy, hate, have* (= possess)*, know, like, love, prefer, seem, understand.*

With these verbs, use present perfect simple for duration:
How long *have* you *had* your car?
I*'ve belonged* to the club for about six years now.

PRESENT PERFECT SIMPLE

The present perfect simple is used to talk about actions or events completed at some point before now, but with a connection to the present. It is also used when talking about the number of times between the past and now.

I think Roberta*'s been* to Milan. Ask her where to go.
I'm not very good. I*'ve* only play*ed* once before.
I *haven't spoken* to him all year. (not once)
They*'ve won* the European cup six times.
I*'ve told* him hundreds of times, but he never listens.

The present perfect simple is commonly used with the adverbs *yet, already, always, never, ever* and *just.*
I haven*'t* decid*ed* what to do *yet.*
They*'ve already* asked Bill – and he said no.
She*'s always done* her best ~~at school.~~ (and she still does)
I*'ve never* lik*ed* swimming in the sea. (and I still don't)
I*'ve just* manag*ed* to get hold of some tickets for the game.

When we give details of events, we use past tenses.
A: Have you ever done a parachute jump?
B: I have, actually, yeah. I *did* one a few years ago. A friend *wanted* to do one to raise money for charity and *asked* if I would join him. It *was* an amazing experience

With the present perfect continuous and simple, we use *since* to show when an activity, intention or feeling started – and *for / all* to show the period.

I've been playing *since I was a kid*.
He's wanted to go there *ever since he first saw it on TV*.
It's not a new restaurant. It's been there *for ages*.
She's been trying to call you *for the last hour*.
I've been planning to visit them *all week / month / year*.

Exercise 1

Complete the sentences with ONE word in each space.

1 I've been working there as a volunteer .... over six years now.
2 I haven't seen him .... morning. He must be off work.
3 She's been seeing a counsellor .... the accident to try and deal with the trauma.
4 I've .... been interested in golf. I don't know why, really, because I like other sports like rugby.
5 Don't tell me what happened! I haven't seen the highlights .... and it's more exciting when you don't know the score.
6 I've .... seen that film, but I wouldn't mind seeing it again. It's brilliant.
7 I've .... loved playing cards – ever .... I was a child.

Exercise 2

Complete the conversations using the ideas in brackets and the present perfect simple or continuous.

1 A: .... to buy the tickets for the game yet? (you / manage)
   B: No. .... all morning, but I can't get through. (I / call)
2 A: .... *The End of the Day* yet? (you / see)
   B: No. .... to for ages now, but .... the chance. Is it still on? (I / mean, I / just / not / have)
   A: Yeah, it is. I won't say anything if you're going to see it, but it's good.
3 A: So why .... to leave? It's a bit sudden, isn't it? (Wayne / decide)
   B: Not really. .... about it for a while. .... the right job to move on to – and now he .... it, he's off. (he / think, he / look for, he / find)
4 A: I played tennis with her yesterday. She's really good, considering .... a few times. (she / only / play)
   B: I can imagine. .... good at sports. She's just got that natural fitness and coordination. (she / always / be)

Glossary

highlights: the highlights are the best moments of a game that they show on TV
can't get through: if you can't get through, you try, but don't succeed in speaking to someone on the phone
off: if someone says *I'm off* or *I must be off,* they are leaving.
considering: we use *considering* to show that we are thinking of a special circumstances or facts when giving an opinion

06 ACCOMMODATION

MODIFIERS

Modifiers make the following word weaker or stronger.
The area is *a bit / quite / fairly / pretty / rather* rough.
(= makes the adjective weaker)
The port area is *very / really / extremely* rough. (= stronger)
It was *absolutely / really / completely* deserted (= stronger)
The place was *a bit of* a dump. (= makes the noun weaker)
The place was a *complete / right* dump (= stronger)
I *hardly* know him. (= almost not)

The choice of modifier also depends on the kind of word that follows.
A bit usually goes with negative adjectives, so don't say:
~~It's a bit nice.~~   It's quite nice.
A bit can't be used with nouns.
~~He's a bit idiot.~~   He's *a bit of an* idiot.
A bit of a / an makes a negative noun softer / less critical.
He's *a bit of a moaner.*   The situation is *a bit of a mess.*

A bit too makes positive adjectives negative. It means things are excessive, but not by much
It was *a bit too hot* for my liking.

Very doesn't normally collocate with extreme adjectives that already contain the idea of very. Use *really* or *absolutely* with adjectives like *boiling, delicious, stunning, filthy, spotless, freezing,* etc.

Do not use *absolutely* with normal adjectives like *hot, nice, bad, cold* or *good*. Use *very* or *really* instead. We often use *not very / not particularly* with positive adjectives to soften a complaint.
It's *not very warm* in my room.
It *wasn't particularly clean* when we moved in.

hardly goes with these words:

hardly any	hardly anyone	hardly anything
hardly anywhere	hardly ever	

We don't normally use *hardly* on its own with a noun.
~~There was hardly entertainment.~~
There was *hardly any* entertainment.

hardly doesn't go with other negatives.
We ~~hardly didn't go~~ to the beach.
We *hardly went* to the beach.

Exercise
Rewrite the sentences using the word in brackets so they have a similar meaning.
1 This coffee is really weak. (strong)
2 It was unbearably hot in the tent. (absolutely)
3 The beach was almost deserted. (hardly anyone)
4 Personally, I thought it was rather loud! (a bit too)
5 It wasn't very cheap. (quite)
6 It was quite chilly at night. (not particularly)
7 I hardly know the area. (not / very well)

HAVE / GET SOMETHING DONE

As with the passive, *have / get* something done is used when the person who did an action is unknown or unimportant. However, we use *have / get* something done to emphasise both the object and the person who the thing belongs to. Compare:
My bike was stolen from outside the shop.
I had my bike stolen. (= I was the victim)

My house is being painted.
We're having our house painted next summer. (= We have decided and are paying someone to do it)

Get is more common with some verbs, *have* with others. There are no rules for this. The best way to learn is by seeing examples. Look at how the structures are used in different tenses:
It was a mess! They *were having some work done* on the roof.
I *should have my hair cut.*
I *had to have my picture taken* for the college website.
I'*m going to get my hair dyed* blond next time I have it done.
I'*d never have my hair cut* that short! It wouldn't suit me.

Exercise
Complete the conversations by reordering the words.
1 A: of / straightened / getting / thinking / hair / I'm / my. I'm sick of this hairstyle.
   B: Really? I'd love to have curly hair like you.
2 A: photo / get / should / framed / that / you. It's really nice.
   B: Do you think so? Maybe I will, then.
3 A: The dentist said have / going / the / taken / to / have / I'm / to / tooth / out. I'm dreading it.
   B: I can imagine. I hate going to the dentist, but what choice do you have?
4 A: Someone broke into the car and stolen / their / had / they / their / all / and / money / passports.
   B: Oh no! That's awful. So what did they do?
5 A: I'm going to have to stop the car. The engine's overheating.
   B: I told you should / we / have / it / had / checked before we left.

07 NATURE

NARRATIVE TENSES

Past simple

The past simple describes finished events – often ones that follow each other. These events can be linked together using words such as *and*, *and then*, *after that*, *after*, *before*.
When the rain *started*, we *went* home.

Past continuous

The past continuous shows an action was unfinished when another action – often in the past simple – happened.
I *met* my wife when I *was living* in Slovakia.
I *had* an accident while I *was driving* to work.

Past perfect

The past perfect shows something happened before an action that has already been mentioned.
I'd only *answered* two questions by the time he *finished*.
When I *got* to work, I realised I'd *left* my keys at home.

With *before*, *after* and *until*, both past simple and perfect can be used with little difference in meaning.
Apparently, it *rained / it'd rained* for weeks before we *arrived*.
We waited until the rain *eased off / had eased off*.

Continuous tenses are sometimes used to emphasise the duration of an activity. Notice the time phrases.
It was raining the whole time we were there.
We were waiting for hours for the fog to lift.

Exercise

Correct the mistake with narrative tenses in each sentence.

1 The thunder was so loud I can't get to sleep.
2 The sun was burning hot and I got really sunburnt because I have forgotten to put any cream on.
3 I was getting caught in a storm when I was walking home, so I stopped in a café until it'd blown over.
4 It got dark, so we decided to go home while we could still see the path.
5 The roads were really treacherous because the snow was melting a bit the day before and then had frozen overnight.
6 I went away on holiday and when I had got back the slugs had eaten all the flowers in my garden!
7 The fog was coming down suddenly and we got completely lost and had to phone for help.
8 It absolutely poured down in the morning and by the time we arrived, the campsite still didn't dry out, so the whole place was a mudbath.

Participle clauses

Participle clauses can follow a noun. They define the noun in the same way that relative clauses do. Clauses that use present participles (the *-ing* form) have an active meaning – and clauses that use a past participle have a passive meaning.
... a range of dishes *featuring* the insects (= a range of dishes *that feature* the insects)
... experiments *aimed at* combating illnesses (= experiments *that are aimed at* combating illnesses)

Participle clauses are much more common in more formal written English than in spoken English.

Exercise

Complete the sentences below by adding the correct form of the words in brackets.

1 The suffering .... by vivisection is just horrendous. (cause)
2 Supplies are slowly starting to reach the areas worst .... by the flooding. (affect)
3 There have been calls for a ban to be placed on beef .... from any areas affected by mad cow disease. (import)
4 The low numbers of young people .... part in sport or .... regular exercise continues to be a cause for concern. (take, do)
5 The government has promised to help rebuild all the properties .... in the recent forest fires. (damage)
6 City Farms is a new project .... by the local council and aimed at putting kids in contact with animals. (fund)
7 The police have said that some of the animals .... from the laboratories could well be carrying diseases. (free)
8 The group .... the protests has issued a statement .... all forms of hunting. (lead, oppose)

Glossary

blow over: if a storm blows over, it ends
treacherous: if roads or conditions are treacherous, they are very dangerous – because of bad weather
slugs: slugs are like snails, but don't have shells. They often eat soft green plants in the garden
mudbath: a mudbath is an area which is full of thick mud
horrendous: if something is horrendous, it is extremely bad or unpleasant
cause for concern: if a situation is a cause for concern, lots of people are worried about it

08 LAW AND ORDER

PRESENT AND PAST INFINITIVES

Verbs that follow modals such as *must*, *might* and *should* are always in the infinitive. The basic infinitive usually refers to present or future situations. Past infinitive – *have* (*'ve*) + past participle – refer to something in the past.

should

They *should help* more. (= it's a better idea if they help, but they are not doing it now)
He *should've done* more to help. (= it was a better idea to, but he didn't do it)

must

You *must be* annoyed. (= I think you definitely are)
It *must've been* awful. (= I imagine it definitely was)
He *must've been kidnapped*. (= I think he was definitely kidnapped because there were no other possible causes)

can't

It *can't be* easy. (= I imagine it definitely isn't)
She *can't have seen* the sign. (= I imagine she didn't see it, because there were no other causes I can think of)

Don't use *must* in the negative when it means *imagine / guess* – use *can't*.
It ~~mustn't~~ *can't be* more than 15 years old.

might / could

He *might be* at a friend's house. (= It's possible he is)
She *might've known* her killer. (= It's possible she knew)

It *could've been* worse. She *could've died*. (= It was possible for it to be worse. It was possible for her to die)

Continuous forms

Look at how these structures are used in continuous forms.
We should get off the phone. He *might be trying* to call now. (= maybe he is trying to)
He *shouldn't have been smoking* in there. (= It was a better idea if he wasn't smoking there, but he was)
I didn't time it, but I *must've been waiting* for over an hour. (= I imagine I was definitely waiting for an hour)
She *can't be earning* much if she's only doing cleaning work. (= I don't think she is earning much)

Exercise 1

Complete each sentence by adding *can't be* or *must be*.

1 It .... very nice, finding out that your girlfriend has been seeing another man!
2 It .... great, getting to travel all over the world.
3 It .... much fun, having to work night shifts.
4 It .... difficult, only seeing your kids once a month.
5 You .... exhausted after such a long journey.
6 You .... any worse at yoga than I am!

Now complete these sentences by adding *can't have* or *must have* and the correct form of the verbs in the box.

be	do	escape	hurt	look	take

7 Your glasses must be somewhere. You .... very hard!
8 This doesn't look right. I think we .... the wrong turning earlier.
9 He tore his knee ligaments. It .... like mad!
10 It .... easy for her, bringing up six kids on her own.
11 I just can't believe they've arrested Kim for blackmail. She just .... anything like that!
12 I saw a parrot in the park. It .... from the zoo.

Exercise 2

Rewrite the words in italics using a modal verb and the correct form.

1 A: The police told me it wasn't worth investigating.
   B: Really? *I imagine you definitely were* furious.
   A: Yeah, I was. *It's possible I will* complain about it.
   B: *It's better you do.*
2 A: *I imagine he definitely isn't* involved in something as bad as that. He's just not that kind of person.
   B: *It's possible he is.* I mean, there's no smoke without fire.
3 A: Did you see that child was found guilty of murder?
   B: I know. It's awful. I blame the mother – *it was a better idea if she did* more to control her child.
   A: I don't know. *I imagine it definitely isn't* easy, bringing up three children on your own.
4 A: *I think it's possible I did* something really stupid. I don't think I turned the oven off!
   B: Well, maybe *it's better if we go* back home and check. We don't want the house to burn down. Sorry. *It was better for me to remind* you before we left.

Glossary

no smoke without fire: we say *there's no smoke without fire* to suggest we think there is a good reason for people saying bad things about someone – even if it's not clear what that reason is yet.

NOUNS AND PREPOSITIONS

We often add prepositional phrases to nouns to define the nouns more.

an argument *about money*
a demonstration *against the death penalty*
a film *by Walter Salles*
a call *for help*
an interest *in history*
a crime *of passion*
an impact *on unemployment*
attention *to detail*
a meeting *with clients*
attitudes *towards women*

Different prepositions can add different information to the noun.

a book *of poetry* (= it contains poems)
a book *about organised crime* (= the subject is crime)
a book *by Gabriela Marquez* (= the author is Marquez)
a book *for Christmas* (= the reason you give the book)
a book *with pictures* (= a feature of the book)
an impact *on unemployment* (= what the impact affects)
the impact *of the policy* (= where the impact comes from)

The prepositions that follow nouns often depend on the verbs used before the nouns.

give a lot of attention to the problem
deflect attention from the real problem

Occasionally, a different preposition may indicate a different meaning of the noun.

earn *interest on* your savings (interest = money)
have an *interest in* economics (interest = a liking)
a *demonstration for* peace (demonstration = protest)
a *demonstration of* how it works (demonstration = showing)

Occasionally, two different positions can be used without changing the meaning of the noun.

ideas *on / about* how to improve safety
an argument *over / about* something stupid

It's possible to have two prepositional phrases.

There is a lot of concern *among parents about rising crime*.

We can sometimes use compound nouns instead of using a prepositional phrase after the noun.

crime by young people = youth crime
robbery in the street = street robbery
theft of the details of your identity = identity theft
service for the community = community service
rate at which ex-prisoners re-offend = re-offending rates

Keep a record of compound nouns and nouns with prepositional phrases in your vocabulary notebook.

Exercise 1

Complete the sentences with the noun preposition combinations.

awareness of	access to	decrease in
involvement in	ban on	recipe for
addiction to	anger at	damage to

1 Police have arrested a leading politician for his .... a corruption scandal.
2 The singer Manny Biggs has admitted himself into a rehab centre for treatment for his .... drugs and alcohol.
3 The government is considering a complete .... the ownership of guns.
4 Better .... the Internet could help solve many of the problems that currently affect the third world.
5 The demonstration against rising prices of water, turned into a riot resulting in widespread .... cars and buildings.
6 There has been some .... the police handling of the incident last week in which a man was shot.
7 Can you give me the .... that soup you made?
8 There's actually been a big .... over the last few years .... the incidence of street crime.
9 Nowadays, there's much greater .... the need for recycling and energy conservation.

Exercise 2

Choose the correct preposition in each sentence.

1 a I'm afraid there's no room *in / for* the class for another desk and chair.
  b We've got room *in / for* one more person in our car.
2 a Police have discovered a terrorist threat *of / to* the president.
  b The airport has increased security because of the threat *of / to* terrorism.
3 a There's a demonstration *against / of* racism being held next week.
  b The students are going to put on a demonstration *of / for* what they've learned at the end of the course.
4 a What's the name of that film *with / about* Jet Li that came out last year? He was great in it.
  b It's an interesting film *with / about* gun crime.
5 a The police have set up a meeting *about / with* the local residents *about / with* burglaries in the area.
  b The survey looked at attitudes *towards / among* young people *towards / among* politics.

09 CAREERS AND STUDYING

CONDITIONALS WITH PRESENT TENSES

We use present tenses in *if*-clauses to talk about things that are generally true – or that are likely to happen in the future. We can use the present simple / continuous or the present perfect simple / continuous.

I get paid extra if I *work* overtime. (= always / whenever)
If you*'re having* problems (= now / at the moment), you can always talk to me.
If you*'ve finished* that (= already), could you make me a coffee?
It's impossible to concentrate properly on what you're doing if you*'ve been working* too hard (= from the past to now).

The result clause can express typical consequences (present tenses), give advice (*should*), express plans (*be going to* + verb), express possibility (*can, might*) – or talk about promises or definite results (*will* + verb).
If we miss a deadline, we *don't get* paid.
If you need any more help with anything, just *ask*.
If it's that bad, you *should think about* leaving!
What*'re* you *going to do* if you don't get the promotion?
If I get this promotion, I *can* finally *buy* a place of my own.
I *might call* you if I'm struggling with my homework.
If they invest more in education, it*'ll help* the economy.

There are several fixed expressions used in *if*-clauses.
If nothing goes wrong, we're going to move in the spring.
If the worst comes to the worst, I'll have to get a factory job.
If all else fails, I'll just have to work part time while I study.

Exercise 1

Match 1–8 with a–h to make complete sentences.
1   If you're really not feeling very well,
2   Our Munich office should open in the autumn
3   If you fail three subjects,
4   I'm going to be in big trouble
5   There's no guarantee we'll keep our jobs
6   If I get the grades I need,
7   I might actually have to beg my uncle for a job
8   If I haven't heard from them by Thursday,

a   I'm going to do medicine at university.
b   even if the company has been doing well this year.
c   if everything goes according to plan.
d   you should phone in sick.
e   I'll have to phone and chase them up.
f   you have to repeat the whole year.
g   if this report isn't finished by Friday.
h   if the worst comes to the worst.

> ## Glossary
>
> **phone in sick:** if you phone in sick, you call where you work and tell them you are too ill to come in today
> **chase up:** if you chase something up, you ask someone who should've done something why they haven't

CONDITIONALS WITH PAST TENSES

We use the past simple / continuous in *if*-clauses to speculate about unreal / unlikely present or future situations and actions. Use *could* as the past form of *can* and *had to* as the past form of *must*.
If I *had* loads of money, I'd give up work entirely.
I would go with you if I *could*, but I can't.
I love it here, but if I *had to* move for my job, I would.

Note: past tenses can also describe real situations that often happened in the past. In these sentences, *if* means *whenever*.
If I we *had* a tight deadline, we often *worked* all night.

We use the past perfect simple / continuous in *if*-clauses to speculate about changing past events / situations.
I wouldn't have got the job if I *hadn't known* the boss.
If he *hadn't been working* so hard, he might've noticed.

Use *would* + a present infinitive to talk about the definite imagined consequence of an action in the present or future.
I*'d quit* if I could afford to, but I need the money.
If I hadn't met her, I *would* probably still *be living* at home.

Use *would* + a past infinitive (see page 67) to talk about a definite imagined consequence in the past.
I *would never have become* a CEO if I hadn't worked hard.
If I was better at maths, I *would've studied* physics.

Could shows possibility and *might* / *may* show less certainty.

Exercise 1

Complete the text with ONE word in each gap (*didn't, hadn't*, etc. count as one word).
If it hadn't [1]............................ raining that day I might [2]............................ have seen the advert. Normally if it was dry, I [3]............................ to work by bike, but that day it was pouring down and I was late, so I took the metro. I was working for a TV company at the time and it was good, but I saw this ad and it said 'Imagine if you [4]............................ in your job for the rest of your life, how [5]............................ you feel? [6]............................ you think you'd contributed to the world? Would you [7]............................ made your mark?' It really made me think and it led me in a completely different direction. I became a nurse. I liked the TV work, but I don't think it [8]............................ have been so rewarding, even if I [9]............................ continued to do it. And I doubt I'd [10]............................ so happy now, if it [11]............................ been for that ad.

10 SOCIALISING

FUTURE PERFECT

The future perfect talks about a 'past in the future'. It is used to say that something will end at – or before – a particular point in the future. The form is *will / won't + have* + past participle. This structure is only used with a limited number of verbs. We often use *by* with the future perfect to mean *at* or *before*. There are lots of time phrases starting with *by*: *by this afternoon, by the time we get there, by the time you've finished, by the end of the year.*

Can I call you back around four? I*'ll have finished* looking through the contract by then.
I *won't have had* time to read through the proposal properly until Monday at the earliest.

We can also use *should + have +* past participle to show that we think something will happen before a certain point in the future, but are not 100% sure.
I *should've finished* by about six or so.

We also use the future perfect to say what we think has almost certainly happened by now.
They*'ll have left* by now. (= I'm 99% sure they have left)
They *won't have left* yet. (= I'm 99% sure they haven't left)
It *won't have landed* yet. (= I'm 99% sure it hasn't landed)
You *won't have heard* of it. (= I'm 99% sure you don't know it)

Exercise 1

Choose the correct form.

1 *I'm going / I will have gone* to Estonia on Thursday.
2 *I'll have lived / I'm going to live* here for two years in June.
3 It's absolutely pouring down now, but they said it'll *ease off / have eased off* during the afternoon.
4 Hurry up! The film *will probably have started / will probably start* by the time we get to the cinema.
5 *I'm helping / I'll have helped* a friend move house tomorrow, but *we're finishing / we should've finished* by five, so call me then.
6 It said in the paper that by the time you're 60, *you're going to spend / you will've spent* nine whole years watching TV! How depressing is that?
7 I'm from a tiny little village in the south. You *will've / won't have* heard of it.
8 That's really odd. The parcel really *will've / should've* arrived by now. I sent it over a month ago.

Glossary

settle in: if you settle in, you get used to a new way of life, job, etc.
eases off: if rain eases off, it becomes lighter and slowly stops
parcel: a parcel is something wrapped in paper or in a big envelope that you send through the post

QUESTION TAGS

Add question tags to statements to get responses, to check things are true and to make polite requests. Question tags are formed using an auxiliary + a pronoun. For positive sentences, use negative tags.
It's really warm, *isn't it*?
We are going to wait for him, *aren't we*?
It was a great game, *wasn't it*?
Terry lives near there, *doesn't he*?

With negative statements, use a positive tag.
The meeting shouldn't take too long, *should it*?

Positive tags are often used to make polite requests.
You couldn't save my place in the queue, *could you*?

We also use these tags:
Let's start, *shall we*? (polite way to make suggestions)
Pass me the salt, *will you*? (makes commands more polite)

DON'T add question tags to questions.
Are you doing anything this weekend, ~~aren't you~~?
Do you want to go and get something to eat, ~~don't you~~?

Other kinds of tags are becoming very common:
You know where the cathedral is, *yeah / right*?
It's really good, *no*?

It's OK to use these forms in speech, but some people think they sound uneducated.

Exercise 1

Decide which two sentences with tags are correct. Change the other four so they are correct.

1 A: Would you like a coffee, wouldn't you?
   B: No, I'm fine, thanks. I've just had one.
2 A: You knew him quite well, isn't it?
   B: Yeah, we went to college together.
3 A: You couldn't lend me a euro, could you?
   B: Sorry, I haven't got any change on me.
4 A: You weren't at the last class, you were?
   B: No. I was ill. Did I miss much?
5 A: Lovely weather, isn't it?
   B: Fantastic.
6 A: Haven't you heard of Shakira, have you?
   B: No. Why should I have?

Exercise 2

Replace *yeah?, right?* and *no?* with more formal tags.

1 You've been to university, no?
2 It's a fantastic place to visit, no?
3 You know where to go, right?
4 We're going to meet them later, yeah?
5 He shouldn't be here, no?
6 They can't come tomorrow, no?

11 TRANSPORT AND TRAVEL

UNCOUNTABLE NOUNS

Uncountable nouns are things that cannot be counted in English. They have no plurals. We do not use *a / an* before uncountable nouns. Here are some of the most common. Many may be countable in your language.

accommodation	information	progress
advice	luck	scenery
behaviour	luggage	traffic
chaos	money	trouble
experience	music	weather
furniture	news	work

Many concepts or abstract nouns are uncountable: *peace, wealth, motivation, happiness.*

With uncountable nouns, we often use the following quantifiers: *some, no, plenty of, not much, (not) enough, a good / great deal of, hardly any, (not) any (at all), little, more, less.*

Lots of nouns can be both countable and uncountable. There is usually a difference in meaning.

fruit: We grow all our own fruit. (= general fruit to eat)
A tomato is actually a fruit! (= one kind of fruit)

Exercise 1

Choose the correct form.

1 Can I get *a coffee / coffee*, please? Black – one sugar.
2 She's upset. She just needs a bit of sympathy and *understanding / an understanding*.
3 That was *a really lovely dinner / really lovely dinner*.
4 They have *a very happy marriage / very happy marriage*.
5 It's important to have *understanding / an understanding* of the local culture when you travel.
6 Have you had *a dinner / dinner* yet?
7 I don't drink *a coffee / coffee*. It makes me too hyper!
8 *Marriage / A marriage* is less important than it used to be.

Exercise 2

Decide which six sentences are incorrect. Then correct them.

1 My hairs are getting really long. I need a haircut.
2 There are lots of accommodations in the town.
3 They breed sheep on a big farm out in the countryside.
4 There weren't that many peoples in class today.
5 The news this week are so depressing!
6 Sorry I'm late. I had some troubles with my car.
7 The tourist board gave me some really useful advices.
8 I forgot to bring any paper with me today.

EMPHATIC STRUCTURES

To emphasise a feeling and to avoid a long subject before a verb, we often move the subject to follow the verb. This involves changing it slightly. Look at the patterns below.
People not queuing at the bus stop annoys me.
It annoys me *when people don't queue at the bus stop.*
It annoys me *that people don't queue at the bus stop.*

Driving on the left for the first time is scary.
It's scary *when you drive on the left for the first time.*
It's scary *driving on the left for the first time.*

We often use *The thing that / what* + verb + *be* for the same reasons. This is even more emphatic. This structure emphasises both the subjects and the objects of the verb.
The way people drove so close behind *really scared me.*
What really scared me was the way people drove so close behind.

I love driving in the mountains on winding roads.
What I love is driving in the mountains on winding roads.

Look at the different patterns after the verb *to be* :
What I hate is *people* bee*ping* you when the lights have only turned green one second ago.
What made me laugh was *the fact (that)* he hadn't even realised there was a hole in his trousers.
The thing that angers me is *the lack of* investment.
What surprised me was *the amount of* traffic there was.

Exercise 1

Complete the sentences with the pairs of words.

what + going	it + sitting	what + amount
it + when	what + number	the thing + way
it + finding	the thing + lack	what + fact

1 .... really annoys me .... people park on the pavement and you have to walk in the road.
2 .... that scares me is the .... some people swerve in and out of the lanes on the motorway.
3 ....'s so boring .... in traffic jams all morning. I'd much rather take the train.
4 .... that concerns me most is the .... of pollution there is in the city centre.
5 .... gets on my nerves is men .... on about how women can't drive. It's such rubbish.
6 ....'s great is the .... of speed cameras there are now. It's really cut down on accidents.
7 ....'s so confusing .... your way round town because of the one-way system.
8 .... I found confusing was the .... of signposting.
9 .... made me angry was the .... that he didn't apologise when it was obvious it was his fault.

12 HEALTH AND MEDICINE

SUPPOSED TO BE -ING AND SHOULD

be supposed to be -ing
When we have arranged something for the future, we usually use the present continuous or *be going to*.
I'*m meeting* a friend later. We'*re going to see* a film.
We'*re going* to the beach on Sunday. Do you want to come?

If you now can't – or don't want to – do what you arranged, use *be supposed to be -ing*.
I'*m supposed to be meeting* a friend later, *but* I think I'm going to cancel. I'm feeling a bit rough.
We'*re supposed to be going* to the beach on Sunday, *but* I'm not sure we will now. The weather forecast is dreadful.

should / shouldn't
Should and *shouldn't* show we have a positive feeling or expectation about a future event.
It *should be good*. I'm sure you'll have a great time.
He *shouldn't find the exam too difficult*. I'm sure he'll pass.

Don't use *should / shouldn't* when you expect something bad.
I'm afraid the injection ~~should~~ *is going to / will be* painful and you might be sore for a few hours afterwards.
~~You shouldn't~~ I doubt *you'll* like it.

Exercise 1
Choose the correct structure.
1 I'll give you some antibiotics for the infection. It *should / shouldn't* clear up in a few days.
2 I'm *going / supposed to be going* away tomorrow, so I won't be in the office.
3 I'm just popping out to pick up my prescription. I *should / shouldn't* be long.
4 My brother's got to have some dental work done. It *should / is probably going to* be quite expensive.
5 We're *supposed to be having / having* a meeting tomorrow, but there are so many people down with flu, I think we'll have to cancel it.
6 I've e-mailed instructions how to find us. It's quite a distinctive building as well, so you *shouldn't have / you're not supposed to be having* any difficulties.
7 *I doubt anyone will be / There shouldn't be anyone* in class today because of the bus strike.
8 Look at the weather! It's awful and the kids are *supposed to be playing / going to play* tennis today.

> ### Glossary
>
> **pop out:** if you pop out / in somewhere, you go there for a short time
> **down with flu:** if someone goes – or is – down with flu or some other virus, they catch it and have the illness
> **distinctive:** if something is distinctive it is noticeably different from other similar things

DETERMINERS
Determiners are words that go before nouns or pronouns to show which things you mean. Some determiners are only used with singular things: *a, an, each, every, another, this, that.*
Is it possible to see *another consultant*?

These determiners are only used with plurals: *these, those, (a) few, other, many.*

These determiners are used with plurals or uncountable nouns: *both ... and, all, some, much, little, half.*

These determiners are used with all kinds of nouns: *my, his, their,* etc.

These determiners are only negative – *neither, no, any.*

Determiners don't normally have *of* between them and the noun they refer to – unless used with another determiner.
both of my parents.

With pronouns, determiners are usually followed by *of*.
both of them

Most determiners can also act as pronouns. They can be used instead of a noun.
I like *both*; *Those* are nice.
However, some can't act as pronouns: *a, no, my.* (You have to use *one / some, none, mine.*)

Use *none of* + a plural noun / pronoun to mean 'not a single one of'. We use a singular or a plural verb form (singular is more formal).
None of the people I spoke to knows much about the problem.

Exercise 1
Correct the mistakes in each of the sentences below.
1 I didn't like neither of the two treatments, personally.
2 They said they had none record of my appointment.
3 Half the class have flu and most of the others students soon will have!
4 Each the three operations lasted about five hours.
5 So many persons make themselves ill through stress.
6 Both of my brothers never go for check-ups.
7 Every doctors I saw failed to diagnose me properly.
8 The all hospital was absolutely spotless.
9 It's just good to know what all the options is.
10 They just haven't invested money enough.

13 LIFE EVENTS

BE ALWAYS / CONSTANTLY + -ING / I WISH + WOULD

We usually use the present simple to talk about habits.
He's so soft. He *lets* her get her own way all the time.

However, we use the present continuous + *always / constantly* to emphasise that a habit never stops or has no exceptions.
She's so spoilt. *She's constantly getting* what she wants!
They're so aggressive. *They're always getting into* fights.
I'm constantly cleaning up after him.

Don't use the present continuous to emphasise things that never happen.
She's such a slob. She ~~is never doing~~ *never does* any exercise.

Be always + -ing usually shows you find something annoying, but it can also emphasise unusual things you like.
He's very romantic. *He's always buying* me roses and writing me poems and things like that!

Use *I wish + would(n't)* + verb to show you want people to behave differently.
I wish the kids would help out more. (They don't usually)
I wish he wouldn't shout so much. (He shouts a lot)

Use *I wish + he / she was(n't)* – or *were(n't)* to describe how we want people's character to be different.
I wish he was / were less strict. He punishes us too hard.
I wish she wasn't / weren't so lazy. She never does anything.

Exercise 1
Find the six mistakes and correct them.
1 I wish he wouldn't tidy up sometimes. He's so messy!
2 He's so stubborn. He's never admitting he's wrong!
3 He's so manipulative. He always trying to make me feel guilty.
4 They're constantly talking and disrupting the class.
5 I wish he is more assertive and that he'd defend himself a bit more.
6 She's so cheerful. Always she is smiling and laughing.
7 I wish they wouldn't argue so much. It's upsetting.
8 I really wish her not to go on about her boyfriend all the time. It just gets very boring.

Exercise 2
Write full sentences using the ideas below.
1 He / constantly / interrupt her / when / she / talk
2 I wish / she / turn her music down / while / I / study
3 I wish / he / speak to me as if I / child
4 I really wish he / so mean / and that he / buy the cheapest thing all the time
5 They / always / joke / and / mess around

PAST PERFECT SIMPLE AND CONTINUOUS
Past perfect forms emphasise that something happened before another event in the past.
I was fired because I'*d complained* about the boss.
A: Weren't you surprised when they split up?
B: No. They'*d been arguing* a lot. (before they split up)

However, we often then go back to use basic past forms when we add further details.
A: Weren't you surprised when they split up?
B: No. They'd been arguing a lot anyway and then *she found out he was having* an affair. (all before splitting up)

Past perfect simple
Use the past perfect simple to emphasise single events that happened before a past time or event that has been mentioned. The past perfect simple is often used to talk about how many times something happened. It often goes with the words *by the time, before, after* and *already*.
He'*d had* a couple of big rows with his boss before he decided to leave.
You know why he got sacked, don't you? He'*d been* late every day for a week before it happened!

Past perfect continuous
The past perfect continuous works in a similar way to the present perfect continuous (see page 93). It describes things that happened over a period of time up to the time of a particular event in the past. It is often used to talk about how long something happened for. It is often used with expressions that show duration such as *for a while* and *for ages / months / years*.
We'*d been thinking about* moving for a while and then one day I went past this house that was for sale and fell in love with it.

Certain verbs tend not to be used in the continuous forms including *agree, be, believe, depend, disagree, doubt, forget, hate, like, mean, mind, owe, prefer, realise*.

Exercise 1
Complete the sentences by putting the verbs in brackets into the past perfect simple or continuous.
1 When I found out I .... , I was speechless. I just couldn't believe it. (win)
2 Apparently, they discovered she .... money from them for months. (steal)
3 I suddenly realised I .... to bring my keys. (forget)
4 She .... from the illness for some time, but she .... anyone about it. (suffer, not tell)
5 We finally realised we .... the turning and .... in completely the wrong direction for half an hour! (miss, go)
6 I .... the business more or less single-handedly for ages, but they .... to give me a pay rise, so I quit. (manage, refuse)

14 BANKS AND MONEY

PASSIVES

We use passives to focus attention on who or what an action affects and when it is unclear or unimportant who performs the action. Form passives using the verb *to be* + the past participle.

My wages are usually *paid* into my account on the 22nd.
A new security system is being installed at the moment.
Your new card was sent out to you last Monday.
They said *cash withdrawals were being made* in Morocco.
The cheque has been cleared, but *you will be charged* for this.

In passive sentences, we often don't mention who performs the action – because it's understood or it's unknown / not important. In passive sentences, to show who or what performed the action, use *by*.
I was offered yet another credit card *by my bank* last week!
The dollar has been strengthened by the news.

We can use the *be* + *-ing* form of the passive after certain verbs and after prepositions.
He strongly denied *being involved* in the scandal.
I have absolutely no interest in *being sold* insurance!
I'm scared of *being ripped off!*

Intransitive verbs (verbs that don't have an object) are never used in the passive form. These include *become, happen, die, lack, rise, fall, wait, arrive, cry, disappear*.

Exercise 1

Complete the sentences by adding the correct active or passive form of the verbs in brackets.

1 I only realised that my card [1]......................... last Saturday when I was doing my shopping in my local supermarket and the transaction wouldn't [2]......................... . I [3]......................... to go through security checks and had to speak to someone from the bank on the phone. They informed me my card [4]......................... . (clone, go through, ask, block)

2 His business had serious cash flow problems last year and he [1]......................... huge debts trying to keep things going. In the end, he [2]......................... bankrupt. All his employees [3]......................... redundant, his house [4]......................... and he [5]......................... penniless. (run up, go, make, repossess, leave)

3 A politician has been accused of [1]......................... in a money-laundering scandal. Michael Hurley, 46, allegedly [2]......................... over £1.3 million from a local council account to a secret account in Belize. He [3]......................... last week after a lengthy police investigation. If found guilty, he could [4]......................... to up to ten years in jail. Mr Hurley [5]......................... all charges against him. (involve, transfer, arrest, sentence, deny)

WISH

The verb *wish* refers to hypothetical things – things we want, but which are impossible. As such, it is followed by past forms.

wish + past simple / could / would

The past simple is used to talk about things in the present that you would(n't) like.
I *wish I was* better with money. I'm always in debt.
I sometimes *wish I had* a car, but I can't afford one.

could

We use *could* to refer to abilities we would like.
I *wish I could help*, but I've got people over for dinner.
I sometimes *wish we could stop* working, but we can't.

would

We use *would* to refer to habits (see page 148) or to people / things 'refusing' to do something.
I *wish the government would invest* in schools more.
I *wish he wouldn't waste* his money the way he does.

Don't use *mustn't* with *wish* – use *didn't have to*
I wish I ~~mustn't~~ *didn't have to go*, but I've got to work.

Use *hope* and present tenses for future possibilities – not *wish*.
I *hope interest rates go up* soon. I have a lot of savings.

wish + past perfect / could've

The past perfect simple or continuous refers to regrets about the past and to things in the past we now want to be different.
I *wish I'd invested* the money instead of spending it.
I *wish we'd never sold* that painting. We sold it for £6,000 and it's worth ten times that figure now.

could've (done)

We use *could've (done)* to refer to past possibilities.
I *wish I could've done* something, but it was impossible.
I really *wish I could've gone*, but I was just so busy.

Exercise 1

Complete 1–5 with the correct form of the verbs in brackets.

1 A: I wish I .... do my tax return!
   B: Isn't it worth getting an accountant? (have to)

2 A: I wish we .... about it earlier.
   B: Oh well. We didn't (think)

3 A: I wish the government .... taxes.
   B: Yeah? I think we should be paying more! (cut)

4 A: I wish I .... my holiday abroad months ago.
   B: I bet! It's so expensive now that our currency has collapsed. (book)

5 A: I wish I .... It sounds like you had a great time.
   B: Yeah, we did. Still, next time, yeah? (can come)

15 FOOD

LINKING IDEAS

and, after, once, until, then, afterwards

And, when, after, once and *until* join two events within a sentence. *Then, afterwards* or *after that* connect the ideas of two separate sentences – unless preceded by *and / but.*

Wash the chickpeas *and* (*then*) put them in water to soak.
Wash the chickpeas. *Afterwards*, put them in water to soak.

Once can mean 'after'. It's often followed by perfect tenses. *Until* shows what happens up to a particular point in time.

Once the onions turn brown, take them off the heat.
Fry the onions slowly *until* they are brown.

then, so, as, if ... then

Then shows what happens next, whereas *so (that)* and *If ... then* show the reason for / result of an action.
Marinate the meat for an hour and *then* grill it slowly.
Marinate the meat for an hour *so (that)* it doesn't dry out.

As can mean 'because'. It goes with the cause and links to the result. *So* goes with the result.

however, although, despite

Although and *despite* join ideas within a sentence.
However usually connects the ideas of two sentences.

provided, unless, in case, otherwise

Provided can replace '*if you make sure*'. *Unless* means '*if ... not*'. *Otherwise* shows the result if you don't do something and often starts a new sentence. *In case* is used to show that you a prepared for something that might happen.

during, for

Use *for* to show duration. Use *during* with a noun to show when another event happened.
Boil the broccoli *for* just three minutes.
He had a phone call *during* dinner and had to leave.

Exercise

Complete the sentences with appropriate linking words.

1 I don't buy these biscuits very often .... I find them so addictive. .... I've had one, I have to finish the whole packet!
2 He let the milk boil over, ... the fact I asked him to keep an eye on it – and .... , I had to clean up the mess!
3 I'll pack some snacks .... we get hungry, ... you don't have to bring anything.
4 Leave the beans to soak .... at least six hours. .... , they'll be almost inedible.
5 They'll cook whatever you want .... you book in advance and you can eat as much as you want .... you burst!

REPORTING VERBS

When we report what people said, we often just summarise their main ideas – rather than reporting their exact words. The verbs we use to do this give some indication of the general content of what was said. Reporting verbs are used a lot in newspapers and on the news.

Some reporting verbs are always followed by the same pattern, whilst others can be followed by a variety of different patterns.

Verbs often followed by *to-* infinitive:

agree	decide	promise	threaten
claim	offer	refuse	

Verbs often followed by *-ing* :

admit	deny	recommend
apologise for	insist on	suggest

Verbs often followed by person + *to-* infinitive:

advise	ask	invite	remind	urge
encourage	persuade	tell	warn	

Lots of reporting verbs can be followed by a noun or a clause:
The rebel groups have *declared a ceasefire.*
The president has *declared (that)* from now on the 1st of April will be a public holiday.
The manager today *confirmed his departure* from the firm.
Public health officials have *confirmed (that)* the death of three people in Elgin was caused by food poisoning.

Many verbs can be followed by different patterns. A good dictionary will help you see these patterns.
Officials have *blamed the food shortages on* the drought.
A chef has been *blamed for* causing the death of a diner.

Exercise

Find the six mistakes in the verb patterns and correct them.

1 The restaurant has been warned that further breaches of food hygiene regulations will result in closure.
2 My grandmother always insists to make her special apple pie every time we go and visit her.
3 A guy was smoking at a table nearby and my dad demanded him to put the cigarette out! I was so embarrassed.
4 A friend of mine suggested me to start keeping a food diary, recording what I ate and when.
5 The bill came to 400 dollars, and then the waiter informed that he'd already added a ten per cent tip!
6 My son is three now, and he just totally refuses eating anything healthy at all!
7 In the end, the waiter offered giving us the starters for free as we'd been waiting so long!
8 I was going to have the chicken soup, but the waiter persuaded me to try the pumpkin ravioli instead.

16 BUSINESS

FUTURE CONTINUOUS

Use the future continuous to talk about things you have arranged to do in the future, especially when you now want to talk about another thing that will happen during this action.

I'll be popping out to the café in a while. (= already arranged / decided) Can I get you anything? (=while I am doing this)

I'm going to be talking to the area manager later, so I'll raise your concerns with her.

If we want people to do things for us, we often use the future continuous to ask (or talk) about plans. It sounds polite.

A: *Are you going to be seeing* Max later? I promised I'd get this report to him today.

B: Yeah, I should be. Do you want me to take it with me?

The future continuous is also used to talk about something that will be in progress at a particular time – or over a particular period of time – in the future.

I can't make Friday. *I'll be attending* a conference in Bolton.

That's a good question. *I'll be talking* about that later on.

You're not going to be doing any sport for a while after the operation.

Exercise

Match the questions in 1–8 to the follow-up comments in a–h.

1 Will you be translating the website content into any other languages?
2 Will you be using your laptop this afternoon?
3 Will you be sending the parts by courier?
4 Do you know when they'll be launching the product in the USA?
5 Do you know if they're going to be taking any new staff on during the summer?
6 Are you going to be going past the canteen?
7 When are they going to be releasing their sales figures?
8 When's she going to be starting her new job?

a Because we really do need them ASAP.
b Because I must remember to ring and wish her luck.
c Because that could be one way of breaking into some overseas markets.
d I'll be quite keen to see how they've done this year.
e Because if you're not, is there any chance I could borrow it?
f Because if it's not going to be for a while, I might buy one when I'm over in Japan next month.
g Because my son's going to be looking for a job then.
h Because if you are, I'd love a coffee!

EXPRESSING NECESSITY AND ABILITY

Must and *can* aren't used in different tenses and don't have infinitive or *-ing* forms. Use forms of *be able to* or *have to* instead.

It's a problem the company *is going to have to deal with*.

We'll soon *be able to offer* the same prices as our competitors.

It's a real pain *not being able to access* my email.

I'll be glad *to not have to study* for exams anymore.

I *haven't been able to contact* the warehouse today, I'm afraid.

To show something makes another thing possible, we can use *enable somebody to do something*, *allow somebody to do something* or *let somebody do something*.

The report has *enabled us to improve* all areas of our service.

The device basically *allows you to avoid* traffic jams.

The investment should *let us keep* our best staff!

To show something makes an obligation, we can use *force somebody to do something* or *make somebody do something*.

High overheads *forced us to relocate* to a less central area.

The crisis has *made us reassess* our whole approach.

We can use *force* in the passive instead of *have to*.

The company *was forced to* close down its main plant.

Exercise

Complete the second sentence in each case so that it has a similar meaning to the first. Use the word in brackets in each case.

1 We've been able to step up production thanks to the new investment.
   The new investment ....
   production. (enabled)
2 With this device, you can monitor how much electricity you're using.
   The device .... how much electricity you're using. (let)
3 We've reached the factory's capacity, so we can't expand at the moment.
   Without a new factory, ...
   expand. (won't)
4 We had to abandon the project in the end. We .... abandon the project in the end. (forced)
5 They only found out because he forced me to tell them.
   They wouldn't have found out if he .... them. (made)

FILE 1

Unit 1 p. 12 Reading
Group A

Rags to riches

You could call this the Cinderella story. To begin with, our hero is a nobody, generally bullied and abused by the people around them. However, we learn about a talent or a secret dream they have, which is often shared by a 'dark' rival. Early in the story, an event provides an initial breakthrough for the hero, suggesting they can reach their goal. However, the hero then suffers a series of setbacks, which sends them into despair. Subsequently, usually with the help of a friend, they begin to change and to believe in themselves as individuals until they finally face their rival and show how superior they are. At the end of the story, the hero gets their riches and usually also gets their 'prince charming' or princess.

The quest

The hero in this case is living in the place that is under threat – often because something inside the society itself is corrupting it. The hero is visited by a ghost or has a dream and is told to go on a long, difficult journey in order to seek the thing that will save their community. The hero sets off with some friends and along the way they have to fight monsters, resist the temptation to join some dark force, or pass through a dangerous area. They are usually helped by some wise old man, beautiful woman or spirit. Having been through lots of ordeals, the hero finally gets to their destination only to find they have to do three tests or deal with some other difficulty before reaching their goal. Having passed these final tests, the quest is complete, the kingdom is saved and they often also win the hand in marriage of the prince or princess.

Glossary

be bullied: if you are bullied, you are repeatedly scared or hurt by people bigger and stronger than you.

rival: a rival is a person / team / company that you are competing with.

breakthrough: if you make a breakthrough, you start being successful at something – or achieve something.

despair: despair is the feeling that things are terrible and that there is nothing you can do to change them.

quest: a quest is a long and difficult search for something.

corrupt: if a society or person is corrupted, they have been encouraged to do dishonest or immoral things.

resist temptation: if you resist temptation, you manage not to do something you want to do, but which could be bad for you.

ordeal: an ordeal is a very bad experience you have for a period of time

FILE 2

Unit 4 p. 31 Reading
Student A

You are going to try and persuade Student B to give money to help fund the Millennium Villages mentioned in the article. Think about how you will explain what Millennium Villages are and how they are helping.

FILE 3

Unit 11 p. 77 Conversation practice
Student B

You work for Right Car Rentals. Student A is going to collect a car they have booked online from you.

Decide if you have any special offers this week.
Point out that the car runs on diesel – not petrol.
Try to sell some extras. You get 15% commission if you do!
Decide how much to charge for the following extras:
- GPS
- Additional insurance to cover for damage to tyres and windscreen
- Comprehensive insurance to cover damage to the vehicle, injury or loss of life, theft of property, etc.
- A baby seat (for children under 2) or a booster seat (for children from 2 to 8)
- Cover for any additional drivers

FILE 4

Unit 8 p. 57 Speaking
Student A
You are the presenter

Talk to the student who is the guest to see what role they have chosen. Then introduce your guest and introduce the questions below for the other students in your group to comment on and debate. Manage the 'calls' of the different students, ask for comments from the 'guest' and move the debate forward. You might want to add your own ideas occasionally or think of your own questions.
- Is prison life too comfortable nowadays?
- Would it be better if prisoners were made to do hard labour?
- A lot of people argue that the only thing that really makes any difference in society is the death penalty. What do you people out there think?
- Isn't the vast majority of crime simply a result of poverty?
- Wouldn't it be better if criminals were forced to explain their actions to their victims or their victims' families?

FILE 5

Unit 12 p. 85 Speaking
Student B

1 There are two cows chatting in a field. The first cow says. "This mad-cow disease is really worrying. They say it's spreading fast." The other cow replies. "It doesn't bother me – it doesn't affect us ducks."

2 A doctor is consulting a colleague. "I have this patient who is suffering form a Jimbomba – it's a rare tropical disease. It's very contagious."

"Ah yes. Interesting, I had a patient who suffered from that some years ago?"

"Really? What should I do?"

"I recommend a diet of pizzas and pancakes."

"Pizzas and pancakes. That's a pretty radical solution. Will it really cure them?"

"Probably not, but it's the only food that'll fit under the door."

3 "Doctor, Doctor I'm on a diet and it's making me really irritable. Yesterday I actually bit someone's ear off."

"Oh dear! That's a lot of calories!"

FILE 6

Unit 8 p. 57 Speaking
Student B
Choose one of the following roles.
- You are a representative of an organisation that opposes the death penalty.
- You are a representative of an organisation that wants to find alternative solutions to prison wherever possible.
- You are a representative of a victims group that believes that punishments aren't hard enough.
- You are a representative of the government. You believe that everything in the prison system is basically fine.

FILE 7

Unit 14 p. 99 Conversation practice
Student A
For three conversations, you are the customer.
1 You want to open a new account.
3 You want to take out a loan – decide how much.
5 You want to transfer some money overseas.

For three conversations, you are the bank clerk.
2 Student B wants to apply for an overdraft. You can do this, but there will be a charge.
4 Student B wants a new cash card. You can't produce one now. One can be sent out within two weeks.
6 Student B thinks they have been the victim of fraud. They do not have insurance and the bank can't refund any losses.

FILE 8

Unit 4 p. 27 Conversation practice
Read your role-play card below and choose which set of things you want to say. Add another opinion. Write notes on why you might think each opinion. Then have a conversation with your partner starting *What do you think of the government?* Agree or disagree with your partner's response and explain your opinions. If the conversation stops, keep it going by asking: *So what do you think of ... the opposition / their policies on education / the economy*, etc.

Student A

You think:
The government is incompetent.
They are soft on crime.
The president is a bit corrupt.
The opposition have some good ideas, but their leader is a bit weak.

....

OR

You think:
The government is doing a lot to improve education.
They have made some mistakes.
Some parts of the economy are doing badly.
You really don't like the opposition leader.

....

Student B

You think:
Your president has a good image on TV and in the world.
The economy is fine.
The government's given too much power to different regions.
The opposition leader is an idiot.

....

OR

You think:
You don't really like the government's foreign policy.
You don't really trust the president.
It's good that the opposition wants to cut taxes.
You're personally doing well and live in a nice area.

....

FILE 9

Unit 7 p. 50 Reading
Group B

WORK ON RESEARCH LAB HALTED

Building work on an animal research laboratory funded by Oxford University has been stopped following several months of threats and harassment by members of extremist animal rights groups. The company involved in the construction of the lab has pulled out of the project amidst fears for the safety of both site workers and the firm's board members.

The £18 million centre was intended to allow experiments aimed at combatting illnesses such as cancer, heart disease and diabetes to be carried out. The project has attracted negative publicity since it was first announced, with demonstrations against it being held quite regularly. Recently, however, it seems that a small radical group opposed to the use of animals in any kind of scientific research has launched a campaign of intimidation. Only last week, the addresses of university staff were published online, leading to concerns that they might now be targeted.

Animal rights groups see vivisection as cruel, unreliable and unnecessary. However, leading scientists have claimed that the research the lab aims to do will provide invaluable insights into the treatment of all manner of illnesses. Work on the building will apparently resume once new builders have been found.

UNLIKELY RECIPE FOR SUCCESS

A Mexican restaurant in Dresden, Germany seems to have found the secret of success: maggots! Since adding a range of dishes featuring the insects to their menu, Espitas restaurant claims to have been almost constantly fully booked.

Despite being a popular source of protein in many countries, in Germany maggots are more commonly associated with decay and death. This didn't stop restaurant owner Alexander Wolf from adding the insects to his menu earlier in the year. Apparently, the initial idea was little more than a joke, but the response was overwhelmingly positive. 'Most are disgusted, but try them out of curiosity or for a dare', noted Mr. Wolf, 'and are amazed at how good they taste. 'Many people come back again, and usually bring more friends with them'.

The restaurant now offers everything from maggot salads to maggots in ice cream, fried maggots with corn and cactus to maggot cocktails. Interestingly, all the maggots are imported from Mexico, as German maggots are not deemed tasty enough.

Following on from recent successes, Mr. Wolf now plans to introduce other traditional Mexican dishes such as ant eggs and grasshoppers.

FILE 10

Unit 12 p. 85 Speaking
Student A

1 A priest was asked to inform a man with a heart condition that he'd just inherited $10million. Everyone was afraid the shock would kill him. So the priest went to the man's house and said, "Joe, what would you do if you were left $10 million in a will?" "Well, father, I'd give half of it to my church." At which point, the priest dropped dead!

2 A man in a bar falls off his stool. Some guys decide to be nice and help him home, so they pick him up off the floor, and drag him out the door. On the way to the car, he falls down three times. When the get to his house, they help him out of the car and he falls down four more times. They ring the doorbell, and one says, "Here's your husband!" and the man's wife says, "Where are his crutches?"

3 "Doctor, Doctor. I think I need glasses." "You certainly do, Sir. This is a hairdresser's!"

FILE 11

Unit 4 p. 31 Reading
Student B
Student A is going to ask you for money to help fund the Millennium Villages mentioned in the article.

You are not sure if giving aid to poor countries is a good idea for the country – or for you personally.

Think of reasons you might give for not contributing and questions you might ask to find out more information.

FILE 12

Unit 1 p. 12 Reading
Group C

Comedy

Obviously, comedies are about making people laugh, but nearly all comic stories share common themes. A couple or a group get separated because of a misunderstanding or because they are unaware of their true needs or characters. Through a series of events, the characters start to realise who they truly love and / or how they have behaved badly. These events involve the heroes wearing disguises at some point, pretending to be someone different, and further silly misunderstandings that result in a terrible mess. In the end, everything is resolved. Any baddie who refuses to change is exposed for what they are and is laughed at or punished in some way, while the couple get together – often in the form of a wedding – whilst everybody else lives happily ever after.

Tragedy

Tragedy is a bit like the Overcoming the Monster story, but seen from the monster's perspective. At the beginning, we see a noble or talented person who, despite being successful, feels their life is incomplete and still wants something more. They are presented with an opportunity to fulfil their desires, but this generally requires breaking some kind of law. At first, they get away with this crime, but new obstacles soon appear and they are forced to commit further, often more violent, crimes until the situation gets totally out of control. The hero has become a monster and is finally destroyed either by committing suicide or by someone seeking revenge.

Glossary

get separated: if you get separated from people you are with, you accidentally lose them – often in a crowded place.

disguise: a disguise is something you wear to change the way you look – so that people won't recognise you.

resolve: if problems are resolved, a good solution is found.

be exposed: if a person is exposed as a liar / cheat / bad person, etc. the truth about them is finally revealed – for all to see.

fulfil your desires: if you fulfil your desires, you achieve what you wanted to – or get what you really wanted.

get away with: if you get away with a crime or with doing something wrong, you are not caught or punished for it.

obstacles: obstacles are problems or difficulties that stop you from getting where you want to be – or getting something you want.

seek revenge: if you seek revenge, you want to hurt, punish or kill someone – because they have done something similar to you.

FILE 13

Unit 16 p. 115 Speaking
Pair A

Discuss how you'll present each product. Give each one a name. Think of the retail price and how much profit you'll make on each one. You might want to explain how each one works and why it's better than competitors – if there are any. Think about how much money you want Pair B to invest and why. What stake of the company will you give them in exchange? Negotiate if they offer you something.

1 A special brush which lets you brush your hair and remove knots without pain

2 A gadget which allows you to pick up Satellite TV signals and play it through your computer

3 A chain of specialist chocolate stores

When the other pair present their products, ask questions about the product, the market, how much they will be earning in a year / two years / three years, etc. If you like the product, offer to invest in their company. Negotiate what percentage of the company you want in return – and specify any other conditions.

FILE 14

Unit 12 p. 85 Speaking
Student C

1 A hypochondriac went to the doctor. "Doctor. You've got to refer me to a consultant. I've got liver disease." "How could you possibly know that," replied the doctor. "There's no discomfort and no outward signs of illness with liver disease."
and the patient says, "You see! Those are my precise symptoms."

2 A man went to his doctor for a check-up. After examining the man, the doctor said, "Well, I've got some bad news and some good news. The bad news is you've got hepatitis, but the good news is you've also got Alzheimer's, so you'll forget all about it!"

3 "Doctor, Doctor. Have you got something for a bad headache?" "Of course. Just take this hammer and hit yourself on the head. Then you'll have a bad headache."

FILE 15

Unit 3 p. 20 Vocabulary

a hammer   a drill   a saw   a torch   a stepladder   a nail   a screw

glue   rope   string   bucket   cloth

a dustpan and brush   mop and bucket   washing up liquid   a corkscrew   a tin opener   a lighter

a rubber   correction fluid   a stapler   scissors   paperclips   bulldog clips

sticky tape   a needle   washing powder   a needle and thread   an iron

pegs   elbow/knee pads   a plaster   a bandage

FILE 16

Unit 1 p. 12 Reading
Group B

Rebirth

This plot is similar to tragedy in that the 'hero' is essentially someone who becomes isolated, mean or heartless. This happens because they are influenced by some evil figure, are badly treated by someone or are wrongly accused of something. The pain of this leads into a downward spiral of hatred and obsession. Sometimes these influences are revealed later in the story through flashbacks to their earlier life. Unlike the main character in a tragedy, however, the 'hero' is finally saved because they come into contact with a younger, more innocent person who makes them see the deadness of their life. The hero changes and begins to live again.

Voyage and return

In the voyage and return story, the heroes find themselves transported to another world, without really knowing why. At the beginning of the story, there's usually something wrong with the hero – they're bored or innocent, or arrogant, etc. Then, by chance, they're thrown into a different world. This could be a fantasy world, another country, or simply a very different social setting from the one they are used to. At first, they find things difficult, but this new place quickly becomes enjoyable, offering lots of possibilities. However, after a while, the hero becomes trapped or corrupted by the place, and it may threaten their life. The hero finally manages to escape, often by recognising flaws in their own character or how they have hurt other people.

Glossary

isolated: if you become isolated, you end up on your own, with no friends to support or to help you.

be accused of: if you are accused of doing something wrong, someone says that you did it.

downward spiral: if you enter a downward spiral, you go into a situation that gets worse and worse.

flashbacks: flashbacks are the parts of books / plays / films where you see what happened in an earlier time.

be transported: if you are transported to another place (or time), you are moved there somehow.

corrupted: if a person becomes corrupted by a place, it influences them in a bad way and makes them do dishonest or immoral things.

flaws: your flaws are the faults in your character (or appearance).

FILE 17

Unit 3 p. 21 Conversation practice
Student A
Look at the four situations below. Think about what you need to ask your partner for in each of these situations.

1 The strap on your bag has broken.
2 You've dropped your ring and it's rolled under a cupboard and you want to try and get it out.
3 You've dropped a bottle of oil on the floor and it's smashed.
4 You knocked over a flower vase in the house you're staying in and a bit of it has broken off.

FILE 18

Unit 16 p. 115 Speaking
Pair B
Discuss how you'll present each product. Give each one a name. Think of the retail price and how much profit you'll make on each one. You might want to explain how each one works and why it's better than competitors – if there are any. Think about how much money you want Pair A to invest and why. What stake of the company will you give them in exchange? Negotiate if they offer you something.
1 An exercise machine for dogs
2 A special Caribbean sauce for barbecues
3 A special box for shoes that enables you to remove smells instantly

When the other pair present their products, ask questions about the product, the market, how much they will be earning in a year / two years / three years, etc. If you like the product, offer to invest in their company. Negotiate what percentage of the company you want in return – and specify any other conditions.

FILE 19

Unit 14 p. 99 Conversation practice
Student B
For three conversations, you are the customer.
2 You want to apply for an overdraft. Decide how large.
4 You have lost your card and need a new one.
6 According to your bank statement, €1500 were withdrawn from your account last week in Belgium. You've never even been to Belgium!

For three conversations, you are the bank clerk.
1 Student A wants to open an account. You need to see sufficient relevant ID.
3 Student A wants to take out a loan. You can't lend this much to someone with such a bad credit rating.
5 Student A wants to transfer money overseas. This is fine, but there will be a 5% commission charge.

FILE 19

Unit 11 p. 77 Conversation practice
Student A

> You are going to collect a car you have booked online –
> a 5-door hatchback. You are travelling with your partner
> (who might do some of the driving) and your 5-year-old
> daughter (who hates being in cars).
>
> The car rental assistant may try to sell you some extras.
> Ask about them and decide if you want them or not.
>
> Think of three other questions you will need to ask.

FILE 21

Unit 3 p. 21 Conversation practice
Student B
Look at the four situations below. Think about what you
need to ask your partner for in each of these situations.
1 You've got some new shoes which are rubbing on the
  back of your heels and you don't want your heels to
  get sore and bleed.
2 On a picnic, the tab on the top of a tin/can has
  broken off so you can't open it easily.
3 A screw on your glasses has come loose and the arm
  of the glasses has fallen off.
4 You need to change a light bulb, but you can't reach
  the light even if you stand on a chair.

FILE 22

Unit 15 p. 105 Conversation Practice

FILE 23

Unit 15 p. 104 Vocabulary

 almond

 mint

 tomato

 grapes

 brocoli

 plum

 raisin

 turnip

 hazelnuts

 octopus

 parsnip

 coconut

 trout

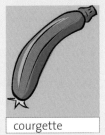 courgette

 parsley

 eel

 rosemary

 fig

 ginger

 orange

 kidney bean

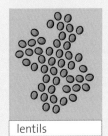 lentils

 sweet potato

 corn cobs

 oyster

 peach

 cabbage

 pumpkin

 radish

 celery

 pepper

 fennel

 spring onion

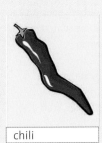 chili

 salmon

betroot

UNIT 01

🔊 1.1

1 Yeah, at the weekends, of course. I go shopping, go to the cinema, go clubbing sometimes. I don't tend to during the week, though, because I've got to get up early for school and I've got homework, and basically my parents prefer me to stay at home.

2 Yeah, all the time. I take my mp3 player with me everywhere – it's, like, glued to my ears! All kinds of stuff as well – rock, pop, even some classical.

3 Not as much as I'd like to, because I really love it – especially musicals. I mean, I do go now and again, but the seats are so expensive I can't afford to go more than a couple of times a year.

4 Very rarely, to be honest. I guess I might in the summer – if it's very hot. I find it a bit boring, just going up and down the pool. It's not really my kind of thing – and I'm not very good at it either

5 Probably less than I think I do, if you know what I mean. It's always on in the background, you know, but I don't pay much attention to it most of the time. I will watch a big game if there's one on and the occasional film, but apart from that, most of it's rubbish.

6 Yeah, I guess so. I usually play football on a Wednesday and I go running now and again. I generally cycle to college as well – unless it's raining.

7 No, not as a rule. I tend to wait for films to come out on cable as I've got a nice, big, flat-screen TV at home. Oh, and I download quite a lot of stuff too.

8 Not as much as I used to. I was addicted to The Sims for a while until my parents banned me. I would sometimes play for five hours a day! I play other games now, but my parents control it a bit more.

🔊 1.2

1 I don't tend to during the week, though.

2 Yeah, all the time! I take my mp3 player with me everywhere.

3 Not as much as I'd like to because I really love it.

4 Very rarely, to be honest. I guess I might in the summer

5 I don't pay much attention to it most of the time. I will watch a big game, if there's one on …

6 Yeah, I guess so. I usually play football on a Wednesday and I go running now and again.

7 No, not as a rule. I tend to wait for films to come out on cable.

8 Not as much as I used to. I was addicted to The Sims for a while, until my parents banned me. I would sometimes play for 5 hours a day!

🔊 1.3

A: Do you go to the cinema much?

B: Yeah, a fair bit, I suppose. I tend to go most weeks.

A: Really? That's a lot.

B: Yeah, I guess so. I'd go more if I could though! What about you?

A: Not that often, no – not unless I really want to see something that I know isn't going to come out on DVD for a while.

B: Mmm. So what kind of things are you into?

A: I don't know. All sorts, really, but I guess mainly action films.

B: Such as?

A: I don't know. I really liked the first Blade films, X-Men, stuff like that.

B: OK. Did you see Old Boy last night? It was on TV.

A: Yeah, I started watching it, but I turned over.

B: You didn't like it?

A: It was so over-the-top, just so disgusting and then the plot! I don't know. It was all a bit too weird for my liking.

B: Really? I love that film – the look of it, the music everything. It's just amazing. I think it's the fifth time I've seen it.

A: Really? As I say, it was OK, but it's not really my kind of thing. Too much like horror really.

B: I suppose so.

A: So apart from Old Boy, what kind of stuff do you like?

B: Oh, all kinds of things. As I say, I go most weeks, so you know... action films, comedies, foreign films – anything, really.

A: Have you seen Gold Diggers?

B: Yeah. Have you?

A: No, but I've heard it's good. I was thinking of going to see it.

B: I don't know. It IS good, but it's pretty heavy, I found it quite disturbing, really. It's not the kind of thing you can watch and just switch off.

A: Oh right. Maybe I'll give it a miss then.

🔊 1.4

Now if you follow me through into the next room, we come to a far more modern piece of work, dating in fact from 1971. On the surface, this may strike you as a fairly conventional, life-like portrait. To the left, there's a young woman standing in front of an open door, and looking directly at the viewer, whilst to the right there's a young man sitting in a chair, with a white cat seated on his lap, pointedly looking away. Through the open door, we can see a balcony and beyond that the green garden of their town house. There are some flowers in a vase on the table, next to a book, and there's a phone and a lamp on the floor. Finally, to the very left of the picture, we see part of an abstract painting hanging on the wall.

However, beneath all of this, the work is actually a very ambiguous, multi-layered piece, heavy with symbolic meaning and with history. Called Mr and Mrs Clark and Percy and painted by David Hockney, the work was recently voted one of Britain's top 10 favourites and a knowledge of the behind-the-scenes story might help to explain some of the tension and drama in a piece which continues to fascinate us.

The couple in the painting are textile designer Celia Birtwell and fashion designer Ossie Clark, shortly after their wedding, at which the artist himself had been the best man.

The piece is loosely based on the 15th century work, the Arnolfini portrait, by Jan van Eyck, but the positions of the male and female characters have been reversed. The suggestion is perhaps that it was Mrs Clark who was the dominant partner in this particular relationship. The lilies on the table represent female purity, while the cat on Mr Clark's lap symbolises infidelity and jealousy. The roots of this symbol lie in the fact that Mr Clark had frequent affairs both before and during their five-year marriage. This played a part in the couple's eventual divorce three years later and may explain part of the friction that seems apparent between the two sitters. We have the feeling that we have suddenly interrupted an intimate moment – a heated discussion, perhaps – and are not exactly welcome.

As a footnote, sadly Ossie Clark later fell into bankruptcy and addiction and his life ended tragically when he was murdered by an ex-lover in 1996, a fact which lends a disturbing edge to the portrait. Celia Birtwell, meanwhile, continued to be one of Hockney's regular models for many years and to this day remains a successful designer.

🔊 1.5

1 Interestingly, the painting used to have a different title.

2 Actually, no-one knows who the painter was.

3 Sadly, she died at the age of only 35.

4 The painting sold last year for $18 million, but, amazingly, Van Gogh himself sold none in his lifetime.

5 Incredibly, Mozart was only 6 when he started performing in public.

6 The painting was damaged in a fire and, unfortunately, it couldn't be restored.

UNIT 02

🔊 2.1

M = May, I = Ivana

M: What a lovely day!

I: Yeah, it's nice, isn't it? It's been a really warm autumn.

M: So where are we?

I: Well, the bit we've just been through, with all the high-rise blocks, is what we call New Belgrade. It's the big up-and-coming area as all the new businesses are relocating here. And I don't know if you can see it or not, but just behind us, over to the right, is the Arena, where all the big concerts and sports events are held. It's one of the biggest entertainment venues in Europe.

M: Yeah, I think I did catch a glimpse of it.

I: That's where they held the Eurovision back in 2008.

M: Oh, OK. So I've seen it on TV, then.

I: And now we're crossing over the River Sava into Old Belgrade.

M: Wow! The river looks wonderful.

I: Yeah, it's great. In the summer, we often go out on little boats or have dinner down by the waterside.

M: Oh, that sounds lovely.

I: And just down there, there's a little street called Gavrila Principa Street, where Manakova Kuca – Manak's House – is located. It's an ethnological museum and it houses an amazing collection of old national costumes and embroidery and stuff.

M: OK. I'll check that out if I have time. What's that building over there?

I: Oh, that's St. Mark's Church.

M: Wow! That's a stunning building. How old is it?

I: Not that old, actually. It was built in the late 1930s or something, but it's on the site of a much older church. It contains the tomb of Stefan Dusan, who was perhaps the greatest Serbian emperor ever.

M: Oh, OK.

I: And if you want to walk around here later, you're quite close to the Kalemegdan Fortress, one of the most historic buildings in Belgrade. There's the Victor Monument up there as well, which was erected after the First World War. It's one of the city's most famous landmarks.

M: Right. Well, I'll have to remember to take my camera with me up there, then.

I: And now we're coming up to Dedinje, which is one of the more affluent parts of the city. It's where all the celebrities and the old aristocratic families live – and a lot of the embassies are based here as well.

M: The houses certainly do look very grand.

I: Yeah, they're amazing, aren't they?

🔊 2.2

1 This year we're introducing a new ride called Hell and Heaven. The riders are strapped into seats and sit for anything between ten seconds and two minutes until, without warning, a door opens beneath them and they plunge 20 metres down into total darkness. Then devil figures appear and they're subjected to bursts of heat before suddenly getting shot back up into the light and up a 50-metre tower where they hang before dropping again. It's due to officially open in June, but I've taken part in the trials and I can tell you it'll really set your pulse racing.

2 A: What shall we go on next?

   B: Let's go on this one.

   A: No way! It's boring! Look at them – just floating along.

   B: It's nice. It's got tunnels and falls too. Look – you get splashed there.

   A: Yawn! Come on. Let's go on Dragon Kahn again.

   B: Can't we have a break? And there are no height restrictions on the boats either, so we can all go – your brother included.

   A: It's so annoying – why can't he be taller!!

   B: Erm, it's called biology! Now stop moaning. You'll spoil things.

   A: It's so unfair.

3 You've got to come with us next time. It's so cool. Oh, oh there's this one ride, yeah, it's just amazing. You go in this car really high up and you get really nervous, you know, with anticipation 'cos it goes quite slowly and I was holding really tight and going "This is gonna be awful, I wanna get off" and we got to the top and it just falls – falls really steeply – like almost vertical – and I just screamed and screamed and then we came up again and suddenly I'm going 'Wow, this is fantastic!" and it has all these loops and twists and turns and you go upside down and everything. It's amazing!

4 The company is applying for planning permission for a park with ten slides and four pools, so we're launching a campaign to stop it. There's already been a drought and this'll worsen the situation in the future. We understand the need for tourist attractions, but we want local government to investigate other, sustainable alternatives, such as horse trekking and climbing. We've nothing against a park with slides – just not ones that'll put a further strain on water resources.

5 I'm dreading some bits. I went on a rollercoaster once and just got really bruised because of all the twists and turns. Still, I'm going to go to the medieval show anyway. It includes jousting, where they wear armour and try to knock each other off their horses. That should be good. Then I might just walk around the grounds, which are supposed to be really pretty.

6 A: Oh man! I think I'm going to be sick!

   B: You shouldn't have eaten before.

   A: Well, it looked quite tame, but all that spinning around made me dizzy. One sec...

   B: I'll get you a tissue.

🔊 2.3

... you get really nervous, you know, with anticipation 'cos it goes quite slowly and I was holding really tight and going "This is gonna be awful, I wanna get off" ...

🔊 2.4

1 Have you ever been there?

2 I'm thinking of going there in the summer.

3 You should have seen him when he got off the ride.

4 I thought he was going to be sick!

5 I will take you because I'm going that way anyway.

6 I am going to leave now because I've got to finish some work.

7 Do you want to do that first or shall we leave it until later?

UNIT 03

 3.1

Conversation 1

A: What's the name of that stuff you use to put posters up?

B: Can you be a bit more specific?

A: Yeah, sorry, I mean that stuff – it's a bit like chewing gum or something, but it doesn't actually feel that sticky.

B: What? You mean blu-tac?

A: Yeah! Is that what they call it?

Conversation 2

C: It's, um ... what do you call those things climbers use? They're made of metal. They're like a hook.

D: What? You mean the thing you use to connect yourself to the rope?

C: Yeah, they have a sort of springy gate thing. You see people using the small ones as key rings sometimes.

D: Yeah, yeah. I know exactly what you mean – I don't know! Do they have a special name – aren't they just clips?

3.2

A: I brought you a present.

B: Wine?

A: No! I know you don't drink. No, it's Californian grape juice! I had some at a friend's the other day and it was really delicious.

B: Really?

A: Apparently, they have all sorts of varieties.

B: Yeah? Well, thanks! Shall we have some now?

A: Sure! Have you got a corkscrew?

B: Ah, that's a point, actually. I'm not sure I have actually. Let me have a look. There's so much stuff in these drawers. Most of it's rubbish. I really should clear it out. Mmm. I don't think there's one here. Can't you use a knife?

A: I don't think so.

B: You need a stick or something to push it down. Would a pencil do?

A: It wouldn't be strong enough.

B: What about a wooden spoon? You could use the handle.

A: Yeah, that should do. Let's see... Oh no!!

B: Oh, it's gone everywhere!

A: Sorry! Have you got a cloth?

B: Yeah. I think we need a mop and bucket as well.

A: Sorry.

B: Don't worry about it. These things happen. You might want to rub some salt into that shirt or it'll leave a stain.

A: Really?

B: Well, it works for other things.

3.3

S = Sales Assistant, C = Customer

S: Who's next, please?

C: Oh hello. I wonder if you can help me. I was given this tie for my birthday a couple of weeks ago and I believe it came from your store. I was wondering if I could possibly get a refund on it as it's... well, it's just not very ME, if you know what I mean.

S: OK. It was purchased two weeks ago, you say?

C: Yes, that's right. Give or take a day or two.

S: Right.

C: But this is the first chance I've had to come in to the store. I was too busy working before.

S: And do you still have the receipt for it?

C: Um . . . no, I don't, no. As I said, it was a present.

S: So – without meaning to be rude – how can you be sure it actually came from us?

C: Well, it was from my girlfriend and I did see her coming home the day before my birthday with a bag from your shop, and I did also see exactly the same ties for sale in your menswear department a minute ago, so I'm assuming it must have come from here.

S: Well, to be honest, we can't really take it back without proof of purchase. Would you happen to know how your girlfriend paid for it? Do you know if it was by cheque or by credit card or . . . ?

C: Look. I honestly haven't a clue. I obviously wasn't with her when she bought it, was I!

S: OK. Please try not to get quite so upset, sir. I'm just trying to do my job here.

C: No, I know. I'm sorry. It's just that ninety pounds is an awful lot of money for a tie – and it does seem a terrible shame if I'm never going to wear it.

S: Indeed, but I'm afraid that under the circumstances, I'm not going to be able to offer any kind of refund or exchange. I suggest you go home and try to find a receipt of some sort. Perhaps your girlfriend kept it?

3.4

S = Sales Assistant, C = Customer (as above)

1 C: But I know I won't be able to get hold of the receipt or any other proof she bought it here without letting her know and she'd be so disappointed, she really would. She's had so many other problems recently – I really don't want to upset her. Please, is there really nothing you can do?

S: I am sorry, sir. It's just that we're not actually legally obliged to accept returns of this kind at all, so there's really nothing else I can do to help.

C: Oh well. I suppose I'll just have to force myself to wear the tie once in a while. Thanks for your help, anyway.

2 C: Yes, but that would mean having to tell her I've been trying to get a refund on the stupid thing!

S: That's not strictly our problem. I'm afraid, sir.

C: No, of course not. It never is, this kind of thing, is it?

S: I'm sorry you feel that way, sir, but I've done all I can for you.

C: Well, it's just not good enough, is it? Do you think you could call the manager, please? I've had just about enough of this.

S: I'm afraid the manager is out at the moment. Would you like me to give you her number?

C: When do you expect her back?

S: It could be any time today.

C: Oh, that's just marvellous, that is!

S: I should tell you, though, that she'd probably tell you exactly what I've just told you. No proof of purchase, no refund.

C: Great! Well, thanks a lot for your help! That's the last time I ever come here! I'll take my business elsewhere in future.

3.5

1 A: Do you happen to know how long the guarantee lasts?

B: I'm not sure, actually, but it's usually at least a year.

2 A: Sorry. Do you know where the toilets are?

B: If you go up the stairs, the Ladies' is on your left.

3 A: Excuse me. Do you know if you sell wire?

B: Yes. There should be some in the hardware department on the second floor.

4 A: Hello. I was wondering if I could speak to the manager?
   B: Certainly. I'll put you through now.
5 A: Would you happen to know when the sofa will be delivered?
   B: It says on the computer it should go out tomorrow.
6 A: Sorry to bother you, but do you think you could bring me the next size up?
   B: Of course. I'll just grab you one from the racks.

UNIT 04

4.1

A: So what do you think of your president?
B: Oh, I can't stand him. He's so arrogant.
A: Really? Whenever I see him on TV he comes across as being OK.
B: Ah, it's all marketing. You hear some people say he's boosted our standing in the world, whatever that's supposed to mean, but he's done nothing for people like me – just put up tuition fees for students.
A: I know. I saw. It's three thousand euros or something a year now, isn't it?
B: More than that!
A: Really! I don't know how you manage. The cost of living there's so high.
B: Tell me about it! I'm going to be so far in debt by the time I graduate, I'll be paying it back for years.
A: Is it easy to find a job there?
B: Well, this is it. Unemployment's shot up recently. It's really worrying. If you ask me, they've been so concerned with supposedly 'green' laws like banning plastic bags, they've totally ignored the economy and now it's a complete mess.
A: So when's the next election? Can't you vote against them?
B: It's next year, but I'm not going to vote.
A: No?
B: No. They're all as bad as each other. The opposition are so busy fighting among themselves that they're not going to make any difference.
A: I know what you mean, but there must be someone worth voting for. I mean, like our government has done a few controversial things – stuff I didn't agree with – but, you know, they've done good things as well. I mean, the economy's really booming.
B: Yeah? Maybe I should think about emigrating there after uni.
A: You should. Honestly, there's such a skills shortage that companies are paying really good money now. They're desperate for people.
B: You don't think the language would be a barrier?
A: Not necessarily. Quite a few multinationals have set up there recently and they use English and there are other jobs, and you'd pick our language up. They've actually done a lot to cut back on bureaucracy too so it's much easier for foreigners to get work than it used to be.
A: Yeah? I'll have to think about it. It'd be nice to escape my debts, anyway!

4.2

1 The government will today launch a new initiative aimed at getting vulnerable young people off the streets and into hostels. The move is a response to growing concern about the number of teenagers sleeping rough on the streets of the capital, many of whom, it is feared, are in danger of becoming involved in drugs and other criminal activity.
2 A senior executive at one of the country's leading law firms is today almost half a million euros richer after winning her case against her employers, McLintock and Rice. Judith Fenton had claimed she was denied promotion as a direct result of telling colleagues she was pregnant. The court ruled in her favour and she was awarded compensation of four hundred and eighty-seven thousand euros.
3 Police are today conducting investigations after a young Asian student was attacked near the city centre by a group of white youths late last night. The attack was captured on CCTV and a senior policeman has announced he believes it may well have been racially motivated. The 19-year-old victim is still being treated in hospital and is believed to have suffered several broken bones.
4 A tiny pressure group has claimed victory over one of the country's richest men. Multi-millionaire Ronald Stamp had been planning to build a hotel and entertainment complex on a privately owned beach on the north-east coast. However, following protests by local residents, the group Save Our Seaside took legal action to prevent what they claimed would amount to "vandalism on a huge scale" – a claim that was yesterday upheld in court.
5 A woman from East Sussex last week became the country's youngest grandmother. At the age of 29, Tracy Bell is now the proud granny of a baby boy, Kevin. Bell's daughter, Caroline, aged 14, said she had initially been too scared to break the news to her mother, and had waited until a doctor had confirmed she was indeed pregnant. Mrs. Bell, however, seems resigned to the situation, stating that as she is already bringing up five children, one more will make little difference.

4.3

A: Did you see that thing on the news about that woman who's been suing the firm she works for?
B: I was just reading about that, actually. She won, didn't she?
A: Absolutely. It was shocking what happened to her. It was such typical double standards!
B: Well, maybe – but it was a lot of money. I'm not so sure about it all, to be honest. If you ask me, if you're in that kind of situation, you have to decide what you want. Either you try and get promoted or you focus on having kids. You can't have everything in life, can you?
A: That's such rubbish! You can't really believe that. This is the twenty-first century! Surely a woman's allowed to have children and a career!

4.4

They told her, 'You either have kids or you can get promoted.' (x2)
I mean, they can have a career and a family. (x2)

REVIEW 01

R1.1

Venice was absolutely amazing. You would've loved it. I stayed with Nina, who I'm sure you remember from uni. It was really kind of her to put me up – and it meant I didn't have to struggle with trying to find a hotel, which would've been almost impossible! The city was completely packed with tourists for the whole ten days, and prices really shoot up.

R1.2

1 At a time when people are struggling to make ends meet, my party finds it incredible that the council are choosing to invest in an art gallery. We should be facing the challenge of soaring

unemployment, energy shortages, education and poverty. We understand that they see it as boosting tourism and creating jobs, but we certainly don't see it as the best way to spend taxpayers' money so we shall be voting against the proposal.

2 Even if it's just putting up a picture, always ensure you have good quality tools and materials. Cheap paint and brushes will give you a cheap finish and tools that aren't sharp will lead to frustration. The basic kit you need is a drill, hammer and saw. You should also get a power screwdriver if you want to save yourself a lot of time and energy. You can hire other tools to do more sophisticated jobs. Always wear protective gear to avoid injury and staining your normal clothes.

3 I have to say, not everything is that easy to put together, and I think that's why some of the things are brought back. People make an impulse purchase and when they get home they struggle to follow the instructions. So we have to have quite a strict policy: we replace any parts that are missing and we only give refunds if products break after they've been constructed correctly or are already damaged – scratched paint or whatever.

4 You look at some of the paintings and you wonder how they did it, because they look so life-like, down to every little detail. I could never do that! You can understand why people want to go up close – you want to reach out and touch, but I have to tell them to stand back. It can be pretty dull at times and if you're in a room with dark, sombre paintings, it can affect your mood. Mind you, I was monitoring the Matisse room the other day and it's great, all those bright cheerful colours

5 Our auction of celebrity artworks was a huge success, raising enough money to buy twenty thousand bed nets to protect against malaria. It also raised awareness of our organisation and what we do and we hope to build on that. Although the conflict is undermining some of our efforts to distribute aid in the country, we're confident we will continue to improve basic health care and improve child mortality among those living in poverty.

UNIT 05

🎧 5.1

Conversation 1
A: What are you up to later?
B: Oh, I'm going to a belly dancing class.
A: You're doing what?
B: Belly dancing. You know, like …
A: Yeah, I know what it is. I just had no idea that you did that.
B: Well, I don't really. It's actually the first class.
A: Oh OK. So why belly dancing?
B: I've been thinking about doing something to get a bit fitter and I've never liked sport particularly. I find jogging and swimming and stuff like that a bit boring, you know – and then I saw this class advertised and I thought it'd be fun.
A: Yeah, I guess so. I should really do something as well. I've put on five kilos since January.
B: Really? It doesn't look it. You've got a lovely figure.
A: Well, I don't feel like I have!   And I'm really unfit. I had to run for the bus this morning and it took me about ten minutes to get my breath back!
B: Well, why don't you come with me?
A: I don't know. I think I'd feel a bit self-conscious.
B: Come on! You can't be worse than me. I'm totally uncoordinated! It'll be a laugh.

A: Well, maybe.

Conversation 2
C: Are you around this weekend at all?
D: No, I'm going to a fencing workshop all day Saturday.
C: You're going where?
D: This fencing workshop. It's like a master class with this top Russian fencer.
C: Wow! I didn't even know you did fencing? How did you get into that?
D: Oh, we actually used to do it at school. In PE, we had the option to try out all kinds of sports and I just really got into it and then I joined a club and then I started competing a bit more seriously, you know.
C: I had no idea. Well, what about Sunday? I'm going to have a wander round the flea market in the morning.
D: To be honest, I think I'm just going to have a lie-in and chill out at home. I'll be exhausted after Saturday.
C: Fair enough. Just the thought of doing that kind of exercise makes me sweat!

Conversation 3
E: What're you doing this evening? Do you fancy meeting later?
F: No, I can't. I've got my ... um ... my um knitting group tonight.
E: You've got what?
F: My knitting group.
E: Since when?
F: I've been doing it for about 6 months now. I took it up because I was giving up smoking and a friend suggested doing it. She said it'd give me something to fiddle with instead of cigarettes, so I joined this group and it's been really good. I feel so much healthier now and I actually really like the knitting. I just find it very very relaxing.
E: OK, but isn't it just full of old women, this group?
F: No, not at all. Well, I mean, I am the only man, but most of the women are quite young.
E: Ah.
F: What? What's 'Ah' supposed to mean?
E: Nothing.

🎧 5.2
A: I've got my knitting group tonight.
B: You've got what?

A: I'm going to a fencing workshop all day.
B: You're going where?

🎧 5.3
1 I should've joined a gym years ago.
2 I shouldn't have eaten so much.
3 You should've gone to bed earlier.
4 I shouldn't have been substituted.
5 He should never have been sent off!
6 We should've gone somewhere else.

🎧 5.4
C = Chloe, M = Molly, K = Kyle
M: I must go and send my cousin an email in a minute.
C: Oh, OK.
M: I've been meaning to go round and see him, because he's not been

well, but Kyle's a bit reluctant to drive me round there because it'd mean spending time with my uncle.

C: Really? What's wrong with him?

K: He's just mad, that's all.

M: He's not, he's just …

K: Annoying?

M: No!

K: Crazy? Exhausting?

M: Chloe – just ignore him. Kyle – you can be so horrible sometimes.

K: Listen, Chloe, the last time we went to see him he had a thing about handstands. We were sitting outside a café, just having a coffee and chatting and he suddenly just got up and did a handstand – right next to all the tables! He kept it up for about half an hour!

C: That does sound a bit odd. How old is he?

M: About 50.

C: 50!

K: I told you! He's crazy.

M: He is not! He's just one of these people who can't sit still. I mean, he's always loved sport and when he does something new, he really gets into it. Like he took us ice-skating once. Do you remember?

K: How could I forget?

M: I mean, we were exhausted after about an hour, but he just kept on skating – and we watched him going round and round for another hour.

K: It was like he'd just completely forgotten we were there! And what about the hang-gliding?

C: Hang-gliding?

M: Yeah, he used to go hang-gliding. Obsessed with it, he was. He went practically every weekend for about three years.

K: Until he had an accident. He fell something like 1000m without a parachute.

C: You're joking!

M: No, it's true.

C: So what happened?

M: Well, he'd borrowed someone else's glider for some reason and they didn't have a parachute, but he went up anyway. And he was caught in really bad weather and the hang-glider broke and he fell.

C: And he wasn't badly injured?

M: Well, he went through some trees, which broke his fall. He had hairline fractures in his shoulder and his neck and some minor cuts and bruises, but basically he was OK. He was incredibly lucky he didn't die.

C: Absolutely!

K: Anyway, then we saw him about three weeks later roller-skating in the park, even though he still had his neck in a brace!

C: But he did give up the hang-gliding after that?

M: Not exactly, no. He tried it once more – to overcome any fear. I mean, he just wanted to prove to himself he could do it, but since then… no. The last few years he's been really into windsurfing. He's actually always liked it – he did it when he was younger – but the last few years, that's been his main obsession. He lives on the coast, so he goes nearly every day.

C: Right. I'm starting to think Kyle might be right!

K: And you haven't heard all of it. For the last few months he's been rubbing lemon juice into his skin and his hair every day! He says it gets rid of dandruff and he was going on and on about how amazingly healthy it is.

M: OK, OK! It's true. He is a little bit mad, but he's a nice guy and he's fun to be with.

K: In small doses!

UNIT 06

6.1

Conversation 1

A: Have you ever been to Hungary?

B: Yeah, I went to the Sziget Festival a couple of years ago.

A: You went where?

B: The Sziget. I don't know if I'm pronouncing it right, but it's an enormous music festival in Budapest. It's held on this island in the middle of the Danube.

A: Oh right. So where did you stay?

B: We camped on the festival site. It was a bit of a nightmare, actually, because it absolutely poured down while we were there. The whole place was flooded and we got completely soaked – tent, sleeping bags, everything. Everything ended up covered in mud. It was crazy.

A: Couldn't you stay somewhere else?

B: Well, we actually did in the end. We met these really nice Hungarians who lived in the city and they put us up for a couple of nights.

A: Wow, that was generous! So would you go again?

A: Absolutely. We had a whale of a time in spite of the weather. I hardly slept the whole time we were there. There was so much going on.

Conversation 2

A: Did you go away in the holiday at all?

B: Yeah, I went to Turkey.

A: In August? Wasn't it a bit hot?

B: It was boiling, but then I love the heat – and you get quite dry heat there.

A: I guess. So did you enjoy it?

B Yeah, it was brilliant. We stayed in this absolutely amazing place on the south coast – right on top of the cliffs, overlooking the ocean.

A: Sounds nice.

B: It was. Wait, I've got a picture of it somewhere on my mobile.

A: Let's have a look. Wow! Look at that sunset. That's stunning!

B: I know. It was like that nearly every night.

A: That's great. Were there any other places nearby? It looks as if it's in the middle of nowhere.

B: It was a bit cut-off, yeah. It was a few kilometres along this winding track to the nearest village – well, town – but they had a minibus to take people there in the morning and to bring them back in the evening.

A: Wasn't that a pain, having to rely on the bus? Didn't they run more often than that?

B: No. It was a bit of pain, if I'm honest, but considering how cheap the place was, it was fair enough. I mean, you could walk back if you really couldn't bear to hang around and there was a little bay you scramble down to from the hotel. It was a great place as there was hardly anyone there. It was also actually really nice just chilling out, drinking tea and chatting to the other people in the hotel. It was cool.

A: Mmm. I think I'd get a bit restless after a couple of days. I don't really like being stuck in one place.

6.2

1 It was quite near the beach
2 The beach was quite crowded
3 It was a bit overwhelming
4 The surrounding area's quite nice
5 The food was pretty good

 6.3

Conversation 1

A: I have a booking under the name of Bergen.
B: Hmm. I'm sorry sir. We have no record of any reservation.
A: That can't be right. I spoke to someone just over a week ago.
B: Well, did you receive a confirmation by email or text?
A: Should I have?
B: That's our normal procedure, yes.
A: No. I haven't had anything.
B: Well, I'm afraid there's nothing I can do.
A: Haven't you got any rooms available?
B: I'm afraid not.
A: Oh, that's great, that is.

Conversation 2

C: Hello. I was wondering if you could help. My room's not very warm. Is there any way I can turn down the air-conditioning?
D: I'm afraid it's all controlled centrally.
C: Can't you do anything about it? I mean, you seem to have it on full blast. It's absolutely freezing!
D: I'm sorry, but we haven't had any other complaints about it.

Conversation 3

E: What do you mean you're not going to give us our deposit back?
F: Look at the state of the place. It's filthy!
E: Well, it wasn't particularly clean when we moved in.
F: And what about the washing machine? That'll need to be replaced.
E: That's hardly our fault. It's ancient. It was already falling apart – and I hardly think it's worth a whole month's rent.
F: Well, it's the combination of things. When you take everything into account – the stuff which is broken and missing, the mess – it all adds up.
E: What? To over a thousand pounds? You're taking the mickey! I can't believe you think we're going to pay that! It's ridiculous!

Conversation 4

G: I warned the landlord that boiler was a health hazard again and again.
H: I know. I remember you telling me ages ago.
G: They promised to fix it, but they just kept putting it off. Honestly, I'm furious about it!
H: I'm not surprised. Still, you were right to have it checked and to get it repaired. I mean, you could've suffocated while you were sleeping.
G: Well, you hear about carbon monoxide poisoning all the time, don't you?
H: It doesn't bear thinking about.
G: The thing is, though, I'm completely out of pocket now.

 6.4

One often hears that something was a culture shock – most often when people arrive in a new country, but also when they enter other kinds of new environments. However, it is usually described as being similar to jet lag – something which you experience for a couple of days and then get over – all you need is a good night's sleep! The reality is, however, that undergoing any big change – whether it's moving house, changing jobs or going to university – will bring about a 'culture shock'. Far from being a single event which is quickly forgotten, it is a process which may take several months – even years – to fully recover from. Psychologists more commonly call this process acculturation and highlight four distinct phases that nearly everyone goes through. These are elation – the joy and wonder you first have, where everything is so new and different; resistance – when things settle into a routine and you start to see everything which is bad in your new situation. You look back through rose-coloured glasses on your life before the change. This resistance is then followed by the transformation phase, where you swing more to the other extreme and start looking down on your previous existence and its culture. You may refuse to mix with people you used to know or who speak the same language. You might put them down when you do. Finally, people reach a state of integration where cultural differences are acknowledged and accepted and people appreciate both their own heritage and their new life.

That's the ideal situation, according to psychologist Perry Graves. "Everyone goes through the initial stages, but not everyone finishes the complete cycle. This can cause problems because they often don't recognise the phases of acculturation. For example, some people drop out of university in their first year, saying they don't relate to the middle class values or that it has nothing to do with reality and so on. In reality, these opinions are actually a symptom of the resistance stage. In other cases, people get stuck in a transformation phase, which may stop them moving on to new experiences or lead to them cutting themselves off from their roots, from people they've known for years and years. That can lead to a deep sense of unhappiness and to feelings of frustration."

UNIT 07

7.1

A: We got caught in this incredible storm on our way to visit friends in Rome.
B: Yeah?
A: Yeah, it was amazing! One moment we were in sunshine, the next we saw like a line on the road ahead and we drove through it and it was hail! Incredible – these enormous hailstones just started bouncing off the car! They were like as big as golf balls.
B: Really?
A: Well, maybe I'm exaggerating a bit, but they were pretty big and it was pretty scary.
B: I bet.
A: And then the lightning started. It was lighting up the whole sky. In the end, we pulled over to the side of the road till it all blew over.
B: Right.
A: And then it cleared up again – almost as quickly as it'd started.
B: It's amazing, isn't it? It actually reminds me of a time I was in Israel. We were visiting this town called Acre. Actually, I guess we should've realized because it'd been boiling all day – very humid and sticky – and then in the evening we were just taking a walk along the old walls – you get this great view across the bay to Haifa.
A: Uh huh.

B: And anyway suddenly we saw this incredible forked lightning across the bay followed by a faint rumble of thunder, and it just continued. It was so spectacular; we were just, like, transfixed watching it because, you know, it was still dry where we were. It was amazing – I could've watched it for hours, but then suddenly it started spitting and then just two seconds later the heavens opened and it started pouring down.

B: Oh no.

A: And of course we hadn't brought an umbrella or anything, so we just ran to the nearest café we could find and honestly it can't have been more than a minute but we got absolutely soaked. I must've poured like a litre of water out of my shoes.

B: No? Seriously?

A: I swear – sitting there in the café I think it was the wettest I've ever been!

7.2

Conversation 1

A: Oh dear! Those don't look very healthy.

B: I know. I bought them to cheer up the flat a bit. You know, a bit of colour and greenery, but they just look depressing now! It's strange. I've been watering them every day.

A: Maybe that's it. The soil's probably too wet. I think it rots the roots.

B: You're joking! You mean I'm drowning them?

A: I guess so!

Conversation 2

C: What are these flowers? They're lovely.

D: They're a menace!

C: What do you mean?

D: They just so invasive! They take over the whole place. None of the other plants can survive – and they're really difficult to get rid of as well.

C: But they look so nice.

D: Yeah, but they're not native to this country and they're destroying the local varieties.

C: That's too bad. I still like them, though.

Conversation 3

E: I wanted to take them something to say thank you for having me to stay and so I bought some flowers.

F: Fair enough.

E: Anyway, I handed them over and you know that feeling when you know you've put your foot in it, yeah? She kind of gave me this tight smile and nodded, but, you know, they were quite a big bouquet.

F: You kind of expect something different, yeah?

E: Exactly. Anyway, she said something to her husband and he took them away and there was a bit of an awkward silence and then we just carried on with the evening.

F: How weird!

E: Yeah. I thought so, but then I was telling someone about it and they told me people there only give those flowers when someone's passed away!

F: Oh no!

E: It was like I was cursing her or something – hoping she'd have a funeral!

Conversation 4

G: You're going to do what?

H: Gather mushrooms. Isn't gather right?

G: Yeah, yeah – gather, pick whatever. It's just, I don't know, I've never met anyone who does it.

H: No? Everyone does it here in Poland. Why don't people do it in Britain?

G: Well, it's dangerous, isn't it? Don't you worry about picking the wrong one and poisoning yourself? Some of them are lethal, aren't they?

H: We're brought up doing this. We know from when we're children what's OK and what's not. And it's good – you feel more connected with nature. Last time we went we saw a deer – really close.

G: Yeah? Wow! It sounds great.

Conversation 5

I: Here, take this. It should help.

J: What's in it?

I: It's just a herbal tea my gran makes. It's basically fennel seeds and leaves with a touch of lemon and honey. She swears by it.

J: I've never had fennel.

I: It's nice. It's got an aniseedy kind of taste. It's great. It'll really settle your stomach.

7.3

1 They're really difficult to get rid of.
2 It shot out of the bushes.
3 We waited till it all blew over.
4 It's beginning to ease off.
5 We were brought up doing it.
6 My gran swears by it.
7 It almost knocked me off my bike.
8 Were you affected by it?
9 The company has pulled out of it.
10 Experiments are being carried out on them.

UNIT 08

8.1

Conversation 1

A: How was your holiday?

B: Fine – apart from getting robbed.

A: Oh, you're joking! What happened?

B: Well, it was stupid, really. I should've been more careful. I was sitting in a café and these lads came up to me with a map asking for directions. I said I didn't understand and they walked off. Then I suddenly realised my bag was gone.

A: Oh no!

B: I'd left it under my chair and one of them must've grabbed it while they were talking to me.

A: That's terrible! Did it have much in it?

B: Fortunately not. My purse was in my pocket.

A: Still, it can't have been very nice.

B: Yeah, it was a bit upsetting, but I didn't let it spoil the holiday.

A: Well, that's good.

Conversation 2

C: What're you reading about?

D: Oh, it's about that girl who got stabbed outside her school.

C: Oh, I know. It's awful! They really should do something about kids carrying knives.

D: I know. Apparently, she might've been involved in some kind of gang.

C: Oh really. So do they know who did it?

D: I don't think so, but I mean, someone must've seen it – it was broad daylight.

C: I know! I guess people could be just too scared to come forward and talk to the police.

D: Hmm. It must be awful for the parents, losing a child.

C: Absolutely! Did you see them on TV last night?

D: No.

C: It was dreadful. Really upsetting.

Conversation 3

E: That's ridiculous!

F: What?

E: Did you see this thing about this guy being arrested for holding his ex-girlfriend captive?

F: No. Doesn't sound that funny.

E: Well, it is kind of because he did it to get her to do his ironing and the washing-up!

F: The ironing? You are joking, aren't you?

E: Well that's what it says here. Says he seized her in a pub, dragged her into his car, drove her home and forced her to do his ironing.

F: And this was his ex-girlfriend.

E: Yeah. Not that that should make any difference.

F: Absolutely. But you wonder, what was he thinking?

E: He's just a dinosaur. You can see why she dumped him!

 8.2

Now, many of you may have seen the remarkable video clip showing hundreds and hundreds of Filipino prisoners – all dressed in orange uniforms and dancing to Michael Jackson's *Thriller*. This ... um ... experimental approach to physical fitness has attracted worldwide attention and was apparently all the brainchild of Byron Garcia, a security consultant at the Cebu Provincial Detention and Rehabilitation Center in the Philippines. The dancing is compulsory and has, it is claimed, dramatically improved discipline in the prison.

So, the question is, is this something we can learn from over here. Would our prisons be better places if we introduced mass dancing hours? And if not, why not? And does anyone have any other ideas on how can we make prisons work better? We want to hear what you think, as ever.

 8.3

G=Gary, D=Doreen, N=Nigel

G: OK, I think we have our first caller. Yes, hello. Doreen in Birmingham.

D: Oh hello, Gary. Yes, well, what I wanted to say was that I think we've got it all wrong, the way we're doing things.

G: Why's that, then, Doreen?

D: Well, they're like holiday camps, aren't they, prisons today. These people, these CRIMINALS, they're animals! They've done horrid, wicked things and yet they're living in there better than some of us are living out here on the outside. TVs, they've got, video games, mobiles, all manner of technology . . . visits from their wives, all sorts. They lead a life of luxury, most of them.

G: Well, that's certainly one way of looking at things.

D: It's true, I'm telling you! So I think the idea of free dance classes – well, it's ridiculous! The world's gone mad, Gary.

G: And what would you like to see instead, Doreen?

D: What I want is a return to the good old days. I want them punished. Make them work Gary.

G: That's not a bad idea, Doreen. What kind of thing did you have in mind? Making clothes, perhaps? Or cleaning the streets?

D: Breaking rocks would be better. Just hard, hard, nasty, dirty, physical work. Breaking rocks in the sun, that's what I'd have them all doing.

G: OK. Well, Doreen. I can't say I'm with you on that one, but thanks for taking the time to call. And our next caller is . . . Nigel. Nigel in Manchester. Hello.

N: Oh hello, Gary. Good morning. Yes, well, firstly, I'd just like to say that – with all due respect – Doreen doesn't seem to know what she's talking about. Anyone who thinks that prisons are fun needs their head examined. And as for the suggestion that breaking rocks would help – well, God save us all! The way I see it, the main problem with prisons today is that we place too much emphasis on punishment and don't pay enough attention to rehabilitation – to helping these people lead useful, independent lives of their own once they are released.

G: Nigel, I couldn't agree more. I could not agree more.

N: And as a result re-offending rates are appalling! Young offenders go into prison for the first time and they make contacts, meet other, more professional, criminals and they come out and go on to commit ever more serious crimes.

G: I know what you mean, Nigel.

N: What I'd like to see, Gary, is inmates, prisoners, learning skills that'll help them avoid a life of crime once they've been released. Fine, make them do work that's useful for society while they're inside, or give them dance hours or whatever, but also teach them how to read and write, teach them computer skills, teach them how to learn. It's the only way we'll ever break this vicious circle of crime and prison and crime again.

REVIEW 02

 R 2.1

volunteer work

a master class

crosswords

racket sports

a comic fair

a fitness fanatic

a goalkeeper

injury time

rock climbing

a camping van

a health hazard

a forest fire

hailstones

identity theft

a street robbery

the death penalty

community service

a rehabilitation centre

 R 2.2

Building work on an animal research laboratory funded by Oxford University has been stopped following several months of threats and harassment by members of extremist animal rights groups. The company involved in the construction of the lab has pulled out of the project amidst fears for the safety of both site workers and the firm's board members.

R 2.3

1 When the race started, the conditions were ideal; the water was beautifully calm, but there was a good breeze. We all set off and to begin with, we managed to keep up with the others, but before we knew it, it really started blowing and we found ourselves heading towards the cliffs! We tried and tried, but just couldn't get control of the boat. In the end, we had to be rescued.

2 When we first inherited the place, it was totally filthy and the roof leaked. I was overwhelmed and thought we should get the work done by someone, but my husband decided to tackle it himself. He's been slaving away, working on it for months. I wouldn't have had the stamina or patience, but he's fit and he's always liked going round flea markets and repairing old things, so he doesn't mind. And it's looking really good now.

3 I took it up after I tore my knee ligaments when I was fouled playing football. It was horrible! I nearly passed out with the pain. After the operation, I had to lie in bed for six weeks and not move my leg, so my mum gave me some wool and needles and showed me how to do it. I felt a bit self-conscious at first. I associated it with my gran, or girls sewing, but, you know, I really got into it and I'm actually quite good at it too. The first big thing I did was to make a jumper for my mum.

4 I was really looking forward to it. It was quite a good match, but in the second half, the away team were awarded a dubious penalty. It really looked as if the attacker dived. When they scored the penalty, it sparked some crowd trouble: people smashed up some seats and threw them on the pitch. We left then before it got any worse, but I heard afterwards that someone had been stabbed – absolutely terrifying!

5 We hook up with some friends who are really into it and we often go for dinner afterwards. To be honest, we're not that good. I think we're both a bit too clumsy. We sometimes actually bump into the other couples. However, we are getting better and we're certainly getting into shape, because you work up a bit of a sweat. The Latin music's good too.

Unit 09

9.1

Part 1

M = Melissa, R = Richard

M: So how're you finding your job? Is it going OK?

R: Oh, it's all right, I suppose. It's not what I want to do long-term, though.

M: No? How come?

R: Oh, it's just so menial! I'm not using any of the skills I learned at university – and my boss is just dreadful! I seem to spend most of my time running round making him cups of tea and photocopying things and if I ask about doing other stuff, he just tells me to be patient and then starts going on about how he did the same when he started at the company.

M: Well, maybe it's true.

R: Oh, I don't know. I was talking to this girl who joined at the same time as me and she said she was learning loads in her department – being really stretched, apparently. It makes me think it's maybe more about me!

M: Oh, I am sorry! If it's that bad, maybe you should think about handing in your notice!

R: I don't know. I guess it might get better if I just give it a bit more time.

M: Well, you'd think so. I mean, it is a big company, isn't it?

R: Mmm, but maybe that's it, you see. Maybe it's a bit too big. Anyway, I can't see myself staying there long term.

M: No? Well, if you do decide to make a move, you're bound to get lots of offers.

R: I don't know about that, but it's nice of you to say so!

M: It's true!

Part 2

R: Well, anyway. What about you! How's your job going?

M: Oh, you probably won't want to hear to this, but it's great, yeah. It's going really well.

R: Well, I'm glad at least one of us is happy, anyway!

M: Yeah, it's amazing. I've been getting loads of on-the-job training – and they've been letting me go into college one day a week as well, to improve my skills. It's been really stimulating. I've also been meeting clients quite a bit. Oh, and I gave my first big presentation last week.

R: Wow! ... sounds amazing. Did it go OK?

M: Yeah, it went brilliantly. I've got my first business trip coming up next month – to New York. And I'm applying for promotion at the moment too.

R: Really? Already? Do you think you'll get it?

M: Hopefully, yeah, but you never know, do you?

R: Oh, you're bound to. From the sound of it, you're their star employee. I can just see you in five years' time, running the entire firm.

M: Ha!

R: And if the worst comes to the worst, I'll end up knocking on the door of your office, begging you for a job!

9.2

And finally, it's official – the paperboy is a dying breed. For the first time, there are more adults delivering newspapers in the United States than young people. The steady shift from youth carriers to adults over the last few years is down to a number of factors: newspapers want deliveries to take place in the mornings rather than afternoons after school hours and more adults – particularly retired people – are grabbing the opportunity to earn some extra income to supplement their salaries or pensions. There are also those who blame the economic boom of the early noughties – families could afford to buy more things for their kids, and so many kids settled for the comfort of a sofa and Playstation rather than take to the streets to earn pocket money.

Many delivery companies say adults are more reliable and provide a better service, but there are those who are saddened by the changes. Bud Keynes, managing director of the Milwaukee Herald: "Doing a paper route when I was 13 was my first experience of business. It taught me responsibility, how to manage my time and communicate with people. More than once, I got soaked or froze to death or got chased by dogs, but it was character building. Too many young people these days enter what is a very competitive job market lacking those basic business skills that you get from being a carrier."

9.3

If you haven't heard of the Bologna Process yet, then the odds are that you soon will. And no, before you ask, it's NOT a new way of cooking pasta! Instead, the Bologna process is a voluntary initiative that is changing the face of education across Europe – and that's starting to have a knock-on effect elsewhere as well.

What I'm going to try and do today is tell you a bit about the initiative before moving on to explore what it involves in more detail.

Named after the Italian city where the idea was first put forward, the Bologna process aims to create a European "higher education area" by making academic degree and quality control standards more compatible and easier to compare with one another.

Now, for many people across the EU, any mention of Europe-wide initiatives is terrifying! There have been countless ridiculous media scare stories about unelected bureaucrats in Brussels telling us what size bananas we are – and aren't – allowed to eat or about football supporters supposedly being forced to wear earplugs at matches, due to crazy health and safety measures. Obviously, for some traditionalists, the idea of any kind of standardisation is too much for them to bear.

However, it seems to me that almost anything is better than the way things were. Under the old system, credits were sometimes awarded to students based simply on the number of hours they'd done. This led to some countries refusing to recognise qualifications from others. Under Bologna, credits will be based on learning outcomes – or what students have actually achieved – rather than length of study. There will also be greater emphasis placed on project work, practical experiments, research, presentations and so on.

This will mean both students and academic staff can move around the Euro zone more easily, without always having to explain their qualifications! It should also mean that Europe becomes a more attractive destination for non-European students.

The main change happening is that most European countries are getting rid of the four- or five-year degree courses they used to offer and instead are starting to adopt a British and Irish style system of three-year degrees. These are then followed by two-year Master's degrees and three-year doctoral degrees – or PhDs.

Many countries have introduced radical reforms, changing not only degree and Master's courses, but introducing tuition fees, restructuring departments and allowing universities to have much greater autonomy, decentralising the curricula, allowing the creation of private universities, and so on.

Of course, these changes have not gone unchallenged – and what I want to do now is to consider the negative responses more fully. Public reaction has been particularly heated in Greece, where there have been massive demonstrations against Bologna, sit-ins and even riots. France has seen general strikes – and even the UK is worried that it will now lose its appeal, as it is no longer the only country to offer shorter degree courses!

UNIT 10

🔊 10.1

N = Nina, L = Linda, V = Vita

N: So how much longer have you got?

L: Three more days. By four o'clock Friday we'll have finished every single one. I can't wait!

V: Me neither. The Physics one yesterday was a nightmare.

L: I know! I'm sure I failed it.

N: You must be sick of it all.

V: I am. If I revise much more my head's going to explode!

L: Just keep telling yourself: three more days, three more days.

N: So shall we go out and celebrate on Friday, then?

V: That sounds like an excellent idea.

L: Yeah, I'd be up for that as well. Do you have anywhere in mind?

N: I thought that Equinox might be fun.

L: Where's that?

N: Oh, don't you know it? It's the big disco on the main square in town. It's great.

V: If you like that kind of place! I have to say, it's not my kind of thing. I can't stand the music down there and besides – it's full of horrible guys.

N: Oh! I thought it was OK when I went there, but if you'd rather go somewhere else, that's fine by me.

L: Well, personally, I'd quite like to get something to eat at some point, if that's all right with you.

V: Yeah, that sounds good. Any thoughts on where?

L: Well, Rico's is always a good bet.

V: Oh, it's such a rip-off, that place. Last time I went there, I spent something like sixty euros. Can't we go somewhere cheaper?

N: How about that Brazilian place near the station?

V: Guanabara? Yeah, that'd be fine with me. Linda?

L: Yeah, whatever. I'm easy. They have music later on down there, don't they?

N: Yeah, they do salsa after ten.

V: It sounds ideal. So what time do you want to meet? Seven? Seven thirty?

N: I'm working till six and it'd be nice if I could go home first, so could we make it eight? I'll have had time to get changed and freshen up a bit by then.

V: Yeah, fine.

N: And I'll phone and book a table – just to be on the safe side.

L: OK. I'll ring a few other people and see if anyone else is up for it – and see you down there.

N: OK. Brilliant. Bye.

V: Bye.

🔊 10.2

Conversation 1

A: Sorry, but you couldn't pass me the salt, could you? Thank you. They look nice.

B: They are. They're lovely. Have you tried that aubergine dip? It's gorgeous.

A: Hmm. I have to say I'm not that keen on aubergines. There's something wrong with them as a vegetable.

B: You're joking! Aubergines – they're the king of vegetables! Although strictly speaking, they're a fruit, of course.

A: Mmm.

B: They're so versatile. You can fry them, grill them, have them mashed, stuffed, barbecued ... .

A: Right.

B: Did you know that they used to use the skin as a dye? The Chinese apparently used to polish their teeth with it!

A: Sorry, I've just seen my friend Mercedes. I must just go and talk to her. I've been meaning to all evening.

Conversation 2

C: So how do you know Niall?

D: Who?

C: Er .. the person whose party this is.

D: Oh right. Well, he's like the friend of a friend of my flatmate. I don't know why I'm here, really. I feel a bit left out. My flatmate dragged me along because she thought she wouldn't know anyone – and now she's met someone. Oh – that's her over there, with that blonde guy. I think I might just go. How do you know Niall anyway?

C: I'm his fiancée! You did know this is a party to celebrate our engagement, didn't you?

D: No, actually I didn't. Congratulations, though! It's a great party.

Conversation 3

E: I'm glad I'm not the only person who couldn't stand it any more.

F: Tell me about it! It was so stuffy in there, wasn't it? You could hardly breathe.

E: Yeah. They need some air conditioning or something.

F: The speaker wasn't exactly helping either, was he? I thought I was going to fall asleep at one point there.

E: Yeah. He's very dull, isn't he? I think I might just go and grab a coffee instead of going back in.

F: That sounds like a good idea. Do you mind if I join you?

Conversation 4

G: Is this the queue for the toilet?

H: I'm afraid so.

G: I love your top.

H: Oh, thanks.

G: It's quite unusual. Where did you get it?

H: I actually picked it up in a second-hand clothes stall. It was only five pounds.

G: Really? That's fantastic! I never really bother looking in places like that. I mean, there's a second-hand place near me, but the stuff in there always looks in pretty poor condition. That looks brand new, though.

H: I think it's quite old actually, but the stall I got it from is just fantastic – just really nice stuff.

G: Mind you, it's so difficult getting stuff in my size.

H: I can imagine. It must be hard. I've got a friend who's maybe your height and she's always moaning about it as well. That dress is lovely, though.

G: It's great, isn't it? I actually just found this place online. Oh look – it's your turn.

Conversation 5

I: Sorry. I couldn't help overhearing. Did you say Everton beat Chelsea?

J: Yeah.

I: What was the final score?

J: They thrashed them! Five-nil.

I: You're joking! I saw the beginning of the game, but then I had to go out.

J: Are you an Everton fan?

I: No – West Ham.

J: Oh dear! You can't be enjoying things much this year!

I: Ah, it's just a temporary loss of form. It won't last. We're just going through a bad patch at the moment. We'll be all right by the end of the season. We'll finish in the top half of the league.

J: You're optimistic! I can't see it myself.

I: Trust me! It'll all work out OK. Anyway, sorry, I didn't want to stop you chatting.

J: That's OK.

10.3

Conversation 1

A: Miserable weather, isn't it?

B: Yeah, awful. It's been like this for weeks, hasn't it?

A: I know. I can't remember when I last saw the sun. Can you?

Conversation 2

C: You don't remember me, do you?

D: It's Yuka, isn't it?

C: No. It's Naomi.

Conversation 3

E: Excuse me. You haven't got a light, have you?

F: Yeah. Here you go.

E: Thanks.

F: You couldn't lend me a euro, could you?

E: No, sorry.

Conversation 4

G: You missed the class on Monday, didn't you?

H: There wasn't one, was there? It was closed for the holiday, wasn't it?

G: No. Mind you, you didn't miss much. It was quite boring.

H: Well, to be honest the whole course is a bit disappointing, isn't it?

Conversation 5

I: I love that jacket. It's from Zara, isn't it?

J: No, I got it from a shop called Monsoon.

I: Really? You couldn't tell me where it is, could you?

J: Sorry. I've forgotten the name of the road. You know the McDonald's, don't you? Well, it's the next road down on the left.

Unit 11

11.1

A = Assistant, C = Customer

A: Hi. How can I help you today?

C: Hi. I reserved a car online. Here's my voucher and my driving licence.

A: Yep. OK. Let's have a look. Right. We have your car ready, but we're running a special offer this week. You can upgrade to the next range for just two euros a day, so you could have an estate car if you like.

C: It's OK. We don't have much luggage.

A: Are you sure? It's a bit more powerful as well.

C: No, I think something smaller – more fuel-efficient – is OK.

A: Fine. You ordered GPS, yes?

C: That's right.

A: OK. Would you like our additional insurance cover for damage to tyres and windscreen?

C: Isn't that already included in what I paid for online?

A: No. I think it's in the small print – and this is only three euros extra a day.

C: What are the chances of anything going wrong?

A: Well, it's up to you, but better safe than sorry, isn't it?

C: I suppose so. OK, then. It is quite cheap.

A: Fine. Can I just have your credit card? That's for the insurance, the cost of the fuel and also your deposit on the car – which is returnable when you bring the car back.

C: Right, so should I return the tank full?

A: No, there's no need, but it is full now. It's diesel, by the way.

C: OK.

A: So could you just sign where I've marked with a cross? You may want to check the car as well before you leave. There are some scratches here and here and a small dent in the rear door.

C: OK. Great.

A: Have a good trip.

🔊 11.2

A = Assistant, C = Customer

C: Hello. Right Car Rentals.

A: Oh hello. I wonder if you can help me. My name's John Farnham. I was in this morning and picked up a car from you.

C: Oh hello, Mr. Farnham. How's it going?

A: Not that well, to be honest. I'm actually calling because we have a problem with the car. I was driving along the motorway and something flew up at the windscreen and cracked it.

C: Oh, I am sorry to hear that. How bad is it?

A: Quite bad. It's a very big crack. I'm uncomfortable driving with it like this.

C: OK. I totally understand. You'll need to ring our breakdown service. The number's written in the book that came with the car.

A: Oh, OK. I'll do that now. How long do you think they will be?

C: We guarantee they'll be with you within four hours

A: Four hours? Is that really the best you can do?

C: Well, it's usually less. Still, at least you've got insurance!

🔊 11.3

S = Sanjar, L = Lily

S: Lily. What's up? You look really fed up!

L: I just got a parking ticket!

S: Oh no! That's so annoying! Where were you parked?

L: Just round the corner. The thing that's really infuriating, though, is that it happened while I'd gone to look for change for the machine.

S: You're joking!

L: No! I parked my car and then I suddenly realised I only had notes. There was no-one around, so I went off to a shop to get change and when I got back … .

S: That's terrible. Didn't you see the traffic warden?

L: I did look, but they'd vanished. They can't have been there long. I think they must've run away to avoid any arguments.

S: Probably! Couldn't you appeal?

L: It's not worth it. In the end, it's basically my word against theirs.

S: I know. You'd never win that one. How much is the fine?

L: £80! AND I got a speeding ticket the other day after I got flashed by a speed camera! That was another eighty – and three points on my licence.

S: Oh Lily! Poor you! They're so strict on these things.

L: But it's so over-the-top. I mean, I was only doing three or four miles over the speed limit. What annoys me is the fact that people who are essentially honest are being criminalised for these little things.

S: I know! And it's not as though people drive that fast here. You should go to Iran. You take your life in your hands driving there. People, they go so fast, but really close behind you and they don't use their brakes. They just flash their lights!

L: Ooh! It's horrible when people do that. I don't know about Iran, but I have to say, I drove through Paris last year and that was terrifying. There were like six lanes and everyone was swerving in and out of the lanes. I got cut up a couple of times and I had to brake, but then I got beeped at!

S: You see! That kind of thing doesn't happen so often here. People really are more polite here. The thing that amazed me when I first came here was the fact that people actually stopped for pedestrians at crossings. That hardly ever happens back home! You have to be really careful not to get knocked over.

L: It can't be that bad, can it? Drivers here can be very inconsiderate and I've had plenty of people swearing at me in London.

S: Believe me! It's nothing compared to Tehran. Sometimes there you're not even safe on the pavement! People ignore stop signs, shoot through red lights. Honestly, it's anarchy!

UNIT 12

🔊 12.1

Conversation 1

M = Michelle, J = Joop

M: Hello.

J: Oh, hi Michelle. It's me, Joop. Listen I'm just ringing to say we're not coming later. Kaatje isn't feeling very well.

M: Oh dear. What's up?

J: She actually fainted this morning while we were out.

M: You're joking!

J: No. We were in a shop and she suddenly had a dizzy spell and then she just passed out.

M: Oh no! Is she all right, now?

J Yeah, she recovered quite quickly, but still she says sorry she'd rather stay here.

M: Don't be silly! Tell her there's no need to apologise and I understand.

J: Thanks. I will.

M: It's not this bug that's going round, is it? One of my colleagues had it recently and said it left him quite faint and stiff and achy.

J: I don't think so. She hasn't had a fever or cough. In fact, she's been complaining about dizzy spells for a while and she's lost weight. She has been under a lot of pressure at work recently as well.

M: That is a bit worrying. Has she been to see anyone?

J: No, not yet and we're supposed to be going away for a few days. I don't know whether we should stay here and get an appointment or leave it till we come back.

M: Well, maybe all she needs is a break.

J: Mmm. Maybe.

M: I know you're worried, but if it's only a few days … . Why don't you see how she is when you get back?

J: I guess.

M: Anyway, send her my love and tell her I'm thinking of her.

Conversation 2

C = Caitlin, N = Nina

N: Hello.

C: Hello. Nina? Hi. It's me, Caitlin.

N: Hi! Where are you? I was expecting you at 6.

C: Yeah, sorry, but Lachlan's had some kind of reaction to something he ate. We're in Rome hospital.

N: You're joking! Is he all right?

C: Yes, yes. He's fine now. He's with the nurse and they're running some tests.

N: No! What happened?

C: Well, we were in the middle of lunch and he suddenly said he was feeling funny – that he was a bit short of breath – and then I noticed a rash. There were spots breaking out all round his mouth.

Then his lips just started swelling up and he was really struggling to breathe.

N: That sounds terrifying. He is all right now, though?

C: Yes, yes, honestly. We rushed him to the hospital – someone from the restaurant actually took us – and they dealt with him very quickly. He had an injection to reduce the swelling and oxygen to help him breathe.

N: Oh Caitlin. You sound so calm. It must've been awful.

C: Well, I wasn't at the time, but everyone's been so good to us. Anyway, listen, they're going to keep him in overnight – to be on the safe side.

N: Oh, right.

C: Sorry. I know we're supposed to be going to the concert tonight.

N: Don't be silly! Lachlan's health is much more important than a concert. When do you think you'll get here tomorrow?

C: It shouldn't be too late. The doctor's going to come at 9, so if he gives the all clear, we should be at yours by lunchtime.

N: OK. Well, listen. Give him a hug from me and don't worry about rushing to get here tomorrow.

🔊 12.2

A <u>man</u> goes to a <u>doc</u>tor // and <u>says</u> // "Doc. // I <u>think</u> there's <u>some</u>thing <u>wrong</u> with <u>me</u>. // <u>Every</u> time I <u>poke</u> myself // it <u>hurts</u>. // <u>Look</u>!" // And he starts <u>poking</u> himself. // He <u>pokes</u> himself // in the <u>leg</u>. // "<u>Ouch</u>" // He <u>pokes</u> himself // in the <u>ribs</u> // "<u>Aagh</u>" // He <u>pokes</u> himself // in the <u>head</u> // and he literally <u>screams</u> in <u>agony</u> // "<u>Aaaaagh</u>! // You <u>see</u> what I <u>mean</u> <u>Doc</u>? // You <u>see</u> how <u>bad</u> it is? // What's <u>happening</u> to <u>me</u>?" // And the <u>doctor</u> re<u>plies</u> // "<u>Yes</u>, // you <u>seem</u> to have <u>bro</u>ken your <u>finger</u>!"

🔊 12.3

P = Presenter, DF = Damian Frisch, CL = Cindy Leong, CS = Charlotte Staples

P: The incredible boom in medical tourism over the last few years has been one of the more interesting side effects of globalization. For quite some time already, we've been used to the idea of medical staff moving from country to country, while more recently many hospitals have also started outsourcing record keeping and the reading of X-rays to developing countries in an attempt to cut costs. However, what's remarkably new is the ever-increasing numbers of patients from developed western countries who are opting to go abroad for treatment.

It's estimated that before too long over six million Americans and over one hundred thousand Britons will be travelling overseas for private medical or dental work – all done at knockdown prices. Countries such as Mexico, Jordan, Malaysia, India and Thailand all stand to benefit from a trade expected to soon be generating over four billion dollars a year. The question arises, however, as to whether this is a genuine win-win situation.

Damian Frisch is a German lawyer specialising in medical negligence cases.

DF: I don't want to be accused of causing panic. I myself have had dental work done in Poland and it was excellent. However, anyone thinking of going abroad for treatment needs to know they are taking a risk. You have to be very careful and do extensive research before making a decision. Otherwise, you are gambling with your health as well as your money. Fraudulent claims and dishonest money-making schemes are commonplace and are on the

increase – and the regulatory environment in many places is not as rigorous as it should be. In addition to this, many treatments are still experimental and all too often there is no after-care as patients return to their home countries. My advice would be it's better to be safe than sorry – and if something sounds too good to be true, then it probably is.

P: Cindy Leong, the CEO of a hospital in Kuala Lumpur that's particularly popular with foreigners, acknowledges that there are some opportunistic practitioners, but that this should not detract form the reality of the change that is happening.

CL: The old stereotypes of Asia as some kind of impoverished Third World are now very outdated. We boast some of the best doctors in the world and have a wide array of ultra-modern hospitals. On top of that, a few of the operations we offer now are so hi-tech that they are actually only found in Malaysia!

In addition, we offer all-inclusive packages for visitors: we can arrange visas and flights, offer a range of special menus, look after patients' companions, even book holiday resorts for post-surgery recuperation – and all at very reasonable prices. At the same time, of course, 90% of our patients are still local – and they all benefit from our innovations. Furthermore, we ensure that a portion of our profits go towards providing at least a basic level of health care for the poor, so everyone stands to benefit".

RP: Certainly, that's how Charlotte Staples, a bank clerk from Rotherham, England, feels.

CS: I had a hip replacement operation in Jordan last year and I can't speak highly enough of the place. I'd been on the waiting list in England for almost a year and I reached the point where I was becoming a very impatient patient! If I'd gone private here, it would've cost me something in the region of ten thousand pounds. As it was, I got my flight, a ten-day stay in hospital, a pioneering new surgical technique AND a two-week holiday afterwards for just over five thousand. Sun, sand, surgery AND savings!"

REVIEW 03

🔊 R3.1

auto<u>ma</u>tic
claustro<u>pho</u>bic
con<u>ta</u>gious
<u>de</u>solate
<u>frau</u>dulent
<u>glo</u>balised
in<u>fu</u>riating
<u>ir</u>ritable
<u>me</u>nial
pio<u>nee</u>ring
re<u>mar</u>kable
<u>ri</u>gorous
<u>spi</u>ritual
<u>sti</u>mulating
<u>ter</u>minal
under<u>va</u>lued
unpat<u>rio</u>tic
<u>ver</u>satile

🔊 R3.2

Do extensive research before making a decision. Otherwise, you are gambling with your health as well as your money. Fraudulent claims and dishonest money-making schemes are commonplace and are on the increase – and the regulatory environment in many places is not as rigorous as it should be.

R3.3

1 On the way to the wedding, I was overtaking a van on the motorway when this guy suddenly appeared behind me. I had to slam on the brakes and swerve to avoid him and then I spun off the road. I should've looked more carefully in my mirror, but I'm sure he was well over the speed limit. Still, it could've been a lot worse. I was more or less uninjured except for some cuts and bruises. The worst thing was I missed the party.

2 I consult the host and then do everything from setting up the marquee to sorting out catering and running things on the night. There are a lot of logistics so it's a nightmare when the host invites guests without mentioning it to me. Once, we had 300 guests when I was expecting 150. We struggled to cope and it all got a bit out of hand. It wouldn't have been a problem if I'd been told.

3 Of course people should enjoy their parties and barbecues at this time of year, but people don't think of the problems. Most are minor illnesses and injuries – upset stomachs, bumps and burns. Yesterday we had someone with a broken toe caused by dropping a cola bottle on it! However, some are really serious. We've had someone with a fractured skull from slipping on spilt fat, and another with kidney failure after eating half-cooked chicken! We just want people to be conscious of this and take care!

4 Today I'm going to talk to you about the history of social events. People generally assume that parties and the like are the same now as in the past, but they'd be mistaken. To show this, I'd like to begin by giving you an overview of how one social celebration – Christmas – has changed over the last 1000 years. I'll move on to consider why these changes have happened and highlight similar changes in social get-togethers and the concept of parties.

5 I've been working so hard for my finals, I've been stuck inside the library and my room, and I've hardly set foot outside for months. So when I graduate, I'm going to start by throwing a big party for some friends. I've got it all planned. It's in this place on the beach and it's going to be fancy dress. After that, I want to take some time off. I don't want to go straight into a job and just work through to retirement.

Unit 13

13.1

Conversation 1

A: Are you reading that interview with Taylor Fox?

B: No, not really. I was just flicking through. Why?

A: Oh, I just thought it was interesting. Did you know she's got two adopted kids from Malawi?

B: I did, actually. From what I heard, she couldn't have kids of her own.

A: No. As I understand it, she'd already had a son with Scott Blake.

B: She's married to Scott Blake?

A: WAS. They got divorced a while back. She's with Cody Lescott now.

B: Of course! I was going to say. So how come she split up with Scott Blake? He seems really nice.

A: That's the image, but it turns out he's a bit of a jerk. He'd been leading a bit of a double life – he was very popular with the ladies and she decided she just couldn't trust him! That's why they called it a day.

B: You're joking! He comes across as so clean-cut and pleasant.

A: Well, apparently not. It seems – how shall I put it – that he likes to spread the love a lot!

B: I see. Well, she's better off without him, then.

A: Absolutely. You should read the interview. She had quite an interesting upbringing. She just sounds very down-to-earth.

Conversation 2

C: Have you seen Ollie recently?

D: No, not for ages. Have you?

C: Yeah, I saw him last week. We went for a drink.

D: Right. How is he?

C: Oh, he's good. Really good, actually. You know he left his job at Byfix?

D: No! Really? I was told he was doing well there.

C: He was, he was. But he'd actually been thinking about leaving for a while – basically ever since he started going out with Leila.

D: Who's Leila?

C: When was the last time you saw him?

D: It must've been about a year ago. As far as I know, he wasn't seeing anyone then.

C: Hmm maybe. Well, anyway, she's Finnish. They met on holiday. She lives in Helsinki. They were commuting between here and there more or less every two weeks, but in the end, he decided to quit his job and move there.

D: You're joking!

C: No. Apparently, she's got a really good job there so they can both afford to live off her salary

D: So he's just going to be a househusband, then!

C: Yeah, well, he said he'd sent CVs to a couple of companies, but if that came to nothing he was going to retrain as an English teacher

D: Really? Well, that's a change for the better!

13.2

1 The second Monday of every January is called *Seijin No Hi* – Coming-of-Age Day – here in Japan. Everyone who turns 20 that year is invited to attend a special ceremony. 20 is the age you become a legal adult here. People gather at a city hall, a stadium, or wherever their city decides to hold the ceremony. The girls usually wear traditional Japanese outfits, which can cost many thousands of pounds, and guys wear either suits or hakamas, which are kind of like kimonos for guys. There then follow lengthy congratulations speeches from the mayor and other dignitaries, after which everyone goes out and meets old school friends and parties!

2 Traditionally, Moroccan marriages were arranged, but nowadays people choose their own partners. Our parents still have the power of veto, though. Weddings join two families together, so parents are important. Our weddings are elaborate affairs and can last from three to seven days. First, each family has a big party in their own home, and then the groom proceeds to the home of his bride, accompanied by his guests, all singing and dancing and beating drums (or honking their horns!). The bride and groom are then lifted onto the shoulders of the crowd and paraded among their guests.

   Later, the bride changes into a traditional outfit and the party continues. Around dawn, she changes again, and the couple disappear to a hotel for a while. Parties and feasting continue throughout the week, though, as the newlyweds visit friends and relatives.

3 Retirement age here in my country is 65 for men and 60 for

women. We're not legally obliged to stop working then, but we can if we want to, which is always good to know. I actually took early retirement – after my wife talked me into it! To begin with, I found it . . . well, not exactly traumatic, but difficult, shall we say. It certainly took me quite a while to get used to having so much free time on my hands, but now I've finally started getting the hang of it. I get a decent annual pension – about 75% of my final year's salary – so I can't complain. My wife and I both still have our health, which is the most important thing, and we have three grandchildren now as well, who we adore.

4 My grandmother died last year at the age of 90. There were over 3000 mourners at her funeral; everyone was crying and wailing and lots of people wanted to touch her because she died such a good death. People felt that touching her could bring good luck. My grandmother had what we in China call 'a five-blossoms death'. The five blossoms represent things you want to happen in your life. The five blossoms are marriage, having a son, being respected, having a grandson who loves you, and dying in your sleep after a long life. This is the best way to die.

UNIT 14

🔊 14.1

Conversation 1

A: Hi. I'd like to open a bank account, please.

B: Certainly. Do you have some form of identification?

A: Yes, I've got my passport with me. Is that OK?

B: Yes, that's fine, but we also need proof of your current address. Do you have a utility bill – a gas bill or electricity bill or anything – with you?

A: No, I don't, I'm afraid. You see, I'm not directly paying bills at the moment. I'm living in a shared house, a student house, and I just pay a fixed amount every month.

B: OK. Well, do you have any proof of income or a National Insurance number at all?

A: No. This is crazy! I'm a student. I'm not working. I have my passport, my driving licence from back home, three cheques I want to deposit and this letter from my uni.

B: Oh, can I just have a quick look at that? Ah OK, I see. Right, well this should be fine. What kind of account were you after?

A: Just a normal current account.

B: OK. Well, what we can do is give you a three-month trial period on a current account, which will cost you ten pounds a month, and if you do decide to stay with us after that, the thirty pounds will be refunded.

A: This is extortion, really, but what choice do I have?

B: OK. Well, if you can just fill out these forms … .

Conversation 2

C: Hi. I'm flying to Caracas and I need to get hold of some Venezuelan currency. I'm not sure what it's called, I'm afraid.

D: No problem. I'll just check for you. Yes, there we are. It's the bolivar. How much are you after?

C: About five hundred pounds' worth, please.

D: OK. That shouldn't be a problem. Let's see. Oh, I'm awfully sorry, sir, but I'm afraid we're actually completely out of bolivar.

C: Oh, OK.

D: I wouldn't have thought we usually hold that much, anyway, but it looks as if it's all been bought.

C: Ah, that's annoying.

D: I'm terribly sorry. Would US dollars do? As I understand it, they're often accepted instead of the local currency. Otherwise, I'm sure you can just change money once you arrive or make a withdrawal from a cash point there.

C: In theory, yes, but I've been caught out before thinking that. Maybe I'll get some dollars just to be on the safe side.

D: Of course. How much would you like?

C: I'll take three hundred, please.

D: OK. That'll be two hundred and six pounds seventy-five pence.

C: Really? What's the exchange rate?

D: We're currently selling at one forty eight to the pound and then there's 2% commission on all transactions.

C: Right. Well, that's the way it goes, I suppose. Can I pay by Visa?

D: Yeah, of course. Just pop the card in there. And just enter your PIN number. Thanks.

🔊 14.2

1 I'll look into the matter at once.

2 The computers are being very slow today.

3 There must've been some kind of mix-up.

4 I'm afraid our system is down at the moment.

5 I'm afraid there's absolutely nothing we can do.

6 I'm afraid I'm not authorised to make that decision.

7 I'll have a word with my manager and see what I can do.

🔊 14.3

The husband bought bricks and hired builders. Before too long, the pile of silver was almost exhausted, but their mansion remained unfinished. The husband decided to see if the moneybag would produce more silver, so without his wife's knowledge, he opened the bag for a second time that day. Instantly, another lump of silver rolled out. He opened it a third time and received a third lump.

He thought to himself, "If I go on like this, I can get the house finished in no time!" He quite forgot the old man's warning. However, when he opened the bag a fourth time, it was completely empty. This time not a scrap of silver fell out of it. It was just an old cloth bag. When he turned to look at his unfinished house, that was gone as well. There before him was his old thatched hut.

The woodcutter fell to his knees in despair, crying "How I wish I'd never opened that bag. Now everything is lost." His wife came over to comfort him, saying, "Not all is lost. We still have each other. Let's go back to the mountain and cut firewood like we did before. That's a more dependable way of earning a living."

And from that day on, that's exactly what they did.

🔊 14.4

Part 1: Zak

Here's an offer. If you give me one dollar each week, I promise to give you $2.6 million at some point in the future. There's just one catch, when I say 'at some point in the future', I mean at any point within the next quarter of a million years! Tempted? I bet you aren't. So why is it that so many people gamble on lotteries when the odds are nearly 1 in 14 million? Probably because the whole marketing of lotteries downplays the odds against winning and emphasises the dream, the ease of getting money, and the 'good causes' that are funded by the profits lotteries make. But I don't see subsidising things like opera and Olympic sportsmen as a good cause. And it's not good when profits simply go to the government or the company that runs the lottery.

Not only does the advertising of lotteries tend to obscure this tiny chance, it also sends this subtle message – people don't need to work hard or get a good education to become wealthy; all you have to do is choose six numbers and your dreams will come true. And then also consider what those dreams are. Are they for a better society and health care? Peace and understanding? NO! It's a mansion and a Ferrari for me! These are values – anti-educational, money-driven and selfish – that go against society. No doubt Stacy will argue that in fact it's all innocent fun and that the stakes are small, but not only do lotteries damage society in this way, they also bring pain to individuals. Take these words from John, a gambling addict from Sydney, for example: "I sometimes gambled away my whole paycheck and had nothing left with which to pay the mortgage or feed the family. In the end, I'd bet on anything – horse races, rugby, roulette, even what the weather would be like – but it all started with lottery tickets. I wish I'd never seen one."

There's more at stake than we imagine. Gambling destroys people's lives and nine times out of ten it starts with lotteries. They're a tax on the poor and benefit the rich and they undermine social values. They really should be banned.

Part 2: Stacy

Well, that really was a sad story that Zak finished with there, wasn't it? Sad – but, sadly for him, also rather misleading in this particular debate. Of course, compulsive gambling is not something that we should approve of. It not only causes pain to the gambler, but also hurts their family and friends. However, addictive behaviour can take many forms: if it wasn't gambling, it might well be drugs or shopping or work. Banning lotteries won't reduce addictive behaviour – even if it were true that nine out of ten gambling addictions started with the lottery. By the way, I'd be interested to hear the source of that figure – dubiousstatistics.com, I'd imagine. But just for a moment, say it was true, nine out of ten gambling addicts start with lotteries, should we also consider banning cigarettes on the basis that heroin addicts started by smoking? Or prohibit credit cards because some people go on to be shopaholics and run up huge debts? No. In the end, I actually agree with Zak – we should take responsibility for our future wealth. It's just that where he suggests we do that by banning the lottery and investing in education, I believe that people should do it by learning self-control.

Which brings me to his point that the lottery somehow goes against hard work and education. With the greatest respect – that's complete rubbish! People don't spend money on the lottery instead of studying and working hard – it's on top of it. Similarly, lottery dreams don't replace friendship, they add to it. The real equivalent of spending money on a lottery ticket is buying, say, an ice cream. Neither are necessary for living – they provide pleasure. Let's face it, gambling in one form or another has featured in human society since time began because it's fun! The only difference is that, unlike ice cream, the lottery ticket, however remote the chance is, might just possibly bring you the additional benefit of riches.

From that standpoint, it's a sound investment. Now Zak may not find lotteries exciting or wish that he had a Ferrari, but I do – and I can't see that there is anything anti-social in that or anything worth banning.

14.5

1 three point seven million
  three million seven hundred thousand
2 fifteen hundred
  one and a half thousand
3 nought point nought two
  two hundredths
4 two thirds
  two out of three
5 forty percent
  two fifths
6 minus ten degrees
  ten below zero

14.6

1 The exact odds of winning the lottery are 1 in 13,983,816 when there are 49 numbers to choose from.
2 In Italy, food accounts for just under one fifth of a family's budget.
3 In the UK last year, 1.4 million people paid over £500 in bank charges – for example, for exceeding overdraft limits.
4 On average, families spend just 0.015% of their income on books.
5 Over three quarters of all women worry about how they'll pay off credit card bills and loans – far more than men.
6 Only about 1 in 10 men know their current level of debt.

UNIT 15

15.1

A: Mmmm, this is gorgeous!
B: Thanks.
A: What's in it? It's got a bit of a lemony taste.
B: Yeah, that's the lemon grass.
A: Lemongrass?
B: Yeah, it's this … actually I don't know what you call it – a herb or spice. It looks sort of like a spring onion, you know. It's like a greyish-white stick. Anyway, you drop it in the sauce while it's cooking and it gives it a kind of citrusy flavour.
A: You don't eat it then.
B: No. It's got a kind of woody texture – it's pretty tough – so you just pick it out at the end.
A: Right – and the orangey colour … is that from carrots?
B: No. It's pumpkin and red lentils
A: Pumpkin?
B: You know, like a big orange squash – like a melon or something – but rounder and the flesh is harder.
A: Oh yeah, of course. Pumpkin – I know this word.
B: Yeah, so you use that or sometimes I use sweet potato instead.
A: Right. So how do you make it?
B: Oh, it's dead easy. You get a large onion and a couple of cloves of garlic and ginger and you chop them all really finely. I actually sometimes use a food processor. Then you put some oil in a pan and heat it up and you just chuck the stuff in the oil with a couple of bits of lemon grass and I sometimes put in a whole chilli as well – just to spice things up a bit – you know, like to flavour the oil.
A: Right.
B: And then you cook it quite quickly, but you have to keep stirring 'cos you don't want it to burn. Otherwise, it can be a bit bitter.
A: OK.
B: Then you throw in the pumpkin. Oh, I should've said you have to cut it up into cubes.
A: How big?
B: I don't know – about an inch – a couple of centimetres? It doesn't matter that much – you blend it all in the end.
A: I meant how big should the pumpkin be.
B: Oh sorry! Yeah, I don't know they vary so much in size. Biggish, I

guess, but not like the huge ones.

A: OK, and then what? You just add water and boil it?

B: Yeah, more or less. You add lentils – roughly a cupful – and a tin of coconut milk.

A: Oh right. Coconut milk.

B: Yeah, actually I often use less, because I find it a bit much otherwise. And then I add about a litre or so of chicken stock and as you say bring it to the boil and then once it's boiling, you reduce the heat and leave it for fifteen minutes or so – till the pumpkin's soft, anyway – and then just blend it till it's smooth.

A: So when do you take out the lemon grass?

B: Oh right, yeah. Sorry. Basically after it's simmered – at the end. It sort of floats to the surface. You just get it out with a spoon.

A: And the green herbs?

B: Well, you can use different things. I usually sprinkle a bit of chopped parsley, but basil's nice as well. And obviously a pinch or two of salt, although personally I got out of the habit of using too much because my dad's got a heart condition and he can't have too much.

A: Right. Well, it's great.

B: Yeah, I like it. Actually I sometimes do it as a sauce – just everything in reduced quantities – and I cook pieces of cod or chicken in it.

A: Mmm. Sounds great.

15.2

1 One of Johannesburg's most persistent – and successful – fraudsters has finally been arrested and is due to appear in court today accused of defrauding restaurants, a charge which carries a maximum penalty of nine months in prison and a 100,000 rand fine. For over a year, Wouter Gunning, aged 54, had been eating out on a regular basis in many of the city's most exclusive restaurants – and all completely free of charge. It's alleged that as he neared the end of his meals, Gunning would habitually introduce a cockroach into his food – safe in the knowledge that high-end establishments would be so sensitive to the damage that any negative publicity could do that they would invariably waive any charge.

Remarkably, the scam only came to light following a chance conversation between two waiters from different restaurants. Mr Gunning denies all charges against him and will be pleading not guilty on the basis of temporary insanity.

2 In a keynote speech today, a leading scientist will blame the food crises in Africa on the rise of organic farming in developed countries as well as the widespread rejection of agricultural technology in general – and of GM crops in particular.

Sir David King claims anti-scientific attitudes towards modern agriculture are being exported to Africa and are holding back a green revolution that could dramatically improve the continent's food supply.

In the past, Mr King has criticised NGOs and the United Nations for backing traditional farming techniques, which he believes will never be able to provide enough food for the continent's growing population. In today's speech, he'll suggest that genetically modified crops could help Africa mirror the substantial increases in crop production seen in India and China, an idea bound to encounter fierce opposition across the European Union, where GM foods are still heavily restricted.

3 A leading consumer protection group is today calling for a total ban on junk food advertising on television between 6am and 9pm in a bid to tackle rising rates of obesity among children. The group, CHOICE, would also like to see a ban on the use of celebrities, cartoon characters and free gifts to induce under-sixteens to eat fast food.

At present, one in four Australian children is overweight or obese and experts have warned that the proportion could rise to 60 per cent in the next 30 years unless urgent action is taken. The inspiration behind the new campaign lies in Scandinavia. Finland, Denmark and Sweden have all prohibited commercial sponsorship of children's programmes, and all have seen a subsequent drop in obesity rates.

4 New findings published today show that the cost of wasted food to UK households now exceeds £10 billion a year. The average household throws out four hundred and twenty pounds-worth of good food per year, while the average family with children squanders £610.

Researchers also found that more than half the good food thrown out have been bought and then simply left unused. Each day 1.3 million unopened yoghurt pots, 5,500 whole chickens and 440,000 ready meals are simply discarded.

In response to the report, the environment minister expressed her dismay:

"These findings are shocking – and at a time when global food shortages are in the headlines this kind of wastefulness becomes even more appalling. This is costing consumers three times over. Not only are they paying hard-earned money for food they're not eating, there's also the cost of dealing with the waste this creates. And then there are the climate change costs of growing, processing, packaging, transporting, and refrigerating food – just for it all to end up in the rubbish bin."

UNIT 16

16.1

I = Ian, C = Claudia

C: Hello. Claudia Hellmann speaking.

I: Oh, hi, Claudia. This is Ian calling, from Madrid.

C: Oh hi, Ian. How're things?

I: Pretty good, thanks. A bit hectic – as usual for this time of the year – but, you know, hectic is good. Anyway, listen, I'm just calling, really, to try to arrange a good time for a video conference. I think we need to talk through the sales strategy ahead of the coming season and it'd be good if the two of us could get together with Piotr in Warsaw and Eudora in Greece to throw some ideas around.

C: Yeah, that sounds good. When were you thinking of?

I: Well, to be honest, the sooner, the better. Would next week work for you?

C: It's possible, yeah, but is there any way you could wait until the week after that? I'll be visiting Spain for the trade fair so I could fit in a day with you then.

I: Oh, that'd be perfect, yeah. Face to face is always better. What day would work best for you?

C: The Tuesday would be good for me. That's the 24th.

I: OK, great. I can make any time after 10.

C: Brilliant. We can confirm the details by email.

I: OK. I'll pencil it in and I'll see you then.

16.2

C: Hello, customer services.

F: Hi. I wonder if you can help me. I'm phoning to chase up an order I placed with your company some time ago – and that I still haven't received.

C: I'm sorry to hear that. Let's see what we can do. Would you happen to have the order number there?

F: Yeah, I do. It's EIA-290–3969.

C: Right. I'm just checking that now and I can't actually see any record of the transaction. When was the order placed?

F: The 29th of August, so that's over a month ago now. It should be under my name – Fabio Baldassari.

C: Ah, OK. I've got it now. I'm afraid there must've been some kind of mix-up in the system because it doesn't appear to have been sent out yet. I do apologise. I'll get that off to you ASAP.

F: OK. Well, at least that explains that, then!

C: Again, I'm really sorry about that, Mr Baldassari.

F: It's OK. These things happen.

C: Thanks for being so understanding. I've just put that through and it'll be going out today by special delivery so it should be with you first thing tomorrow. That's at no extra charge, of course.

F: Great. Thanks. Would you mind just emailing me confirmation of that?

C: No, of course not. Can I just take your email address?

F: Sure. It's baldassari – that's B-A-L-D-A-Double S-A-R-I - underscore f at meccanica dot com. That's meccanica with a double c.

C: Got it. OK. I'll send that through in a minute.

🔊 16.3

1 at
2 forward slash
3 underscore
4 dot
5 dash

🔊 16.4

1 postmaster at claes geller brink – that's c-l-a-e-s-g-e-double-l-e-r-b-r-i-n-k dot com
2 w-w-w dot study tefl – that's t-e-f-l, dot co dot u-k
3 zip dot oh nine eight dot k-d at mail dot r-u
4 do or die, that's all one word, underscore ninety-nine at sez-nam – that's s-e-z-n-a-m dot c-z
5 u-c-y-l-j-e-double-h – that's double the word and then h – not double h – at u-c-l dot a-c dot u-k
6 h-t-t-p colon and then two forward slashes, w-w-w dot xoomer – that's x-double o-m-e-r dot alice dot i-t forward slash sweet floral albion – that's all one word – forward slash capital s capital f capital a dot h-t-m

🔊 16.5

P = Presenter, KT = Kevin Thomas

P: *Dragon's Den* is soon to enter a new series with would-be entrepreneurs trying to **raise money** by pitching their ideas to five self-made millionaires who provide capital and business expertise **in return for** a stake in their companies. The show, which originates from a Japanese programme called *The Money Tigers*, has become an enormous success, with many other countries adopting similar formats. One of those countries, which may surprise some people, is Afghanistan. Kevin Thomas reports.

KT In a country which has been devastated by war and where the average income is just $1000 a year, starting up a company is a risky business. Yet if Afghanistan, which still **heavily depends on** foreign aid, is ever going to sustain itself, then it's a risk more

investors are going to have to take, according to Damien Evans, a development economist.

"Small and **medium-sized businesses** are easily the biggest employers and if employment there is going to rise as it needs to, then it's these kinds of businesses which will have to be encouraged, developed and expanded. The problem at the moment is not just instability, but **a lack of skills** such as financial planning and marketing strategies among business people. These are still relatively new concepts for many people there."

Which is where "Fikr wa Talash" comes in. "Dream and Achieve", as the programme is translated in English, is loosely based on business programmes such as *Dragon's Den*. The show aims to provide just that sort of basic business education as struggling entrepreneurs present their businesses and plans for expansion, which then **come under scrutiny** from local experts. Unlike the British version though, there are just two cash prizes and the proposed businesses also directly reflect the rather different needs of the Afghan economy. Investors in Britain have backed things such as software that allows you to create a personalised doll with the face of your choice, a men's style magazine aimed at the super-rich, and a website that searches the Internet and alerts users to special offers for online gambling. In contrast, the Afghan programme included proposals to set up a dairy and a jam-making factory.

The winner was Faisulhaq Moshkani, a father of nine who had been running a plastic recycling plant in Kandahar until high fuel costs ultimately forced him to close down. The first prize of $20,000 has enabled him to build a mini-hydroelectric plant to power a new factory. The benefit for the country is that it'll soon be able to produce its own plastic rather than having to import it all from abroad.

But " Dream and Achieve" is not simply about education and development, it's also entertainment. It is one of numerous reality TV shows which have found success in the country, including the **hugely popular** singing contest Afghan Star. TV producer Farzad Amini:

"**Reality TV** is popular all round the world because it's overwhelmingly positive. It gives ordinary people a chance to succeed and this brings hope to the viewers. Afghans are no different, but perhaps TV has greater significance here because of our economic situation and the complex and changing nature of our society".

Second place in "Dream and Achieve" went to a 25-year-old mother of five. Just ten years ago, as a woman, she wouldn't have been able to work, let alone run a business. Another character featured was an ex-warlord who had rejected violence in favour of milk production. Not the kind of background you'd find people having on the British programme and sure signs of a complex and changing society.

P: That was Kevin Thomas reporting.

REVIEW 04

R4.1

1 branch / pass away
2 counsellor / mourners
3 veto / yeast
4 niche / hygiene
5 portfolio / soak
6 stake / waste
7 ward / patch
8 usher / rough
9 fuss / fusion
10 hostile / bride
11 float / rope
12 authentic / dawn
13 grave / glance
14 mortgage / launder
15 alert / entrepreneur
16 commute / texture
17 oven / toll
18 withdraw / resort to

R4.2

Italy has also passed a law which establishes the official ingredients, method, shape and size of pizza. The dough, which has to use natural yeast, must be worked and shaped with the hands and then baked on the floor of a wood-fired oven.

R4.3

1 Internet dating services make finding a partner less of a lottery. The odds of encountering your perfect partner in your normal day-to-day life are actually quite low because most people only have a small network of people they meet, and even fewer that they actually chat to. So you can either compromise with someone who is just nice or you can look for Mister or Ms Perfect at www.webmate.co.pr. So end your search and register today.

2 Every couple goes through rough patches and sometimes they need someone independent to stop tempers flaring. Occasionally, the situation can be caused by an affair that's created distrust, but more often it's other causes that underlie rows – a relative passing away, getting into debt or irritating behaviour that only becomes apparent soon after marriage. We're here to help people reach compromises and move on. We're usually able to dissuade people from divorce, but about 15% do call it a day.

3 It's hard because you know you could be upsetting someone's wedding plans. People often plead with me not to close down the kitchens, but they should see it from my standpoint. If I investigate a place which puts on receptions and I find hygiene standards don't meet the law, then it's not good if I ignore it. And as I always explain, they wouldn't want their guests all suffering from an outbreak of food poisoning.

4 We've done well in the wedding market and last year we made a substantial profit, but growth has been slowing and we feel that it is time to branch out into corporate events, which is why we are proposing a new venture with Launch.com, which specialises in entertainment events that bring publicity and promote brand image.

5 I know it's boring, but to get through life I think it's important to be careful with money. These days, everything costs money. Someone told me a kid costs £200,000. Even dying is getting expensive – an average funeral costs almost £3000. Given that, it's best not to waste money. We had a small wedding – nothing elaborate – and didn't even bother with a honeymoon because we're saving up for a deposit to get a mortgage. And I've set up an account for our future children too!

CREDITS

Although every effort has been made to contact copyright holders before publication, this has not always been possible. If notified, the publisher will undertake to rectify any errors or omissions at the earliest opportunity.

Photos

The publisher would like to thank the following sources for permission to reproduce their copyright protected images:

Alamy – pp66ml (Vstock), 68br (Photofusion Picture Library), 103b (Caro), 113br (Phil Cornelius), 124–125b (Stan Gamester), 130bl (Justin Kase zsixz), 132bl (Eric Nathan); **BBC** – p23 (Mr Trebus); **The Bridgeman Art Library** – pp10 (Ashes, Munch, Edvard (1863–1944) / Munch–museet, Oslo, Norway / © DACS / Index / The Bridgeman Art Library), 11tr (The Portrait of Giovanni Arnolfini and his Wife Giovanna Cenami (The Arnolfini Marriage) 1434 (oil on panel), Eyck, Jan van (c.1390–1441) / National Gallery, London, UK / The Bridgeman Art Library); **Cartoonstock** – pp41br (Neil Dishington), 72bl (Joseph Farris), 77bl (Kes), 22a (Kml); **David Hockney** – 'Mr and Mrs Clark and Percy' 1970–71 / acrylic on canvas / 84 x 120" / copyright © David Hockney / photo: Richard Schmidt; **Dreamstime** – pp40tbl (Bhairav), 46tm (Retina2020), 69br (Iofoto), 79mr (Kubalibre), 103c (Ant236), 107tm (Tingberg); **Fotolia** – pp28bl (Luisafer), 31br (Dale Harrison), 40tml (vuk), 45tl (Andrey Stratilatov), 52d (Valda), 75ml (Michael Langley), 98bl (Paul Prescott), 107tl (Nitipong Ballapavanich), 107tr (Viktor Pravdica); **Getty** – pp56d (Andrea Pistolesi), 66bl (Comstock), 73br (STRDEL / Stringer), 124tl (Apple Tree House); **iStockphoto** – pp8–9t (Robert Kohlhuber), 9br (Nikolay Tarkhanov), 14–15t (Klaas Lingbeek- van Kranen), 17b / 17d (Hans F. Meier), 18a (Robert Creigh), 18d (Reuben Schulz), 18e (Graffizone), 18f (Julie de Leseleuc), 18h (10four), 22c (chocorange), 25br (Justin Horrocks), 26–27t (Juan Collado), 28ml (Joe_Potato), 28br (Andres Balcazar), 29br (Fertnig), 30bl (ranplett), 36–37t (morganl), 39tl (Olga Mirenska), 42–43t (Brian Jackson), 42a (John Gollop), 42b (Torr Priaulx), 42c (Alexander Hafemann), 42d (Brian Raisbeck), 46tl (Paul Fawcett), 47b (best-photo), 48–49t (fotoVoyager), 48a (Tony Campbell), 48c (Sean Martin), 48d (JulienGrondin), 51t (absolut_100), 52–53bg (CHEN PING-HUNG), 52a (brytta), 52c (AVTG), 54–55t (arturbo), 56c (Frances Twitty), 59tl / 110–111t (Jacob Wackerhausen), 59b (biffspandex), 64–65t (LajosRepasi), 64bl (Karl Dolenc), 68mr (Laurence Gough), 70–71t (Sean Locke), 75bl (Robert Simon), 76–77t (Loic Bernard), 79tl (Niclas Hallgren), 81bg (Todd Harrison), 82–83t (Alexander Raths), 86br (Jeffrey Smith), 92–93t (Tatiana Morozova), 92ml (Courtney Keating), 95mr (Christophe Testi), 95bl (ericsphotography), 96bl (Alexander Shalamov), 97c (James Richey), 97b (Hande Sengun), 97d (Dan Brandenburg), 98–99t (ilbusca), 103a (Kriss Russell), 109mr (Monika Adamczyk), 109br (ShyMan), 110br (bluestocking), 111br (Heiko Bennewitz), 112tl (Marcio Eugenio), 112mr (Neustockimages), 114mr (Jean Nordmann), 121br (Mikhail Bistrov), 125t (Alija), 126br (Sara Marlowe), 127bl (Scott Vickers), 127bl (Dona ld Gruener), 127bl (Nicole K Cioe), 162b, 162c, 162e–h, all Writing

Unit photos; **The Kobal collection** – pp12mr (Paramount / Shangri-La / The Kobul Collection), 12br (LucasFilm Ltd / Paramount / The Kobul Collection), 13m (MGM / The Kobul Collection), 13bl (Miramax / Universal / The Kobul Collection); **Shutterstock** – pp17a (condor36), 17c (cheyennezj), 18b (Palto), 18c (Diane Gonzales), 18g (Kevin Britland), 20–21t (26kot), 22b (Ragne Kabanova), 36b (iofoto), 38br (Maridav), 40tl (Thomas Barrat), 40br (Bobby Deal / RealDealPhoto), 48b (Anton Prado PHOTO), 51bl (Orientaly), 52b (Pablo H Caridad), 56a (Marko Vesel), 56b (G. Campbell), 70b(bg) (William Attard McCarthy), 78br (Ljupco Smokovski), 92bl (Andresr), 97t (Volina), 97a (Brian Weed), 104–105t (Baloncici), 113bl (Razvan CHIRNOAGA), 114br (Lizette Potgieter), 123br (KBL Photo), 133br (Zoltan Pataki), 135 (Darren Baker), 135 (Maxim Tupikov), 162a, 162d; **Victoria Chappell** – p79 (cathedral).

Cover photo: istock (Vernon Wiley)

Illustrations: KJA Artists